D0464999

DATE DUE

A Requiem for Karl Marx

A REQUIEM FOR

KARL MARX

Frank E. Manuel

Harvard University Press
Cambridge, Massachusetts
London, England
1995

Copyright © 1995 by the President and Fellows
of Harvard College
All rights reserved
Printed in the United States of America

Library of Congress Cataloging-in-Publication Data

Manuel, Frank Edward.
A requiem for Karl Marx / Frank E. Manuel.
p. cm.
Includes bibliographical references and index.
ISBN 0-674-76326-2
1. Marx, Karl, 1818–1883.   2. Communists—Biography.
I. Title.
HX39.5.M3195   1995
335.4′092—dc20   94-48452
[b]

Designed by Gwen Frankfeldt

Contents

Preface vii

Introit 1

1 The Alien of Trier 3

2 Joanna Bertha Julie Jenny von Westphalen 27

3 The Dioscuri: Old Moor and the General 55

4 Emigré Cannibalism 88

5 The Albatross: *Das Kapital* 101

6 The Arena of Class War 121

7 The Ambiguities of Nationhood 142

8 Utopias: The Approved and the Forbidden 155

9 Enemies within the Gates 181

10 Shearing of the Beard 211

11 Vicissitudes of an Icon 227

Notes 243

Index 251

Illustrations follow page 120

Preface

An autopsy on the corpus of Marx's thought is a hazardous undertaking: its initial presumption may be false—the victim may not be dead; or perhaps Marxist particles have dissolved into the spiritual atmosphere of our times and bonded with so many alien bodies that it is impossible to identify and isolate them. Reverberations of Marx's thought have been felt primarily in the twentieth century, and, despite appearances to the contrary, the seismic tremors are by no means over. Today the mindset imposed by Marx's system provokes inquiry into the elements fostering its original growth and the maladies, present at birth, that have hastened its demise. The requiem before you is no addition to the polemics of Marxologists; it is an essay, a personal expression of wonderment over the fast tempo at which the writings of a nineteenth-century author captured and enthralled the minds of men and women on different levels of society and amazement that only recently have the ideas been declassed and treated as historical relics. The quip that Engels imputed to Marx—"What is certain is that I for one am not a Marxist"—if he ever said it, is not very enlightening about the psychic experience of bearers of the doctrine, many of them now bereft of their credo and their faith. The disfranchisement of Marxism is too new to be weighed in the balance of history, but at least Marx himself, dead for more than a century, can be brought to judgment.

My first encounter with Karl Marx occurred when my father took me at the age of seven to a labor union meeting in Boston. One of the orators, doggedly quoting ad nauseam from Marx and Engels, was finally cut off by an exasperated chairman, who banged his gavel and peremptorily ruled that if Marx or Engels had anything to say they would have to wait their turn and speak for themselves. Not until my freshman year at Harvard in the fall of 1926 was the acquaintance renewed, when I got to read the *Communist Manifesto*. Over the succeeding decades few years have passed without my studying one or another of Marx's writings, or at least perusing a commentary on Marx in celebration or denigration of his argument. Though I was never a true believer, in sympathy or antipathy toward Marx's ideas I have moved with the ebb and flow of attitudes among many Americans of my generation. My ambivalence doubtless resonates in this requiem.

Proposals to write a biography of Marx during his lifetime—there were nibbles at the idea as far back as 1873—never came to fruition. But this Age of Computers has not left its readers wanting in lists of books on Marx and Marxism that make printed bibliographies supererogatory. (I have used the names Marx and Marxism with the same looseness that has characterized Western thought about Christ and Christianity, Freud and Freudianism.) The pressure of a single key is sufficient to prompt a system like the HOLLIS catalog at Harvard to spew forth the titles of four or five thousand volumes on Marx and Marxism, whose number, if united with the products of HOLLIS counterparts in other libraries of the world, must surely be tripled—an uninformed guess. To the many authors I have read in English, French, German, and Italian, including those I have forgotten, I owe a debt of gratitude of unknown dimensions. The result of immersion in this literature is called a requiem in imitation of the great musical scores of Mozart and Bizet and Verdi, who also failed to identify the sources of the divine melodies that coursed through their heads. Alas, my reflections bear none of the marks of their genius.

The *Requiem* is deeply colored by the fifteen hundred-odd letters passed between Marx and Engels and their many correspondents in Europe and the United States. It does not pretend to analyze their published works in detail nor does it engage in the disputes of contentious editors over specific word meanings. The often tragic life of Marx the man is related to his theories of class struggle, revolutionary strategy, and utopia, conceptions interpreted as emanations of his whole being rather than as independent rationalist structures. Marx does not stand alone. While Engels is close by his side as a major protagonist in the drama, Frau Jenny Marx, their three daughters, and an array of enemies are summoned to illuminate the character of the dominant figure. This is a nineteenth-century story, enacted in Germany, France, and above all Victorian England.

The first significant attempt at the publication of the Marx-Engels correspondence, by Eduard Bernstein and August Bebel (Stuttgart, 1913), bowdlerized the texts and made them conform to the moral standards of proper members of the German Social Democratic Party. The French translation of their flawed work in the collection of writings assembled by J. Molitor only perpetuated the crude manipulation of the remains of Marx and Engels. Whole passages were omitted lest they cast a shadow on the image of the Marx who was being turned into a Victorian gentleman, a man without blemish. From all indications, the cleansing process had already been initiated by Engels and the Marx daughters who survived him. Lenin was instrumental in restoring the stricken passages and establishing the canon of Marx's writings. Their publication was undertaken, though not completed, by the Marx-Engels Institute in Moscow, under the early direction of David Rjazanov. The name of the Institute, an official research facility, was gradually inflated until it became the Marx-Engels-Lenin-Stalin Institute of the Central Committee of the Communist Party of the Soviet Union, abbreviated as IMELS, a now virtually forgotten acronym. The Institute's *Historisch-Kritische Gesamtausgabe,* the first volume of which was published in 1927, and the more recent *Werke,* begun by the Institute for Marxism-Leninism in Berlin in 1956, remain the foundation upon which Marxology has rested, though the English translation, *The Collected Works of Marx and Engels,* a cooperative enterprise started in 1975, deserves special mention.

The Internationaal Instituut voor Sociale Geschiedenis in Amsterdam has become the repository of a large collection of original manuscripts and letters by Marx and Engels, along with related documents, that did not find their way to Moscow. The stacks of notebooks into which Marx copied excerpts from his voluminous readings are now being prepared by an international committee that has vowed to maintain scholarly neutrality among socialists, former communists, and professors of no particular persuasion. An International Marx-Engels Foundation, under the patronage of the Amsterdam Instituut, has been collaborating with the Conference of German Academies of the Sciences and the Karl Marx Haus in Trier to assure continuation of a comprehensive historical and critical edition of the works of Marx and Engels, graced with variants—a project launched in 1975 that was interrupted by the fall of the Berlin Wall and the political restructuring of the former Soviet Union.

Since both Marx and Engels were masters of irony and resourceful inventors of cuss words, the flavor of their sarcasm and black humor is often difficult to retain in English. In the fast-changing world of modern languages, epithets like "philistine" have lost their original meaning and their nineteenth-century coating; "Nigger" and "Jüdel" are currently taboo; "Dreck" and "Scheisse" and their numerous compounds, rarely absent from the discourse of the dioscuri, have been drained of their shock-value in a world where obscenities have become hackneyed. Parodying religious rhetoric is commonplace in the writing of Marx the descendant of rabbis and Engels the son of German pietists. For the rest, the *Requiem* is meant for family reading.

With the permission of *Daedalus: The Journal of the American Academy of Arts and Sciences,* parts of two of my essays on Marx, "In Memoriam: *Critique of the Gotha Program,* 1875–1975" and "A Requiem for Karl Marx" (which appeared in the issues entitled "In Praise of Books," Winter 1976, and "The Exit from Communism," Spring 1992), have been adapted and bear witness to a modicum of consistency in my views of Marx over the last two decades. Fragments of my oral presentations of Marx's thought in university lectures may be preserved in the class notes of former students and I trust betray no such uniformity.

Acknowledgment is made also for quotations from *The Collected Works of Marx and Engels* (International Publishers, 1975–) and from a letter (Louise Freyberger to August Bebel, September 2 and

4, 1898) in the archives of the Internationaal Instituut voor Sociale Geschiedenis. I am grateful to Ms. Mieke Ijzermans for courtesies extended during my visit to the Instituut. Thanks are due the Boston Athenaeum for access to its library and for the generous help of its research staff; Brandeis University for the loan of volumes from its Marx-Engels collections and for technical assistance in preparing the manuscript of this book; and Professor Dirk Struik for allowing me to consult his copies of recent works not yet available in university or public libraries.

A word of appreciation to my wife, Fritzie, and to Christine Thorsteinsson, my editor at Harvard University Press, for their help-ful suggestions—and those they refrained from making—to a reluc-tant dragon of an author.

Frank E. Manuel
Boston

A Requiem for Karl Marx

Introit

Requiem aeternam dona eis, Domine
Et lux perpetua luceat eis.

—Latin Requiem Mass

This is a requiem of my own devising for Karl Marx—an unauthorized ritual for a Jew who was born in 1818, was baptized at age six into the Lutheran faith in the Catholic Rhineland city of Trier (then Prussian territory), received his doctorate of philosophy at Jena, turned into a radical journalist and philosophical economist, and, after living in exile for thirty-four years, died in London in 1883, an atheist and leader of the world communist movement.

Icons have no control over their destinies, and Karl Marx has suffered many changes of fortune in the two communist empires that adopted him. In the Soviet Union he often formed part of a trinity along with Engels and Lenin, their giant portraits looming over the reviewing stand in Red Square on May Day and on the anniversary of the Bolshevik Revolution. Marx even penetrated the inner sanctum of Stalin's study: affixed to the wall was a photograph taken in 1876 showing a seated Marx, amply bewhiskered and clad in a neatly pressed frock coat, with his monocle suspended from a string—more a proper English gentleman than a revolutionary shadowed by the police of many nations. By 1990 Lenin's bald head shone in isolation on the backdrop of the solemn assemblies in the auditoriums of the Supreme Soviet and the Congress of Communist Parties, though Marx was still accorded a place of dignity here and there: in the theater of the absurd, Moscow 1990, his picture looked down on Ronald Reagan as he addressed a group of Soviet lawmakers. On the curtain of the assembly of the Republic of Russia, over which Boris Yeltsin presides, only a mammoth Russian flag was spread. Lenin, too, has been dropped—though not everywhere—in the former Soviet Union, and his monumental statue has been toppled in many public places. The embalmed corpse on Red Square still draws the curious.

In China for a time Marx and Engels were squeezed between Lenin and Stalin in official displays; with shifting communist policy, Stalin was deleted from the group, and of late Tiananmen Square is decorated only with the effigy of Mao Zedong. Marx's status was maintained, though pockmarked with ambivalences, throughout the Cultural Revolution, and prominent Chinese officials continued to make pilgrimages to the Karl Marx Haus in Trier, the elegant and commodious home where he was born, now a museum. To its exhibits they contributed a porcelain plate, adorned with a visage of Marx that oddly resembles Mao's. Other communist countries once honored Marx each in its own way, renaming a city, a street, an institute, a university, after him. Abruptly he has begun to vanish—though in China he lingers on.

1

The Alien of Trier

Who runs up next with wild impetuosity?
A swarthy chap of Trier, a marked monstrosity.
He neither hops nor skips, but moves in leaps and bounds,
Raving aloud. As if to seize and then pull down
To Earth the spacious tent of Heaven up on high,
He opens wide his arms and reaches for the sky.
He shakes his wicked fist, raves with a frantic air,
As if ten thousand devils had him by the hair.

—Edgar Bauer and Friedrich Engels, "The Insolently Threatened
Yet Miraculously Rescued Bible," 1842

Trier was the ancient seat of a Catholic diocese, and nineteenth-century travel books describe the many churches, chapels, convents, and monasteries crowded into this city of twelve thousand inhabitants. Visitors gaped at the sombre remains of the Roman Porta Negra, while the more devout marveled at Christ's tunic, which had found its way into the cathedral. In 1844, when Karl Marx was writing his first diatribe against the young Hegelians from whom he was severing connections and wickedly called his attacks on them *The Holy Family,* a Jacob Marx—no relation—was publishing a pious account of the renewed miracles of the Trier tunic. This Marx was a professor in the episcopal seminary, and his book featured testimony on the wondrous cure of the young Countess von Droste Vischering. The next year Jacob Marx's narration was translated into English and malevolently published as an anti-Romanist tract by a Protestant—*History of the Robe of Jesus Christ: preserved in the Cathedral of Trèves, by J. Marx, Professor in the Great Seminary, to which is added an account of the Miraculous Cures Performed by the Said Robe, during its public Exhibition from 18th*

August to 6th October, 1844. Approved by his Lordship, the Bishop of Trèves. According to one report, half a million pilgrims flocked to view the relic, despite the contention of the French clergy that they had the genuine tunic of Christ and that the one exhibited at Trier was a counterfeit.

Karl Marx was born in Trier on May 5, 1818, the second son of Heinrich (originally Heschel) Marx and Henriette Pressburg, who had been married in a Jewish ceremony five years before. Their union was prolific. Of their nine children, three males died early: Moritz-David, the first-born, at four, Hermann aged twenty-three, Eduard at eleven. Karl was the survivor and inherited the mantle of the first-born, the chosen one of God. The females—Sophie, Henriette, Luise, Emilie, and Karoline—lived to a reasonable old age and most of them wed respectable burghers. Only Sophie, two years Karl's senior, had close ties with her brother and served as a go-between in his secret courtship of her friend Jenny von Westphalen, his future wife.

The marriage of Heinrich and Henriette Marx was loving and harmonious, despite the wide gap in their intellectual capacities—he read the *philosophes* and she could not punctuate. Theirs was a traditional Jewish bourgeois family arrangement of the period, with the wife subordinate to her husband, but respected and cherished. Since the two younger brothers of Karl were early recognized as mediocre and the many sisters displayed no special talents, the hopes and aspirations of Heinrich Marx centered on Karl. After Henriette Marx was widowed, she divided her responsibilities more equitably among her children, a changed position in the family constellation that Karl did not easily accept. Marx never dwelt upon his childhood in any of his writings, and the only anecdote preserved from before his seventeenth year is a story his youngest daughter, Eleanor, had from her aunt: he dominated his siblings and used to play a game with them in which he acted as a coachman being pulled by horses. The children suffered his ordering them about because they were rewarded with the fascinating tales he told them.

Since the middle of the seventeenth century, the eldest son in a rabbinic dynasty with roots in central Europe had customarily become the chief rabbi of Trier. Heinrich Marx's father, who had filled that office, was born in Bohemia Mordecai ben Samuel Halevy, and his oldest son, also named Samuel, succeeded him in 1804. "Marx" was a recent family acquisition. In conformity with a Napoleonic decree meant to further Jewish assimilation, the rabbi of Trier in 1808 adopted the name for the whole family, then as now common in the Catholic city (Marx derives from Markus).

Heinrich Marx, a younger brother of the rabbi of Trier, broke with Judaism and became an apostate steeped in the writings of Voltaire and Rousseau. After Waterloo, when the Napoleonic Rhenish department was dissolved and the territory reverted to the Prussian monarchy, a Napoleonic decree excluding Jews from the legal profession was retained, and despite recognition by officials that Heinrich Marx was a loyal subject, he had to become a Christian to safeguard his position in the civil service. Though the overwhelming number of Trier citizens were Catholic, Heinrich entered the Lutheran Church around 1817, since Evangelical Protestantism was the state religion of Prussia, where he was making his career. Citizens of the Rhineland who had been incorporated into the French state had enjoyed most of the political and legal rights of the Napoleonic Code, a dispensation that was particularly welcome to Jews who had inhabited the area for centuries and had previously been denied basic rights by the German princelets and ecclesiastical rulers of the region. Though much of the freedom granted by the Napoleonic Code was preserved after the defeat of Napoleon and the award of the territory to the Prussian monarchy, certain disabilities discouraged Jews from entering the civil service and the legal profession, or seeking academic posts, unless they converted to Christianity.

Jews in Prussian territories responded to the restrictions in a variety of ways. One group developed entrepreneurial skills that won them a place in society without their submitting to conversion, though their business success provoked envy and fanned the flames of endemic Judeophobia. The behavior of these prosperous Jews ran the gamut from strict ritual observance through religious indifference. Even when new converts married Christians, their origins were rarely forgotten, especially by rivals, though generations might have passed. Among the converted and indifferent Jews, the psychic consequences of their ambiguous social position left wounds—in memoirs they sometimes confessed to the desire to tear their Jewish origins from their bodies and rid themselves of the malignant growths they had inherited. Others flaunted their Jewish roots in defiance of their detractors, a cover for their pain. In the course of a lifetime a Jew could assume many poses depending upon his changing status. And there were Jewish rebels and reformers who concocted different solutions for the "Jewish Question," which had preoccupied Jews and Christians since the latter part of the eighteenth century. Among the German Jews were born many of the major revolutionaries of the nineteenth century.

The stratagems of converted Jews were often pitiable attempts to surmount the age-old social and legal barriers. Heinrich Marx had written abject petitions seeking exemption from residual Napoleonic decrees and calling upon the Prussian monarchy to lift restrictions on Jews, who longed to be assimilated with their new Prussian fellow-subjects. In the name of humanity, he begged the Prussian overlords to accept as equals Jews who welcomed the liberality of the new regime, flattering the Prussians as bearers of an enlightenment that would free the Jews from unjust, despotic Napoleonic impositions. The petitions cringed, cajoled, proclaimed allegiance to the newcomers, who, Heinrich was well aware, might be looking for local allies in a Catholic region that had once sworn loyalty to the French emperor. For Heinrich Marx, conversion to the Evangelical state religion was a small price to pay for tolerance and, it was hoped, equality.

Karl was about six when his father had the whole brood received into the same faith. His wife held out until after the death of her father, a rabbi of Nijmegen, Holland, whose origins have been traced to Pressburg (Bratislava). The baptism of the numerous progeny of Henriette and Heinrich Marx took place in a ceremony at their home, followed by a celebration with an array of godfathers in attendance. The conversions of German Jews in this period were rarely acts born of profound religious conviction, and remnants of Jewish identity lingered, particularly in the first generation. The conversion of Heinrich Marx, though disapproved in the Jewish community, did not lead to an absolute breach between the two branches of the Marx family, and after the death of Rabbi Samuel of Trier in 1827, the relations of Heinrich Marx with his brother's widow and their children remained close.

From his father Karl Marx inherited a political tradition that was mixed and often confusing. Heinrich Marx had joined a Trier literary society whose members at the close of a bibulous banquet had sung subversive songs like the *Marseillaise* and the *Parisienne;* but his speech had praised the king of Prussia and expressed the hope that the just aspirations of his subjects would be fulfilled. Although Heinrich Marx had not forgotten the egalitarian laws of the French that governed Trier when it was part of the Rhenish provinces, in a letter to his son he contrasted the liberalism of the Prussian monarchy with the despotism of Napoleon and proposed to him the composition of an ode celebrating the battle of Waterloo; he argued that a victory for Napoleon would have shackled humanity and the human spirit forever. The paternal influence was pragmatic, irreligious, and committed to reason.

The shades of rabbis and the sons and daughters of rabbis hovered about the boy Karl, but they seem not to have touched his person except when death brought the Marxes together to divide bequests. Genealogies trace Karl's rabbinic ancestors back through his grandmother Eva Chaja to Jehuda ben Eliezer Halevy Minz (Mainz), the head of the famous rabbinic seminary in Renaissance Padua who died in 1508—a remarkable line that rivals the family trees of most European monarchs and is probably as authentic. Descriptions of Karl Marx in later years ordinarily referred to him as a Jew. His own scant writings on Jews, considered as psychological rather than political documents, bespeak a strained attempt to erase the stain of his ancestry.

Though baptism did not wipe away the stigma of being a Jew any more than it had after the mass conversions of Spanish Jews in 1391, the handful of Jews residing in Trier conducted their affairs unmolested. The Prussian officials were aliens in Catholic Trier—there were only about five hundred Lutherans in the city—and so were the Jews; they appear to have cohabited in tolerable amity until the 1940s, when the Nazi machine invaded their lives and the rabbi of

Trier was seized and sent to a death camp. After World War II the religious and secular notables of Trier held a memorial service for the martyred rabbi.

Karl Marx never had to wrestle with the religious scruples of his family—the fate of Engels. His mother may have clung to Jewish customs, but she hardly bound her son to a religious world view. His Enlightenment father imposed neither Judaic nor Christian learning upon him. Affirming his deism, Heinrich Marx constantly avowed his faith in the God of Newton, Locke, and Leibniz in letters to his son, and encouraged him to follow in his path. From his mother, Karl may have absorbed Jewish tales on the level of folklore. In the Friedrich Wilhelm Gymnasium of Trier he studied Greek and Latin; if he attended the course of Schneemann, the Hebrew professor, there are no extant papers with even a scribble of a Hebrew letter. The Lutheran Bible was the text that colored his style. At the gymnasium Marx acquired a storehouse of rich Old and New Testament imagery, and at the university a familiarity with patristic literature that stood him in good stead throughout his life. The erudite raillery against rival theorists flaunted in his first book, *The Holy Family,* bears witness that his acquaintance with religious texts was far from superficial. Notations on his university records indicate that his understanding of theology and canon law was at least adequate. One course stands out as a major source of rhetoric for his vision of a future paradise on earth: in the summer term of 1839 at the University of Berlin, he attended Bruno Bauer's lectures on Isaiah, a primary text for messianic prophecy, and for a time he adopted Bauer's heterodox religious views.

Bauer, Marx's first academic mentor, dangled before his disciple the prospect of a scholarly career at Bonn, one of the many illusions that possessed Karl. Though at his father's direction he was studying jurisprudence, young Marx was always flirting with other vocations. At one time or another he fancied himself a poet, a drama critic, a professor of philosophy, and, in a compromise with his father's wishes, a professor of philosophical jurisprudence. His father, a practical man, steadily insisted on the security of a post in the civil service, where Karl could combine his legal and cameralistic knowledge.

The temper of the Trier gymnasium Marx attended was enlightened. In contrast with the low estate into which the school had fallen during the French occupation, under the new Prussian regime it was influenced by Kantian thought, many of whose dicta found their way into Marx's early writings and stamped his moral universalism at an early age. Goethe during his stay in Trier had a long conversation about Kant with a young professor, J. H. Wyttenbach, later director of the gymnasium when Marx was a student there from 1830 to 1835. Though in political skirmishes there were more than occasional lapses in Marx's adherence to the demands of the categorical imperative, the Kantian rules of practical morality were not violated without twinges of conscience. To be human an action had to be universally applicable; the new species-being that Marx would bring into the world was nurtured on Kantian rules, though it was Hegel's dialectic that permeated the method of Marx's philosophy.

Marx has left no record of harassment during his years in the Friedrich Wilhelm Gymnasium; there is a tradition that he was spared the taunts of classmates because they feared his sharp tongue and his talent for composing acerbic verses. The required exercises he presented to his professors were graded according to their merit, usually without enthusiasm. "Reflections of a Young Man on the Choice of a Profession,"[1] an essay of the seventeen-year-old when he was graduating from the gymnasium, is a valiant attempt to find a place for himself in the order of things, before his open declaration of war against the society in which he lived. The essay was marked "pretty good" by his teachers, but its author was faulted for his tendency to resort to extravagant pictorial analogies. Read more than a century-and-a-half later, it seems overflowing with moral prescripts reiterated throughout his life, albeit with changed meanings. In later years Marx could resort to such heavy volleys of contempt and denigration that sometimes his absorption with the tactics of revolution appears to have made him forget the cause for which he was fighting, but this essay of his youth serves as a reminder that there was once a layer of innocence in his soul, a touching naiveté. Written by a Lutheran convert, the composition bears the imprint of his pastor's teaching. Luther is one of the few religious leaders Marx ever cited with approval, long after he abandoned any religious faith he may have had. Once he jestingly praised Luther's sanction of drink; and in *Das Kapital* Luther was called upon to bear witness to the economic transformations occurring in sixteenth-century Germany.

The graduation essay is more than a search for a calling in the Lutheran spirit, though Marx may have been touched by Lutheran pietism. "The force that must guide us in the choice of a career," he wrote, "is the good of mankind and our own perfection." The two goals are not inimical to each other, for the nature of man has been so ordered that he can achieve his own excellence only when he strives for the good and welfare of others. To work for the world remained his favorite motto in old age. There is already an awareness that the choice of a way of life is not completely free even for a youth of seventeen. "Our relationships in society in a sense have already been initiated." Society does not allow absolute freedom; there are limitations that are determinants. The utopian idea of Marx's later anthropology is already implicit: it would be a better world if that choice were free of pre-established bonds. Any direct reference to the handicaps imposed by his Jewish origin is suppressed and the question of freedom is left abstract. Despite impediments there *is* some freedom, he confidently proclaims, but failure to make the right decision can bring on disaster.

Later, Marx would point the way to the optimal social course for mankind, but any given society, like an individual, was hovering on the brink of catastrophe when making critical judgments. At the age of seventeen, he had assimilated both a Judaic and a Lutheran sense of an inner voice that was the only guide to the right path. The Judaic idea of prophecy as transformed for German Enlightenment Jewry by Moses Mendelssohn was coupled with the Evangelical Lutheranism softened by the pietists of the seventeenth and eighteenth centuries. For anyone who has read Luther's *The Jews and Their Lies*, a Jewish Lutheran must appear a monstrous oxymoron. But Western culture has shown a penchant for the most outlandish syncretisms, and young Marx's essay bears traces of both religious strains. The traditional call of divinity, the *Ruf der Gottheit*, has been internalized in a mixed Judeo-Lutheran rhetoric.

Marx recognized that dangers were hidden in the recesses of

consciousness as he searched for the true way. Enthusiasm for a particular calling could be the mere seduction of its external glamour, a mask for the frenzied lust for honor, *Ehrsucht,* and for prestige, *Ehrgeiz.* Kant's moral strictures against *Ehrsucht, Heersucht* (lust for power), and *Habsucht* (lust for possession) had penetrated German secondary schools. Marx may later have become committed for a time to a Hegelian system with its grand dialectical apparatus and a philosophy of history that charted human development in "phases"; but the moral dictates of Kant and the prophets of Israel and the inner voice of Luther's conscience possessed him early on. The economic theory, the scientism, the French Revolutionary rhetoric that he despised but used, all varied from decade to decade in his writings, but they can be construed as superstructures on a moralist foundation dating from his adolescence.

We must be wary of the drives of facile enthusiasm for a goal, Marx admonishes himself. The choice must well up from the innermost depths of a man's being lest he fall victim to a siren's song. Equally dangerous is a departure from reality. Should we choose a goal for which we do not possess the necessary talents we will falter and sink into a mire of self-contempt, the most painful of human emotions. His dwelling on the anguish of self-contempt *(Selbst-ver-achtung)* is arresting; it is intertwined with the confused experience of this young Jew baptized by a father without religious conviction and resentful of his mother and her despised remnants of Judaic practice. Despite the predominantly triumphal tone of the graduation exercise, in one passage Marx gave voice to a strange prefiguration of his own bitter psychic fate: "Self-contempt is a serpent constantly gnawing at one's breast; it sucks the life-blood out of the heart and mixes it with the venom of the hatred of man and of despair."

The adolescent's analysis of the nature of a life purpose would later be transferred from his individual person to all mankind. The analogy between the cycle of a human life and the course of history was so commonplace in Marx's culture that it was trite and virtually inescapable. A narcissistic engulfment of the world fits in with Marx's character. Extraordinary self-awareness in one psychic sphere accompanied by blindness in others, at least on the conscious

= 11 =

level of the written word, is not rare among men of talent. The youth could in the abstract depict the war between the spiritual and the physical elements in his being, and give utterance to the dread that if he did not resolve this conflict in the soul he would be defeated by the turbulence of existence. But if he overcame his inner turmoil he would emerge a hero, indomitable; burdens could not bend him and he would enjoy a bliss that was no shriveled egotistical delight, but a happiness that would be shed upon millions. His fame would be everlasting and when he died his ashes would be moistened with the hot tears of noble men. Later in life, bereft of the immortality of the Jewish just man and unable to accept the Lutheran salvation of the baptized babe, Marx, like his Enlightenment predecessor Condorcet, created an Elysium of his own—the Roman fama of the classical schoolbooks, lathered with romantic sentimentality. The cast of Marx the liberator of mankind was self-molded in his youth.

The image of mourners shedding copious tears over the ashes of their hero can be read in psychological terms. In the course of almost five decades Marx embellished with scientistic decorations this adolescent dream of himself as the savior of humanity. He grasped whatever came along: the science of economics in the English mode, the analysis of social relations in French class terms, the philosophic system of Hegel with its concept of stages in a dialectical development, and the Diderot-Hegel idea of alienation. He would denounce revolutionaries led astray by the quick solution of a coup d'état and would deride rival utopian visionaries after having read and sometimes assimilated them. But in retrospect he remained loyal, after a fashion, to the self-imposed mandate of his gymnasium essay.

Marx's religious exercise, also required for the baccalaureate, lacked the theological refinements demanded by a thorough analysis of the subject posed by the examiners: "Demonstrate, according to the Gospel of Saint John, XV, 1–14, the reason, the nature, the necessity, and the effects of the union of believers with Christ." Marx's commentary was historical, stressing the profound tendency of human nature to elevate itself to God through a higher morality, as exemplified by Plato. The pagans were made to rise from their general moral impurity to a loftier virtue through the union of believers with Christ—more humane and gentler than the Stoics and more noble and pure than the Epicureans. The professor who reviewed the exercise noted that the student's responses were all of a moral and historical nature and omitted specifically religious arguments. Marx was in no sense a Christian theologian, though when convenient he adapted the accepted style to his own doctrine.

Since Marx himself virtually never made reference to his youth, we are dependent on correspondence with his fiancée and letters exchanged with his parents that date from the years he spent at the Universities of Bonn and Berlin. Aside from stereotyped complaints about Karl's extravagance, which was greater than a man in his comfortable but modest position could bear, Heinrich Marx had tried gently to nudge him into a sensible career. His extant letters from 1835 until his death in 1838, when his son was twenty, provide a composite portrait of the young Karl, drawn by a father whose love was all-embracing, even when there were momentary flashes of anger. Scoldings were immediately followed by expressions of remorse, in which it is the father who begs forgiveness from the son. This is the man who had the deepest insight into the creature whom he had brought into the world and in whom he hoped to realize fulfillment where he himself had failed. He appreciated Karl's extraordinary talents before other men did, but was apprehensive of the demonic in his son's character, which he feared would destroy him.

One long letter took on the style of a legal brief in which the father set forth his grievances in numbered paragraphs as if he were in a court of law. He argues, he pleads, he coats his censures with tender affection. The letters of Heinrich Marx during his last illness begin and end with plaintive cries that his philosophical son appears deaf to the entreaties of his mother, who is beset with anxieties. There must be a balance between the head and the heart, and the father fears that Marx's cold intellect is undermining his affective nature. For long months the parents did not hear from him and had to live on rumors.

From Karl in Berlin, after a relatively short sojourn in Bonn, came notices of total absorption in philosophical studies—for a while he devoured everything Hegel had written—and wild attempts at poetic creation that are no better than the standard romantic lamentations of the age, in which death, destruction, and despair are more prominent than pastoral themes. As a token of affection Karl sent his father a collection of his poetry. For a time he continued legal studies, but after six years at Bonn and Berlin he submitted his doctoral dissertation on Democritus and Epicurean philosophy to the University of Jena, where it was accepted *in absentia,* a not uncommon practice in the German system. When he bemoaned his lot to his father—their Jewish origin was unmentioned, though it lurked in the shadows for a young man who hoped to pursue a literary or academic course—Heinrich Marx reminded him candidly of his own difficulties in procuring advancement in the Prussian civil service. At one point Karl set about constructing a philosophical system out of bits and pieces from the books he devoured—lectures did not much interest him—but when he awoke to the realization that his structure was an empty shell he worked himself into a frenzy, dashing up and down the banks of the Spree like a man possessed. On a doctor's advice he took refuge in the countryside around Berlin to recuperate.

While his father was favored with effusions of love during Marx's absence at the University of Berlin, his mother was an object of disdain. She was uncultivated, a Dutch rabbi's daughter in a strange land. In long complaints written in clumsy German, she pestered her son about his personal habits—his eating and drinking, his disregard of her homely hygienic precepts, his neglect of his sisters and brothers, and the general disorder of his life. Her letters, overflowing with love, dripped with saccharine phrases that only annoyed the doctor of philosophy-in-the-making, who was trying to find for himself a unique position among the grandiose system-builders of the Germanic philosophical-theological jungle, all covert pretenders to the mantle of Hegel.

Except for a passing reference to his "angelic mother" in a youthful letter and infrequent expressions of admiration for her stamina, Karl's filial love was lavished exclusively on his father, whose photograph his son always carried with him in later life. After Heinrich Marx's premature death, Karl's mother held tight the purse-strings of her son's legacy, even when he was an exile living in abject poverty. Despite his mother's baptism at the age of thirty-eight,

Marx identified her with the accursed Jewish religion to which she had clung in irritating little ways. Because of his ancestry he would never become a university professor in the Jew-baiting German world. He despised the Jewish stock brokers with whom he was classed, and his hapless Jewish mother—*die Alte,* the Old Lady, for him no term of endearment—became the personification of the ugly traits he attributed to Jews, whose dark skin he could not shed. He was ashamed of her, and through an alchemy we only partially comprehend, the shame turned into self-loathing.

The repression of the plain fact of his Jewish origins and the dislike, even the overt hatred of his mother, were interwoven and became a destructive force that underlay Marx's relations with most human beings he encountered. Although he was not the complete misanthrope, suspicion and contempt were his constant companions, the image of his despised mother looming in the background and crippling his capacity for love. Redemption was in the father and in those who, like him, offered their nurture unconditionally. It was Marx's good fortune to draw close to him two persons who sustained him in his darkest hours, his wife and his friend Friedrich Engels. The enemies were legion.

Hatred of the father has become a platitude of our popularized psychology; rejection of the mother, *die Natur,* nature herself, opens the floodgates to a far more threatening world, and we often avoid dwelling on it. By contrast with the rarity even of veiled allusions to his Jewish origins, throughout Marx's active political life there is a profusion of documents and letters in which he mocked the "Jewish" character of rivals for revolutionary leadership in the communist or working-class movement, especially if they were operating in defiance of his commands. Moses Hess, Ferdinand Lassalle, Eduard Bernstein were objects of his scorn—he called Lassalle a "Jewish nigger." Marx's language caricaturing Jewish usurers and Jewish haggling could easily meld with the refuse-heap of antisemitic literature in the German world. In private correspondence delineations of Jews were thick with scatological obscenities—Moses Mendelssohn was a "shit-windbag." Elsewhere, Jews are almost invariably coupled with the adjective "dirty." He attacked Ludwig Feuerbach for conceiving revolutionary praxis only in its "dirty Jewish manifestation." A casual reference to Polish Jews is joined to a remark that they multiply like lice, and the *New Rhenish Times* Marx edited during the abortive mid-century revolution sneers at them as the dirtiest of all races (April 29, 1849). *Scheisse* and *Dreck* are constantly paired with Jews as a group or as individuals. Even age did not temper Marx's inbred Judeophobia. From Ramsgate on August 25, 1879, he complained to Engels: "Place is full of Jews and fleas."[2]

From Bruno Bauer Marx adopted the labeling of Jews as a "collection of atoms" incapable of historical development, a chimerical nationality. Jews were identified with exploiting capitalists or groveling bootlickers of men in power. *Jüdel,* Jew-boy, was among the milder epithets in Marx's political dictionary. "Baron Izzy"—Ferdinand Lassalle—was the most obnoxious of his Jewish enemies, and Marx heaped ridicule upon him both before and after his death. Mutual name-calling was frequent among radical Jews who differed on philosophical issues. The Saxon editor Arnold Ruge accused Moses Hess of being a Christian who tried to disguise himself as a Jew, to which Hess rejoined that Ruge was a Jew who sought to pass himself off as a Christian. Marx entered the fray, dubbing Hess "Rabbi Moses."

The incapacity of Marxism in later years to cope with nationalism and ethnicity doubtless has many sources; but one of them is the rootless, godless Karl. Any examination that probes beneath the surface of his economic iconoclasm and his political universalism faces his painful struggle with the nature of his Jewish stock. Marx the wandering Jew failed to appreciate the tenacious hold of ethnicity in modern Europe, while his religious and ethnic status as a baptized Jew without a country had devastating consequences for his own psychic economy.

In a letter to Arnold Ruge in Dresden (dated Cologne, March 13 [1843]), Marx made one of his rare references to a connection with the Cologne Israelite community, which had appealed to him as editor of the *Rhenish Times* for support. "I have just been visited by the chief of the Jewish community here, who has asked me for a petition for the Jews to the Provincial Assembly." Surprisingly he added, "and I am willing to do it." He was clearly preparing his strange reply to Bruno Bauer's position set forth in *Die Judenfrage:*

"However much I dislike the Jewish faith, Bauer's view seems to me too abstract. The thing is to make as many breaches as possible in the Christian state and to smuggle in as much as we can of what is rational. At least it must be attempted—and the *embitterment* grows with every petition that is rejected with protestations."[3]

Despite his criticism of Bauer, in the extended piece Marx composed on the Jewish question, *Zur Judenfrage* (1844), he enveloped himself in a similar fog of abstractions. His repudiation of his mother and his self-hate pervade its involuted arguments. Instead of addressing directly the yearning of the German Jews for political emancipation, Marx in this polemic with Bauer embarked on a philosophical disquisition on the poverty of the concept itself. Standing alone, political emancipation for a minority like the Jews implied the reduction of man to an "egotistic independent individual" who in his civil existence had become separated from his moral, social person. Authentic human emancipation involved the incorporation of the abstract citizen into a "species-being," who so orders his social powers that there is no distinction between the political man and the man of everyday life. This ideal species-being would become in Marx's later writings synonymous with the universal communist man. When Marx drowned the concrete Jewish question—the demand for the lifting of specific civil disabilities—in a sea of philosophical reflections, he camouflaged his own Jewish resentment. The anger turned inward against the self, and in the same essay on the *Judenfrage* he took the opportunity to identify the Jewish religion with the worship of Mammon. He mockingly distinguished between the Sabbath Jew and the real Jew of everyday life: the lofty expressions of godliness by the Sabbath Jew were a fraud; the essence of the religion was to be found in the daily behavior of Jews in the marketplace.

The frequent eruptions of carbuncles and furuncles that covered Marx's body from the early 1860s on, his gastro-intestinal and liver ailments, may have been overt physiological manifestations of a submerged psychic pain. Such psychosomatic explanations need not be swallowed whole, but Marx's perennial wrangling with his personal Jewish problem cannot be cast aside. The shame of being a Jew assumed extravagant forms when he attacked other Jews—a patent attempt to hide or disguise his indelible Jewish coloration. If he denounced Jews, constantly unmasked writers and men in power as crypto-Jews, was he not aligning himself with non-Jews, with those inimical to Jews, and thus proclaiming that he was not a Jew and would have nothing to do with that repulsive religion, the official camouflage for Jewish hucksters and their exploitation of the wretched of the earth?

After the death of his father, Marx's estrangement from his mother was virtually complete; relations with his sisters were never warm. The contest with his mother over what was due him from his father's legacy embittered a connection that was already strained, and wove a web of psychological negations that shaped his feelings toward himself and the world. From childhood until death, Karl Marx was a formidable man of rage, bristling with sarcasm, and with few exceptions contemptuous of those with whom he worked. He was also a man of genius, passionate in love and in hate. His conduct toward his mother was brutal to the end.

Marx had finally received a substantial portion of his father's estate through the intervention of an uncle, a Dutch merchant named Lion Philips, husband of his mother's sister Sophie. The name of the Philips Company has survived the vicissitudes of the system whose apocalyptic end his nephew had foretold. The correspondence between Marx and the Philips family reveals Marx the manipulator, who used them as a source of income in the worst of times, and grew distant from them when their aid was no longer necessary. The worldly businessman Lion Philips knew something of Marx's revolutionary activities, but he respected this untamed relative as a writer. For a brief while he acted as a surrogate father. At one period when their relations were lively Marx stayed at the Philips house because of a completely disabling attack of carbuncles, and the "worthy old gentleman" himself applied poultices to Marx's intimate parts. Karl appears to have had a genuine affection for Uncle Lion, and in gratitude for the tender care given him at Zalt-Bommel wrote that, despite the carbuncles and furuncles, he considered the two months he spent in his house one of the happiest episodes of his life. Marx could be a charmer when he set out to seduce, though he found it difficult to flatter and praise a man unless he admired him in some measure.

One incident in the friendship of Marx and Lion Philips pierced Marx's armor of Jewish denial: in a letter he mentioned in passing that Benjamin Disraeli was their "Stammgenosse" (of the same stock). This was perhaps Marx's sole reference to his Jewish origin. Accepting kinship with the prominent English politician and writer whose father, like Marx's, had converted, was another futile attempt to denature himself. To be a "relative" of the famous English dandy was a snobbish effort to be cleansed. When his uncle died, Marx eulogized him as a Voltairean gentleman, a rare example of a note of appreciation about a benefactor, not counting Engels and Wilhelm Wolff, who left Marx his life-savings.

Lion Philips had many children, and this crowd of cousins served as a sort of replacement for Marx's own family of sisters and brothers, on whom he had turned his back. Affectionate letters are addressed to Antoinette Philips, a cousin. There were material rewards for Marx in the relationship, but after Engels arranged to give him an annuity for the rest of his life, the ties with the Philips family were loosened. The son of Lion Philips refused to contribute to a guarantee for the French translation of *Das Kapital,* though he was willing to send his cousin money when he was in dire need. Marx's public identification with the Paris Commune, though in private he had opposed it as foolhardy, made it difficult for Dutch bourgeois to fraternize with the leader of an international movement that aroused terror in the breasts of right-thinking people. After the liquidation of the Commune, socialism and communism could no longer be disguised as deviant intellectual orientations on which one might frown but still tolerate in familial and personal relations.

If to Marx Jews were dirty morally and physically and he was a Jew, his denied origins gnawed at his guts on some level of consciousness throughout his life. The Jew who would not come out of the closet is a stereotype of the modern world. The body's vengeance for the cover-up has assumed many forms. Though a skeptical doctor might well doubt whether the bacteria of a skin disease as common as carbuncles were instruments of Jehovah's punishment for Marx's violation of the commandment to honor father and mother, the son's rejection of the bond between mother and child had grievous consequences. He is loathing his own nature, his own body. The carbuncles are external marks of the sin and can never be made to disappear, not with the swallowing of drops of arsenic in Fowler's Solution, the lancing of the "curs," as he dubbed the boils, or the administration of poultices on the wounded areas. The carbuncles vanished for a while, only to re-emerge in times of psychic distress. The wish that his mother were dead, plainly written in a letter to his protector Engels, was followed within a year by the actual event, and soon afterward by another attack of carbuncles that laid him low.

To "them," the gentiles, Marx was always a Jew despite the ritual sprinkling of the Lutheran baptism. Beginning with a pamphlet published in 1850, Germans were regularly warned by antisemitic writers against the dangerous revolutionaries Marx and Engels, who were planning to establish their Jewish dictatorship in Germany. It was becoming common to point out Marx's Israelite origin. His clumsy riposte was to identify capitalist exploitation with Judaism and to demand the extirpation of both. In their correspondence Marx and Engels seized every opportunity to signal to each other the appearance of a learned book that denigrated the originality of Jewish religious writings. On June 16, 1864, Marx conveyed his delight at the publication of a work by the renowned Leyden professor Rheinhart Dozy on the Israelites of Mecca that stoked the fires of his atheism as well as his denigration of Judaism. The Dutch orientalist had brought out a book asserting that Abraham, Isaac, and Jacob were figments of the imagination; that the Israelites were idolaters who carried around a stone in the Ark of the Covenant; that the tribe of Simeon migrated to Mecca, where they built a heathen temple and worshiped stones; that, after the release of the Jews from Babylon, Ezra invented the myth of the creation and the histories up to and including the book of Joshua, and promulgated laws and dogmas, paving the way for monotheism. Engels responded jocularly with satisfaction that Marx sounded fit again and had not been shaken by Dozy's revelations.

With the object of befuddling the censors, Marx and Engels sometimes used the word "Jews" as a private means of denoting the members of their clandestine revolutionary groups. When they wrote deploring the persecution of Jews in Germany, it was their code for expressing indignation at the arrest of communist party adherents, not a sudden solicitude for the lot of the Jews.[4] The contempt of Engels, the gentlemanly representative of German business in Manchester, was crudely recorded in a letter to a Barmen merchant about the Manchester society founded by Jews to promote German culture: "The so-called Schiller Institute . . . (also known as the Jerusalem Club) has become a purely Jewish institution and between 1:30 and 3, the din there is enough to drive one out of one's mind . . . What's happening is typically Jewish. To start off with they thank God for having a Schiller Institute, and barely are they installed than, apparently, it's not good enough for them, and they want to put up a large building, a veritable temple of Moses, and to move the thing there."[5]

It is hazardous to leap from singling out a major source of inner conflict in the young Marx to ascribing to it the drive behind a philosophical system designed to serve as a battering-ram against the whole of capitalist civilization. But even if the dynamics of the psychological process cannot be accepted in detail, there are plausible elements in the conjecture that the self-hate of Marx, who lived in constant denial of being a Jew, when turned outward was transformed into a universal rage against the existing order of society, and bred a utopian fantasy of redemption. The sequence of a gruesome apocalyptic destruction of the society into which Marx was born, followed by a vision of a future golden age in which there would be neither Christian nor Jew, neither proletarian nor capitalist exploiter, accords with a traditional religious pattern. Buried in Marx's soul was the messianic hope alive in the rabbinic expositors of the prophets of Israel, passed on through generations of rabbis among both his father's and his mother's forebears.

The alien, the stranger, the outsider, Karl Marx, who lived most of his adult life in exile a stateless author—the concise description on his London death certificate—would have been the last to acknowledge his condition in public print. The revolutionary theorist who raised Hegel's concept of alienation to the quintessential denomination of man living in capitalist society never, to our knowledge, ventured to reflect to friend or foe on his own status as the prototype of the alienated Jew. Marx was no tyro at psychological portraiture of those who came within his ken, especially if they were enemies. But with the exception of the essay written upon his graduation from the Trier gymnasium, he avoided an analysis of his own self-image and the religious and social forces that were shaping his nature; the word Jew does not appear in the gymnasium essay texts that have been preserved. His later voluminous correspondence overflows with pontifical utterances about the national characters of the peoples among whom he lived—Germans, Frenchmen, Englishmen, exiled Russians and Poles. With few exceptions, his national character profiles are satirical and derisive. But he shunned an ethnic definition for himself. In a letter to the father of Paul Lafargue, the future husband of his beloved daughter Laura, he identified himself as a Rhinelander, and since he was writing to a prosperous Bordeaux wine merchant, he recalled that he had once owned a vineyard, highlighting his earthy roots and distinguishing himself from unscrupulous Jewish traders.

Later in life the self-loathing of Karl Marx ranged up and down the scale, from outbursts of despair when he wished he were dead through black humor and jesting self-mockery. His model of conduct was the Stoic who would simply maintain a dignified silence in the face of adversity; but he was fully aware how rarely he adhered to his resolve. The lofty symbol for mankind and for himself as the chosen incarnation of the historical moment was Prometheus. Marx found realistic portraits of contemporary bourgeois man in Balzac, a favorite writer, and the human condition in a hostile world was embodied in the bum who deflated philosophical bromides in Diderot's *Neveu de Rameau* (Rameau's Nephew), to which Marx found a reference in Hegel's *Phenomenology of Spirit,* where it served as the source for his concept of *Entfremdung* (alienation). Marx's definition of alienation is deeply immersed in Hegel's transformation of the chief interlocutor in Diderot's dialogue into a symbolic figure of the estranged man of modern times, whose ruthless mockery of his society, accompanied by outlandish antics, becomes an affirmation of a great truth. In 1808 Goethe had published a German translation of Diderot's work, in which the sanctimonious virtues of the Enlightenment were opened to playful scrutiny by the nephew of the composer Rameau and judgments were obfuscated in a jumble of musical phrases mined from the treasure house of excerpts without a beginning and without an end. Schiller, who had been given a manuscript copy of one of the original French versions of *Le Neveu de Rameau* by a young nobleman who had found it in St. Petersburg, showed it to Goethe. When it first appeared in German, the French paid it no heed, but Hegel, the universal philosopher with eyes both in back of his head and in front, took hold of the imaginary conversation and made its hero an exemplar of *Entfremdung*. A copy of *Le Neveu de Rameau* was a prized possession of the aging Marx.

Alienation is an old term in Western culture on which a multitude of meanings have been grafted through the ages. It has been used to diagnose the suffering of the wretch who has denied his God, and in one of its roots in English is related to madness *(alienatus a se);* the doctor who pretends to cure the insane is an alienist. Marx was ever on the *qui vive* for ways of describing the economic process in phrases that would startle and awaken the imagination of readers unaccustomed to the terminology of the dismal science. Man's alienation from his very essence, his labor poured into works over which he had no control, acquired a broad economic-philosophical significance in Marx's portrayal of the modern capitalist system of production. At times alienation preserved the generalized psychological meaning related to Diderot's original intent; and over the years it became banalized as a description of man ill at ease in his own skin and in the social relations into which he had been thrust by the powerful economic processes that manipulated his destiny.

The idea of alienation in the Marxist system assumed universal significance in the analysis of the capitalist mode of production, under which man is cut off from his very being when his labor is swallowed up in the maw of the productive mechanism. The more a man gives of himself, spends his brawn in the construction of the industrial machine, the less control he has over the object of his own creation. In a manuscript of 1844 Marx had already formulated the philosophical essence of his theory: "The alienation of the worker in his product means not only that his labor becomes an object, an *external* existence, but that it exists *outside* him, independently, as something alien to him, and that it becomes a power on its own confronting him. It means that the life which he has conferred on the object confronts him as something hostile and alien."[6]

In the Marxist fantasy-construct of the productive system, the more the individual impoverishes himself physically and psychically, the more manifest the omnipotence of the machine-god becomes. At one time or another Marx resorted both to analogies from primitive religious practices described by travelers and to Feuerbachian anthropologizing of Christianity. In 1842 he read the eighteenth-century Charles de Brosses's description of the cult of fetish gods— primitive man made these little idols and then endowed them with power over the destiny of their creator. The fetishism of commodities, which Marx introduced into *Das Kapital,* was another striking metaphor for the relations of the impotent proletarian with the monster-machine that he had built with his own toil.

This specific usage of the idea of alienated labor is a far cry from the diffuse psychological feelings of estrangement with which the concept of alienation has become associated in popular speech. And yet on the psychic level the ideas have interpenetrated. When by nature man is bound to the body and soul of his mother and for extraneous reasons, whose depth we often cannot fathom, a fracture has occurred, the process of alienation entails consequences as profound as those Marx imagined in the spirit of the alienated worker. When historical circumstances have anchored an individual in his collective, especially one as marked and branded as the Jewish people (call it nation, stock, ethnic group, or religious sect), the rupture of these ties inflicts psychic wounds for which there is no easy healing. It is a matter of relative indifference whether repudiation of membership in the collective is a deliberate act performed with economic gain, interest, or social advancement in mind, or whether the repudiation is the concomitant of forced conversion, or the result of a legally-imposed disability. The torture of a Jew burned in an *auto-da-fè* and the pain of social exclusion are hardly comparable, but in the jungle of the unconscious such distinctions become blurred.

Marx's self-loathing as a Jew was compounded by the realization that he was a German living under the Prussian heel, a feeling that became acute when he traveled through Holland, where he imagined the humblest Dutchman was a self-respecting citizen, unlike the most prominent of Germans. With the accession of Frederick William IV to the Prussian throne in 1840, the hateful despotism stood before the world in all its nakedness, and Marx felt ashamed. But he was young and at one time in the 1840s, when he analyzed this emotion, he discovered in it a favorable portent. German patriotism was a hollow shell, but if the German chauvinists would only experience the first symptoms of shame as they stood despised by the whole civilized world, they would be taking a step toward the revolution. Shame, he concluded, was a sort of anger that turned inward, and if a whole nation were truly ashamed it would become a lion recoiling before a leap into freedom. His Jewish self-hate was never subjected in writing to any such introspective analysis, but he appears to have been aware of the psychological process.

The surrender of his Prussian citizenship in 1843 was the second severance of ties with a collective into which Marx had been born. The cutting-off of his Judaic origins had been imposed upon him in childhood; his repudiation of Prussian citizenship was his own decision and, for the moment, was liberating. Actually, he was no more capable of sloughing his German skin than eradicating his Jewish birth. The politics of the day constantly forced him into assuming an attitude toward Germans and German culture—both of which were being stamped by Prussian hegemony—despite his assimilation of French and English manners. Most of his personal friends and enemies were Germans, and once his revolutionary theory assumed a fixed shape, the fate of the German land mass became the key to the transformation of Europe and the world. In a letter of 1866 to Engels preening himself over the completion of the first volume of *Das Kapital,* he identified his work closely with German culture, though his tone was jesting: "You will understand, my dear fellow, that in a work such as mine, there are bound to be many shortcomings in the detail. But the composition, the structure, is a triumph of German scholarship, which an individual German may confess to since it is in no way *his* merit but rather belongs to the nation, which is all the more gratifying as it is otherwise the silliest nation under the sun!" He then concludes: "I feel proud of the Germans. It is our duty to emancipate this 'deep' people."[7] During the kaleidoscopic changes of the period, Marx was called upon to adopt a position toward every new political intrigue and territorial war among the European powers, and a loyal adherent has often been required to follow him through the labyrinthine reasoning in support of one Prussian policy and rejection of another. In judging passing political developments, however, he had a single criterion, the furtherance of the world proletarian revolution.

Karl Marx knew that he would be rejected by the German university system because of a decree from the outside world that branded him an alien. In the formal surrender of his Prussian citizenship, it was he who in an independent act of will proclaimed himself a foreigner. But in any event he was the tainted stranger. As he embarked upon his revolutionary mission, Marx the citizen of the world considered his state of statelessness one of the inconveniences to be coped with, but since he was no doctrinaire cosmopolitan, he once made an attempt to regain Prussian citizenship so that he could re-enter German politics; and on a later occasion he applied to become a subject of Her Majesty Queen Victoria. Both requests were denied, and he died as he had lived, a man without a country, a circumstance he treated as an annoyance, an impediment to his free movement that he was usually able to circumvent, crossing the Channel under an assumed name to attend secret meetings when he could afford the price of passage. But wherever he wandered, he remained the alienated Jew of Trier.

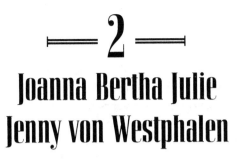

2

Joanna Bertha Julie Jenny von Westphalen

The contribution made by this woman, with such a sharp critical intelligence, with such political tact, a character of such energy and passion,
with such dedication to her comrades-in-struggle—her contribution to
the movement over almost forty years has not become public knowledge;
it is not inscribed in the annals of the contemporary press. It is something
one must have experienced at first hand. But of one thing I am sure: just
as the wives of the Commune refugees will often remember her—so, too,
will the rest of us have occasion enough to miss her bold and wise advice,
bold without ostentation, wise without ever compromising her honor to
even the smallest degree.

—Friedrich Engels at Jenny Marx's grave

Of Karl Marx's friends at the Trier gymnasium we know nothing
beyond his comradeship with Edgar von Westphalen, the odd-
ball son of a prominent Prussian civil servant, Baron Ludwig
von Westphalen. Edgar was no great intellect, but he came to share
Marx's radical opinions, participated haphazardly in clandestine
organizations, went off to America, and then from time to time
turned up penniless in the Marxes' London household—sometimes
when they were themselves in dire distress. When Marx was in
Berlin on one of his quests for literary work he visited Edgar, who
had finally secured a minor official post. In later years Marx considered him a nuisance, but he never scorned him.

Through Edgar, Marx became an intimate in the Westphalen
family, and he was soon taken up by the aging Baron Ludwig, who
appreciated his sharp mind and adopted him as a young friend.
From the baron he learned to admire Homer and Shakespeare. On

their long walks Marx listened to recitations of poetic classics by the Enlightenment gentleman, a practice he followed in later years on outings with his own children. In gratitude Marx dedicated his doctoral dissertation to him.

At the age of seventeen or eighteen, Karl Marx fell in love with the baron's daughter, the belle of Trier, Joanna Bertha Julie Jenny von Westphalen, who was four years his senior. His affections were returned, but not everyone in the House of Westphalen looked benignly on this suitor. Jenny and Edgar were the baron's children from his second marriage and there was a bond between them that allowed for the easy acceptance of young Karl; there was also a close friendship between Sophie Marx and Jenny. The first marriage of Baron Ludwig had produced progeny of a different stripe: Jenny's half-brother, Ferdinand von Westphalen, fancied himself a Prussian of the old school, and the idea of an alliance with a former Jew was distasteful to him. The obstacles he placed in the way of the lovers are hinted at in correspondence; after Baron Ludwig's death in 1842, the ambitious bureaucrat, who later became Prussian minister of the interior, raised difficulties for his half-sister, as a wave of antisemitism swept through the Germanic world. Whatever his personal motives—and there were palpable social reasons for opposing the union—garden-variety repugnance to an alliance with a Jew, baptized or not, was the norm in the circle of Prussian officials of the post-Napoleonic period.

Nor did Marx's mother smooth the path for the young couple after her husband's death. The details of the estrangement between the two families while Marx was at the University of Berlin are veiled, since a letter to Karl on May 29, 1840, in which Henriette Marx burst forth with a litany of complaints against the Westphalens, is partly torn and often illegible. They had slighted her, failed to send condolences on the death of her husband, humiliated her. When Marx's brother Hermann went to visit Jenny, he was received not in the family quarters but in Edgar's room. Mrs. Marx claimed that she had tried to protect her son from knowledge of the sufferings she endured on his behalf. Her wailing and whining pervaded the mangled narrative. Such plaintive letters from his mother only deepened Karl's aversion to her. On more than one occasion he deplored her propensity to "take command." To his father he had confided his most chimerical plans for the future as a professor or a writer, but what could he say to this ignorant woman of whom he was ashamed?

The victim of these family squabbles was Jenny von Westphalen. When Marx became engaged to her during the fall of 1836, his father, privy to their secret, voiced his enthusiastic approval, accompanying his consent with long expositions of the new responsibilities this alliance with a noble family entailed. He seized the opportunity to persuade his son to abandon poesy and philosophical studies, and to turn to practical courses that would assure him a secure status. Heinrich Marx's affection for Jenny, who spent long hours in their house, was not merely a polite formula, as he dwelt on the sacrifices the marriage would mean for the beautiful, good woman whom so many other suitors in Trier had courted in vain. In the meantime, Jenny, waiting for her Karl, who was miles away at the University of Berlin, vowed eternal devotion in letters of passionate love.

Like his son, Marx's father was captivated by Jenny, but he had keen insight into the character of Karl and the fragility of his fiancée, and he was full of anxiety about their life together. "I will not and cannot conceal my weakness for you," Heinrich Marx admitted to Karl in a letter of March 2, 1837,

> At times my heart delights in thinking of you and your future. And yet at times I cannot rid myself of ideas which arouse in me sad forebodings and fear, when I am struck as if by lightning by the thought: Is your heart in accord with your head, your talents? Has it room for the earthly but gentler sentiments which in this vale of sorrow are so essentially consoling for a man of feeling? And since that heart is obviously animated and governed by a demon not granted to all men, is that demon heavenly or Faustian? Will you ever . . . be capable of truly human domestic happiness? Will—and this doubt has no less tortured me recently since I have come to love a certain person like my own child—will you ever be capable of imparting happiness to those immediately around you?
>
> What has evoked this train of ideas in me, you will ask. Often before, anxious thoughts of this kind have come into my mind, but I easily chased them away, for I always felt the need to surround you with all the love and care of which my heart is capable, and I always like to

forget. But I note a striking phenomenon in Jenny. She, who is wholly devoted to you with her childlike, pure disposition, betrays at times, involuntarily and against her will, a kind of fear, a fear laden with foreboding, which does not escape me, which I do not know how to explain, and all trace of which she tried to erase from my heart, as soon as I pointed it out to her. What does that mean, what can it be? I cannot explain it to myself, but unfortunately my experience does not allow me to be easily led astray.[1]

As the years of the betrothal dragged on, the dark side of Jenny betrayed itself in letters to her dear Karl that are difficult to unravel, as she becomes unsure of the permanence of his love. There are intimations that she has been gravely ill; she longs for a spiritual union with him, obliterating everything else in the world, finding solace and happiness in his person alone. Much of the language may derive from the prevailing romantic prose of the time—parallels are easy to discover—and yet there is a unique poignancy in her writing. In response to critical remarks in one of Marx's lost letters she laid bare her feelings, dilated on a woman's frailty, and begged him to be tender, taking into consideration her unfortunate circumstances.

> Oh, Karl, if only I could rest safe in your love, my head would not burn so, my heart would not hurt and bleed so. If only I could rest safe forever in your heart, Karl, God knows my soul would not think of life and cold prose. But, my angel, you have no regard for me, you do not trust me, and your love, for which I would sacrifice everything, everything, I cannot keep fresh and young. In that thought lies death; once you apprehend it in my soul, you will have greater consideration for me when I long for consolation that lies outside your love. I feel so completely how right you are in everything, but think also of my situation, my inclination to sad thoughts, just think properly over all that as it is, and you will no longer be so hard toward me. If only you could be a girl for a while and, moreover, such a peculiar one as I am.

Her turmoil bred fear that for her sake Karl might become embroiled in a quarrel leading to a duel—an incident real or imagined about which we know nothing more. And the dread assumed a bizarre shape in a fantasy of mutilation that obsessed her night and day. "I saw you wounded," she confessed to her beloved in faraway Berlin, bleeding and ill, and Karl, to tell you the whole truth, I was not altogether unhappy in this thought: for I vividly imagined that you had lost your right hand, and, Karl, I was in a state of rapture, of bliss, because of that. You see, sweetheart, I thought that in that case I could really become quite indispensable to you, you would then always keep me with you and love me. I also thought that then I could write down all your dear, heavenly ideas and be really useful to you. All this I imagined so naturally and vividly that in my thoughts I continually heard your dear voice, your dear words poured down on me and I listened to every one of them and carefully preserved them for other people. You see, I am always picturing such things to myself, but then I am happy, for then I am with you, yours, wholly yours.

Apparently Karl had heard a rumor that Jenny was unfaithful to him, that is, carrying on lighthearted conversations with other men, a thought that horrified her as she recollected moments of intimacy with her dear one, when he kissed her and held her close. This letter, written sometime in 1839–1840, confirms that she had been seriously ill but was recuperating. The nature of her malady is obscure; it still took her an hour to read a page, without absorbing it. She begs Karl for a book that could divert her a little, but it has to be a work of a special kind that would exercise her mind. The requirement could not be met easily—"a bit learned so that I do not understand everything, but still manage to understand something as if through a fog, a bit such as not everyone likes to read; and also no fairy-tales and no poetry, I can't bear it."[2] One wonders what she made of the wild, cryptic love poems that Karl sent her before he realized that his literary gifts did not lie in that direction.

A year or more later, the mysterious, lingering affliction still confined Jenny to her bed and to a cautious regimen supervised by her affectionately vigilant mother. Perhaps her malady was recurrent and this was a second episode. Whatever the physical consequences of her illness, her passion for her absent lover was undiminished and expressed itself in cloying phrases. "Just a kiss on each finger and then away into the distance. Fly away, fly to my Karl, and press as warmly on his lips as you were warm and tender when starting out towards them."[3]

In the nineteenth-century German world the marriage of a Jew, converted or not, to a gentile woman was the ultimate declaration of independence from "the religion of Moses and Israel." The chief contemporary Jewish pretenders to the leadership of the proletariat, which was by definition gentile, moved along the same road. Moses Hess married his French mistress Sibylle despite her ill repute. Marx and Lassalle allied themselves with gentile women, distancing themselves even further from their ancestral stock by choosing scions of the German nobility. (No deliberate planned acts to achieve assimilation through such mechanisms are implied; unconscious devices were triggered in the souls of these men that led to the same consequences.) Marx succeeded in winning his Jenny, the daughter of an ennobled German civil servant and the distant relative of a Scottish earl, Archibald of Argyle. Lassalle was killed in the attempt to acquire the daughter of a minor Prussian court official with a title. Often intermarriage made parents vigilant to preserve their new gentile status, an effort to ensure that future generations would be free of the taint of Jewish origins. For two of Marx's daughters, Laura and Jenny, the intermarriage achieved its purpose, as they wed Frenchmen and bore gentile children. The third, Eleanor, lived in common-law marriage with a gentile; while remaining firm in the atheism of her father, she denied him after his death in her own way by agitating among Jewish workers in Whitechapel in the 1890s, and boasting of his Jewish origins. In the early 1840s the acquisition of a noble gentile wife, like Marx's bonding with tall, blond Engels, was a symbolic act whose significance Marx would have scoffed at, though it cannot be stricken from his secret history.

The four-year age difference between Jenny and Karl did not fit the customary marital pattern and leads to speculation about whether he was seeking a surrogate for the mother whom he rejected and she was in search of a son rather than a provider and protector. The age discrepancy and the Christian religion of Marx's bride prefigure the experience of another Jewish disturber of the universe, Albert Einstein, at seventeen the lover of a Serbian girl of twenty-one, Mileva Marić, who married him over the strenuous opposition of their families. Jenny Marx and Mileva Marić, both talented women in their own right, paid dearly for their misalliances and devotion to the child-men in whom they recognized genius.

The young Marx dazzled his elders and sometimes his peers with his brilliance. On first acquaintance Moses Hess, then an autodidact litterateur, wrote dithyrambs about Marx's philosophical genius, which combined the profundity of Leibniz, Spinoza, and Hegel with the passion of the eighteenth-century *philosophes*. Hess, six years older than Marx and already the author of weighty books—*Die heilige Geschichte der Menschheit von einem Jünger Spinozas* (The Sacred History of Mankind by a Disciple of Spinoza; 1837) and *Die europäische Triarchie* (The European Triarchy; 1841)—proclaimed Marx his *Abgott* (idol) and was prepared to sit at his feet if he ever lectured on philosophy. In a few years they were at each other's ideological throats. Karl Köppen, a Berlin gymnasium teacher and the author of works on oriental religion, complained of young Marx's neglect in the language of a rejected lover. The wealthy Saxon litterateur and editor Arnold Ruge, dismayed by the low intellectual level of Germany after Hegel's death, planned to issue German-French yearbooks in cooperation with the bright young man, then in his early twenties. In 1842 Marx contributed to and soon became the editor of the Cologne *Rheinische Zeitung* (Rhenish Times), a bourgeois newspaper Moses Hess organized. Many years were to pass before Engels and after him Lenin proclaimed Marx a genius, but the legend of Marx the philosophical prodigy, perhaps heir to Hegel, had long been in the making. There was something overpowering in the energy, debating skill, passion, of this young man who had not yet published a book of his own and whose only words in print were newspaper articles. His own father had been snowed under by his philosophical plans and poetic raptures, neither of which he could comprehend.

Seven years passed between the secret engagement of Jenny and Karl and their marriage in 1843. On the eve of the union Karl, now editor of the *Rhenish Times,* in a letter to his friend Arnold Ruge proclaimed his love for his bride-to-be and rehearsed the tribulations they had both endured, an account mottled with opaque passages whose meaning is elusive.

> I can assure you without romanticism that I am head over heels in love, and indeed in the most serious way. I have been engaged for more than

seven years, and for my sake my fiancée has fought the most violent battles which almost undermined her health, partly against her pietistic aristocratic relatives, for whom the "Lord in heaven" and the "lord in Berlin" are equally objects of religious cult, and partly against my own family, in which some priests and other enemies of mine have ensconced themselves. For years, therefore, my fiancée and I have been engaged in more unnecessary and exhausting conflicts than many who are three times our age and continually talk of their "life experience."[4]

There is no record that members of the Marx family were in attendance when Karl and Jenny were married on June 19, 1843, in her widowed mother's house in Kreuznach. For an extended period the young couple lived with the baroness on her estate, while Karl filled notebook after notebook with lengthy excerpts from French Revolutionary histories. But a decision to go into exile had already been taken before the marriage. In the letter of March 1843 to Ruge, Marx had complained of his suffocation under Prussian censorship of his newspaper, appeared delighted with the prospect of collaborating on the series of German-French yearbooks that Ruge—sixteen years his senior—had proposed, in which the writers would be free of the shackles of bureaucratic control, and voiced his determination to breathe Prussian air no longer.

In the early 1840s Marx was floundering about without a firm foothold on a career or a philosophical system to sustain him. With Bruno Bauer he toyed with plans for a periodical devoted to the propagation of atheism; in the *Rhenish Times* he had to play the liberal democrat for his Cologne sponsors, a group of burghers vaguely committed to the constitutional reform of the Prussian monarchy; his ties with the Berlin Young Hegelians had not yet been severed. He was carrying on a number of researches simultaneously, promising Ruge contributions on a wide variety of subjects—religious art, the Romantics, the philosophic manifesto of the historical school of law—for a collection that later appeared in Switzerland, *Anekdota zur neuesten deutschen Philosophie und Publizistik* (Anecdotes on the Newest German Philosophy and Journalism). The *Deutsch-Französische Jahrbücher* (German-French Yearbooks), to be published in Paris, where the newlyweds moved in the fall of 1843, seemed a salvation; there Marx saw his first significant writings in print. (Only one volume of the projected series ever materialized.)

In June 1844, while Marx was still in Paris, Mrs. Marx took her sick baby and went off to Trier to visit her ailing mother, who had left Kreuznach and was staying in the home of the Trier tax-collector. To the husband she later addressed as "high priest and bishop of my heart," Jenny wrote a letter in which she poured forth her love in language reminiscent of her amorous effusions during the period of their engagement, when he was in Berlin and she was ill and depressed. The hardships of police surveillance had not dampened her ardor. Her identification with whatever Marx felt and thought was complete; the intensity of her emotion went far beyond the stereotypes of romantic love, as she pleaded for more frequent letters and evoked moments of sensual passion.

Jenny's letter was devoted to a circumstantial account of her sojourn in Trier that centers on the two mothers. Her own mother, who had been generous with gifts and money, was in financial straits, as Jenny's brother Edgar squandered the family fortune at the opera in Cologne, while mouthing revolutionary catchwords and assuring his sister of his tender feelings for her. The thought of an inevitable confrontation with the other mother inspired terror; but in the end, the reception by Mother Marx and her three daughters allayed Jenny's apprehensions. Two of Marx's sisters were gravely ill, and in alluding to Mother Marx's apparent gaiety as "somehow sinister," Jenny repeated sentiments that Marx had confided to her in private and that she had harbored during their lengthy courtship. Despite a return visit to see the lovely grandchild Jenny had borne, Mother Marx remained an object of distaste to her daughter-in-law.[5]

The cordial welcome accorded Jenny in Trier outside of the family circle did not deceive her. She knew that it was due to the word that had spread about her husband's editorship of the *German-French Yearbooks,* a success story that she confirmed by her own elegant and carefully groomed appearance. Their substantial friends hoped that Marx would return to Trier and find himself a permanent post. Jenny played her part with style, and received the citizens of Trier in the grand manner. The erstwhile belle reveled in the radiance of her skin and her modish outfits, and told her husband as much with self-conscious pride. Her feminine vanity never faded, making the disfigurement by smallpox in 1860 unbearable.

Jenny derided the words of admiration that she heard from the "asses" of Trier. She knew that they were treading on unsteady ground and that the mole of revolution would undermine their smug satisfaction with the institutions of the existing society. The strike of the Silesian weavers, about which Heinrich Heine wrote his famous poem *Die Weber,* was a sign of the times. Jenny remained true to Marx's revolutionary credo throughout her life, but after they were forced to seek refuge in England there were periods of bleak despair when she doubted whether they would live to see the advent of a new social order. In the summer of 1844 she was still intoxicated with the freshness of her passion fulfilled, enchanted with her little baby, Jenny, and exultant over the deference shown her by the citizenry of Trier. Yet the deep-rooted anxiety of her persona breaks through. She was full of foreboding, and after narrating the vanities of her social success, she admits to feelings of depression and the fear that her saucy frivolity will be punished.

In the midst of her girlish effervescence Jenny retained her rationalist, critical sense. In her June 1844 letter she even dared to suggest to the formidable Karl that he be more circumspect in his writing, more urbane and witty, because in the end a lighter touch would make him more effective—advice that could have no greater meaning for him than efforts to rein in a growling bear: "Don't write with too much rancour and irritation. You know how much more effect your other articles have had. Write either in a matter-of-fact and subtle way or humorously and lightly. Please, dear heart of mine, let your pen run over the paper, even if it should on occasion stumble and fall, and the sentence with it . . . [L]et the participles take their course and set down the words just as they come of themselves."[6]

The years of exile that followed—the Marxes moved from Paris, to Brussels, to Cologne, back to Paris, and finally to London—were harrowing. Expulsion orders by the police of one country after another were molestations they could not take in their stride, as Jenny sold or pawned their belongings in one place to start up in another. In Brussels Jenny was locked up overnight in a cell with prostitutes while the expulsion proceedings dragged on. Marx wasted his money in radical newspaper ventures and in the purchase of arms for abortive revolutions, believing that the apocalypse was imminent. When the uprisings of 1848–1849 proved to be ephemeral, he was remembered for the militancy of the *Neue Rheinische Zeitung* (New Rhenish Times) he had edited in Cologne, but he soon became another penniless émigré.

On May 20, 1850, without her husband's knowledge, Jenny narrated to Joseph Weydemeyer, an old comrade, one day in the life of the refugee Marxes after their first winter in London. Because wet nurses were expensive, she was determined to feed her newborn Heinrich Guido herself, despite frightful pain in her breast and back. But the little angel absorbed with her milk so many anxieties and unspoken sorrows that he was always ailing. Since coming into the world he had not slept a whole night through. Of late he often suffered violent convulsions, hovering between life and death. In his pain he sucked so hard that he created an open sore on her breast, from which blood would spurt into his trembling little mouth. One day while Jenny was nursing the infant the landlady, to whom they had paid 250 Reichstalers in the course of the winter, came in to demand £5 more. Since Jenny had no money, two bailiffs were summoned who placed under restraint whatever she possessed— beds, linen, even the baby's cradle and the toys of the other children, Jenny born in France, and Laura and Edgar in Belgium. The bailiffs threatened to seize everything within two hours, leaving her lying on the bare boards, with her shivering children and sore breast. Conrad Schramm, a fellow émigré and friend who had been a colleague on the defunct *Neue Rheinische Zeitung* and on the six special numbers in 1850 subtitled *Politisch-ökonomische Revue,* hailed a cab and went in search of help. The horses took fright and he was brought back to the house bleeding.

The next day was cold, wet, and overcast and Karl went looking for lodgings since they were being evicted. When he mentioned four children no one would take them in. With the aid of a friend, Jenny hurriedly sold her beds to settle accounts with apothecaries, bakers, butchers, and the milkman, who, their apprehensions aroused by the scandal of the bailiffs, suddenly besieged her with their bills. The sold beds had already been brought out on the pavement and loaded onto a barrow when English law intervened: since it was long after sunset their removal was prohibited. The landlord bore down on them with constables, declaring that the Marxes might have appropriated some of his property and that they were "doing a flit" and going abroad. In less than five minutes a crowd of two or three hundred people stood gaping outside their door, "all the riff-raff of Chelsea." The beds were then moved back into the house since they could not be turned over to the purchaser until the next morning after sunrise. Finally, the Marxes found two rooms in the German Hotel on Leicester Square for £5.10 a week.

Jenny's purpose in writing had been to press Weydemeyer in Frankfurt for any small sums that may have become available from the sale of copies of the *Revue*. She assured Weydemeyer that, despite their sufferings, her husband had not lost confidence in the future and that she was among the happiest and most favored few since the mainstay of her life was still by her side. Time, alas, would erode the faith of this extraordinary woman, who in 1850 could still conclude her letter with the hope that the coming month of June might be destined by world history to witness the opening of the titanic struggle during which they would all clasp one another's hands again.[7]

In the succeeding years, the dingy rooms the Marxes inhabited in London turned into chambers of death, as Jenny lost three young children and a still-born babe. She remembered moments of joy, and compassion for the now frequently ailing Karl replaced her youthful ecstasy; but there were intermittent seizures of anger and despair when she wished she were dead. An ill-defined neurotic disturbance whose symptoms were already evident in Jenny's letters to her fiancé might have been provoked by the stress of family quarrels, the protracted engagement, and the miseries of exile; the hidden origins of her malaise are unfathomable. For four decades of married life Karl and Jenny hovered on the brink of a volcano that periodically erupted. In the beginning "little Jenny" acted like a child-wife obedient to her adored god or "angel"; at times, she again yearned for a union of souls in which the boundaries separating their two beings would be dissolved; or she played the mother to her "rogue" child, her "bad boy," her "little wild boar." In the course of the years terms of endearment became less extravagant, and the melancholy thoughts that possessed her in her youth erupted in critical episodes over which she had no control.

There were limits to the endurance of this intelligent, long-suffering woman, and after periods of exacerbated irritability she took refuge in illness. Jenny never found a secure place for herself in the presence of the man who, when they married in 1843, she called her "one and only beloved, black, sweet, little hubby." In the worst of times the family built themselves an imaginary world: one girl was Kacadou, another Tussy, or the empress of China, or heiress to the empress. Marx himself was usually Mohr (Moor), or Old Nick, or the Old One. Friedrich Engels was the General—it took years before Marx regularly addressed him as Fred. Mrs. Marx stuck to the formal "my dear Mr. Engels" for a long time, though ultimately she confided freely in him.

March 1851 was a period of utter disorder in the Marx household. A plea for money to Jenny's mother was refused because her son Edgar had been sent off to Mexico with the remains of the family fortune. Marx threatened to draw bills on his own mother and, in order to embarrass her in case of nonpayment, to appear on Prussian territory and get himself incarcerated. But on second thought he abandoned the idea for political reasons: since his enemies were touting it about that the workers were deserting him and that his popularity had waned, such a *coup de désespoir* might be misinterpreted as mere political histrionics. His mother replied in insolent terms and warned him that she would protest any bill drawn on her. Jenny Marx gave birth to a daughter, Franziska, who did not live more than a year. Though the birth had been an easy one, Mrs. Marx, overwhelmed by domestic troubles, became ill. There was not a farthing in the house; the family was constantly harassed by tradesmen demanding their due; and old loans from creditors were called in. In a state of bewilderment, Marx in his correspondence mingled the rehearsal of his financial disarray with rumors from Germany that he had exploited the workers for selfish purposes and aspired to dictatorship. And then the final blow: while he was up to his neck in "petty-bourgeois muck" it became apparent that their housekeeper, Helene Demuth, was more than six months pregnant—that at least is the inference to be drawn from two letters to Engels in which Marx alludes to a *mystère*. Matters had taken a tragi-comic turn, he wrote, but after some hesitation he decided to postpone the complete revelation until he was able to visit Engels in Manchester.

The solution to the *mystère* was openly disclosed to stalwarts of the German Social Democratic Party decades later, when Louise Freyberger described the deathbed scene of Friedrich Engels to August Bebel in a letter written on September 2 and 4, 1898. Freyberger, married to Karl Kautsky in 1883, divorced six years later, and remarried in 1894 to a Dr. Ludwig Freyberger, had been managing Engels' household since the death of Helene Demuth in 1890. Though Freyberger had a reputation for flightiness and intrigue, on first examination her account of the *mystère* is generally plausible.

For nearly fifty years it had been kept secret that Karl Marx committed adultery with the peasant servant-girl Jenny's mother had sent them from her own household, while Mrs. Marx was in Holland begging in vain for a loan from Uncle Lion Philips. Engels, out of consideration for Jenny's health, took upon himself the sin of his revolutionary elder, falsely confessed to paternity of the infant, who was born June 23, 1851, and arranged for foster parents. Only on his deathbed in 1895 did Engels betray Marx's *mystère* to his daughter Eleanor, scribbling on a slate since he was suffering from cancer of the esophagus. Named Freddy, the boy was brought up as an ordinary worker and led a dreary existence after an unfortunate marriage.

The Freyberger letter from which details of the episode are derived exists only in a typescript copy in the Amsterdam archives of the Internationaal Instituut voor Sociale Geschiedenis; there is no record of the whereabouts of the original, and the keepers of the typescript surmise that it was made sometime in the 1920s. Upon close scrutiny details of the story told by Louise Freyberger leave some room for doubt, though if it is considered in conjunction with the later behavior of the three Marx sisters toward Freddy, the paternity of Karl Marx appears to be reasonably well established.

Though Friedrich Lessner and Karl Pfänder, old comrades from 1848 and the early years of the International, and perhaps Laura

Marx and Louise Freyberger, had earlier intimations of Marx's paternity, Engels' Manchester friend, the lawyer Sam Moore, was told the facts a few days before the General's death. When he informed Eleanor Marx, she refused to believe it and said the General lied, that he had always admitted he was the father. Upon further direct questioning Engels repeated his testimony to Sam Moore, adding that Tussy (Eleanor Marx) wanted to make an idol of her father.

According to Louise Freyberger, the General then empowered Moore, her husband Ludwig, and herself to make use of their information only if he were accused of shabbiness toward Freddy, since he did not want his name maligned when it no longer served any purpose. He had intervened simply to protect Marx from a bitter family crisis. Freddy looked ridiculously like Marx, Louise thought, and it would take blind prejudice to see in Freddy's plainly Jewish face and his thick blue-black hair any resemblance to the General. She also claimed she had seen the letter in which Marx originally informed his friend of Helene's pregnancy. Freddy never learned who his father was either from his mother or from the General.

Louise piled on gossipy details of the episode, some of which are suspect.

> When I first came to London and I learned to know Freddy, old Nimm [one of Helene Demuth's nicknames in the family] introduced him to me as her lover and he came regularly every week to visit her, but it is remarkable that he never entered through the visitor's entrance, always through the kitchen. Only when I came to the General's house and he continued his visits did I see to it that he enjoyed all the rights of a visitor.
>
> For Marx separation from his wife, who was fearfully jealous, always presented itself before his eyes. He never loved the boy. The scandal would have been too great. He never dared do anything for the boy. He was put out to board with a Mrs. Louis, I believe she is spelled that way, and he named himself after his foster mother. Only after Nimm's death did he assume the name Demuth. That Mrs. Marx once fled London and went to Germany and that Marx and his wife did not sleep together for many years Tussy knew very well. But it never suited her to give the real reason for this. She worshiped her father and made up the prettiest legends.

In closing, Louise "naturally" gave August Bebel the right to use her letter "if it should be absolutely necessary."[8]

While in their writings Marx and Engels were preparing mankind for the coming of the new man, promising a magical purification of love relationships between men and women once they were emancipated from the sordid cash nexus that governed bourgeois marriage, flesh-and-blood Freddy Demuth grew up in working-class London, a remnant of the old order that Marx and Engels could not in their own lives transcend—*Aufhebung* would have been the pompous Hegelian term. In 1895 Freddy appeared in the railway station from which Engels' body was transported to the crematorium. The sisters, who seem to have accepted the fact of Marx's paternity, on occasion sent Freddy small gifts of money. Only Eleanor established a warm personal bond with her half-brother. The abandonment of this son, his only male offspring who survived, reveals Marx in one of his most cowardly and chilling moments—though one need not credit every word in the Louise Freyberger letter and there are still unanswered questions related to the incident.

It is possible that Mrs. Marx remained ignorant of Freddy's paternity. A single laconic sentence of her reminiscences may be a reference to the birth of Helene Demuth's child: "In the early summer 1851 an event occurred which I do not wish to relate here in detail, although it greatly contributed to increase our worries, both personal and others."[9] Those who visited the Marxes have borne witness to Helene Demuth's intelligence and strength of character. She held the family together through trials that were perhaps common enough among the poor of London, but to which neither the son of the Justizrat Heinrich Marx nor the respected Ludwig von Westphalen's daughter, whose calling card included the identification "née Baroness von Westphalen," were accustomed. "Lenchen," as she was called, was the constant nurse during the frequent illnesses that plagued Marx and his wife. She was praised lavishly in a letter Jenny wrote in the spring of 1861 to Louise Weydemeyer, who had migrated with her husband to America: "In the domestic sphere 'Lenchen' still remains my staunch, conscientious companion. Ask your dear husband about her, and he will tell you what a treasure she has been to me. For sixteen years now she has weathered storm and tempest with us."[10] Letters and memoir notes leave the impression that the Marx household was not a peaceable kingdom. Mrs. Marx complained that as the girls grew up they heeded her less and less; perhaps she was too strict with them, and when they quarreled with her, Lenchen was the person to whom they turned for comfort.

By the end of July 1851 Marx had still not finished his proposed treatise on political economy nor had he found a publisher on the strength of its outlines. He tended to blame troubles at home for the delay, but he was sufficiently self-revealed not to exonerate himself completely in his regular confessions to Engels. "The interruptions and disturbances are too great, and at home where everything is always in a state of siege, for nights on end floods of tears exasperate and enrage me. I obviously cannot do much work. I feel sorry for my wife. The heaviest burden falls on her and, *au fond*, she is right. Industry ought to be more productive than marriage. In spite of all this you must remember that by nature I am not very patient and even somewhat severe, with the result that from time to time my equanimity is lost."[11]

Despite her revolutionary constancy and her role as helpmeet, Jenny was long excluded from intimacy with the friend of the family Friedrich Engels, and in her correspondence with him she was sometimes formal, even austere, while painfully aware that they were living on his bounty. There is more than a touch of disapproval about his Manchester *ménage à trois* with the Irish Burns sisters, and at one party congress she snubbed his mistress. "Mommy," in fact, became the tragic outsider in the Marx household. Not all fragmentary reminiscences are tales of woe, but periodically Jenny's reserve broke down. One incident remains graven on the mind of a reader who might otherwise forget that the Marxist Tower of Babel was erected in the heart of Dickensian London.

At Easter, 1852, our little Franziska had a severe bronchitis. For three days she was between life and death. She suffered terribly. When she died we left her lifeless little body in the back room, went into the front room and made our beds on the floor. Our three living children lay down by us and we all wept for the little angel whose livid, lifeless body was in the next room. Our beloved child's death occurred at the time of the hardest privations, our German friends being unable to help us just then. Ernest Jones [a Chartist leader], who paid us long and frequent visits about that time, promised to help us but he was unable to bring us anything . . . Anguish in my heart, I hurried to a French emigrant who lived not far away and used to come to see us, and begged him to help us in our terrible necessity. He immediately gave me two pounds with the most friendly sympathy. That money was used to pay for the coffin in which my child now rests in peace. She had no cradle when she came into the world and for a long time was refused a last resting place.[12]

The death in childhood of the two males to whom Jenny had given birth, Henry Edgar and Heinrich Guido, was for Karl a far deeper wound than the loss of Franziska; the girls were cherished, but sometimes regarded as a burden. With time, the attachment to his daughters grew very strong, but in his writings Marx continued to treat women as lesser beings.

By September 1852, the Marx family had fallen into the depths of destitution: "My wife is ill, Jennychen is ill, Lenchen has a sort of attack of nerves. I cannot and could not call the doctor because I have no money for medicine. For the past eight to ten days I have been feeding the family on bread and potatoes, and it is questionable whether I can rustle up any more today. This diet was not nourishing in the present climatic conditions."[13] By the end of April 1853 Jenny Marx was beside herself. While Karl was away in the City attempting to negotiate a loan, she took advantage of his absence to write a pathetic letter to "Herr Engels." She recounted her vain efforts to get help from relatives on both sides of the family and from friends on the Continent. Appeals to her sister in Berlin and her mother-in-law in Trier remained unanswered. In desperation she was turning to Engels, openly acknowledging how painful it was for her to address him on money matters behind her husband's back; but after the shamefaced letters she had sent failed to evoke any response, there was no other course for her to follow. Claiming that she could not even depict the extent of their hardships, she nevertheless overcame her reticence to describe how little Musch had managed to get three breads from the baker. To a query as to whether Mr. Marx was at home he had replied, "No, he ain't upstairs!" as he bolted out the door with the loaves under his arm and quick as an arrow ran to their lodgings. Swallowing her pride, Jenny Marx pled: "Can you send us something?"[14] The perennial battle with poverty was alleviated now and then by remittances from Engels and small inheritances from relatives. The death of Jenny's ninety-year-old uncle was hailed as a "very happy event" when "the old dog" left his niece £100.

In 1856 Mrs. Marx took the children to Trier for several months to attend her dying mother and oversee the details of her funeral. Left alone, the Moor assuaged his solitude by writing love letters to his absent wife. One, dated June 21 and addressed to "my darling sweetheart," was a thirty-eight-year-old man's clumsy attempt to compose a message of love in the romantic style of his youth. The effort to communicate amorous feelings and the imagery appear strained. Learned allusions to the Black Madonnas, which he likens to his wife's dark photograph that he has before him, and to Othello—"And love you I do, with a love greater than was ever felt by the Moor of Venice"—sound forced. The stereotyped phrases culminate in an awkward use of Shakespeare's line in Act III, Scene 4, of *Hamlet,* where the prince berates his mother for preferring the new king over his dead brother and commands her to look upon the picture of each. Denigration of the critics who misrepresented Marx's true character is lightened with self-mockery in which his own economic jargon is parodied. "Who of my many calumniators and venomous-tongued enemies has ever reproached me with being called upon to play the romantic lead in a second-rate theatre? And yet it is true. Had the scoundrels possessed the wit, they would have depicted the 'productive and social relations' on one side and, on the other, myself at your feet. Beneath it they would have written 'Look to this picture and to that.' But stupid the scoundrels are and stupid they will remain."

The mock heroic pose is not sustained, as Marx turns to a stilted didactic disquisition on the nature of great passions as distinguished from loves that have become habitual. Distance has made love for his wife grow like a giant. "I feel myself once more a man because I feel intense passion, and the multifariousness in which we are involved by study and modern education, no less than the scepticism which inevitably leads us to cavil at every subjective and objective impression, is calculated to render each one of us petty and weak and fretful and vacillating." In this rare and ponderous monologue on the nature of love, Marx embraces a discourse that makes him sound like Ferdinand Lassalle trumpeting his passion for one of his many ladies. In a theatrical gesture Marx announces to Jenny that he is prepared to abandon love for the Feuerbachian man, for the scientistic conception of the Dutch physiologist Jakob Moleschott, even "love for the proletariat," in favor of "love for a sweetheart and notably for yourself," because it turns a man back into a man again.[15]

Toward the end of this bombastic love letter he catches himself, uneasy lest Jenny smile at the sudden effusion of amorous rhetoric. But the floodgates have opened; he longs for her sweet white bosom, and since he cannot kiss with his lips he must kiss with his pen and frame words. He grows sentimental about the woman to whom he owes the greatest and sweetest memories of his life. As the verbiage continues to pour forth one senses that he is striving to reawaken emotions that have long lain dormant.

Another letter, written on August 8 to his "one and only sweetheart," sends her a thousand kisses and complains of his loneliness, while making odious comparisons with a substitute roommate, the émigré philologist Wilhelm Pieper, who had once served as his secretary and whom he was then sheltering: "I have Pieper sleeping with me in your stead. *Horrible.* In the same room at any rate. *Engels is coming next week.* That's a relief. For 3 weeks I've been as hypochondriacal as the devil."[16] There are not many such outpourings of feeling in Marx's letters, perhaps only in one other, written a few years after his wife's death, when he was alone in Algiers seeking a respite from pleurisy.

After Mrs. Marx's return from the Continent in 1856, money from his mother-in-law's legacy enabled Marx to get out of the old hole on Dean Street and rent a house at 9 Grafton Terrace, Kentish Town, in the borough of St. Pancras. (Jenny's half-brother, Ferdinand von Westphalen, apparently had parted with her portion after a delay occasioned by his initially investing it.) But the problem of making ends meet persisted, exacerbated for Jenny by the emotional and physical strain of a devastating disease that she caught in the fall of 1860.

On November 20, when she had just finished copying the manuscript of Karl's long-winded diatribe *Herr Vogt,* Jenny was stricken with smallpox. Four months later she could describe her sufferings to Louise Weydemeyer with clinical objectivity:

> Severe, burning pains in the face, complete inability to sleep, and mortal anxiety in regard to Karl, who was nursing me with the utmost tenderness, finally the loss of all my outer faculties while my inner faculty—consciousness—remained unclouded throughout. All the time, I lay by an open window so that the cold November air must blow upon me. And all the while hell's fire in the hearth and ice on my burning lips, between which a few drops of claret were poured now and then. I was barely able to swallow, my hearing grew ever fainter and, finally, my eyes closed up and I did not know whether I might not remain shrouded in perpetual night!

When the children, who had been packed off with a few belongings to the Liebknechts, returned home, they could scarcely hold back their tears at the sight of their mother's face, disfigured by scars and a dark red tinge that with black humor she described as "à la hauteur de la mode couleur de 'Magenta'" (at the height of fashion, the color "magenta"). She never quite recovered from the blow to her vanity when she saw her reflection in a mirror: "Five weeks before I didn't look too bad along-side my blooming daughters. Since I was by some miracle still without a grey hair in my head and had still kept my teeth and figure, I was habitually considered to be well-preserved—but how changed was all this now! To myself I looked like a rhinoceros, a hippopotamus, which belonged in a zoological garden rather than in the ranks of the Caucasian race."[17]

Though she had not yet fully recovered, Jenny continued to transcribe her husband's often indecipherable manuscripts and even to conduct correspondence for him with the dispersed members of his revolutionary network. During one period she took dictation in the room that was his study. In her truncated memoir she refers to the hours she spent helping him with his work as among the happiest in her life.

But despite her devotion, Jenny Marx did not follow her husband submissively when the fortunes of their daughters were at stake. She was in charge of their rearing, and in a family dispute her word sometimes overrode the will of the awesome Moor. When Karl was negotiating with Lassalle about a new radical journal they planned to publish in Berlin, she put her foot down and quashed the prospect of leaving London for the Prussian capital, where her daughters were likely to be drawn into the shady circle of Lassalle's friend the Countess von Hatzfeldt, who was enmeshed in a marital scandal that offended Mrs. Marx's sense of propriety. In private Marx could jest with Engels about Lassalle's Jewish "pizzle," or divert his friend with pornographic quotations from French literature, but the Marx daughters were being brought up in a respectable English or German manner and would not be exposed to the influence of Lassalle's decadent Berlin society. Jenny sent the girls to a school that was not free, sewed their clothes, and pawned her own when she deemed it necessary.

In the midst of the abysmal poverty to which the family was often reduced, and constantly dunned by the baker, butcher, grocer, landlord, to all of whom they were in debt, Mrs. Marx, with the aid of Helene Demuth, kept up a semblance of middle-class decency. When visitors like Lassalle came to their flat, she did her utmost to mask the family's real circumstances. But even that egocentric rival of her husband soon became aware of the desperation she tried so hard to conceal.

Jenny's ideological commitment to the revolutionary cause never wavered, and she shared her husband's rage against his detractors in the movement. His enemies were her enemies. She was anguished by his physical suffering during the violent onslaughts of carbuncles and the chronic liver attacks. He tended her during her last years as she lay dying of cancer of the liver. Their long relationship cannot be summed up with a dismissive label. But caught between her memories of childhood gentility and the squalor of existence as an exile, Jenny would recede into states of depression, a condition that had afflicted her since adolescence and that recalls Heinrich Marx's apprehensions. Her periods of distraction were not depicted in detail, and their character is only alluded to in correspondence. They may have had psychic roots deeper than the wretchedness of living in poverty while trying to maintain the pretensions of an aristocracy that was her birthright. The atmosphere in the house was often "forlorn"—Marx's word—and at times he thought he would go mad.

In the fall of 1861 Marx again signaled Engels that his wife's nervous condition had seriously deteriorated. They had pawned everything that was not nailed down. As long as there was a prospect of funds Jenny bravely endured the day-to-day adversities. But the agreements with the *New York Herald Tribune* and the Vienna *Presse* for paid articles were not working out as favorably as he had expected, and his messy arrangements for the printing of *Herr Vogt* had entrapped him in a legal miasma. When Jenny lapsed into a dangerous state for a few days Dr. Allen, the local physician, became alarmed. "He knows, or rather conjectures, where the shoe pinches, but is too considerate to say anything untoward," was Marx's comment to Engels at the height of the "great troubles."[18]

This was probably one of the gravest episodes in the ups and downs of Jenny Marx's psychological sufferings; but her husband's complaints about her illness, never recorded with the precision of the descriptions of his carbuncles, are a constant refrain in his letters to Engels. On June 18, 1862, Marx wrote: "Pouring out my *misère* to you again is very distasteful to me but *que faire?* My wife tells me every day she wishes she and the children were in their graves, and I cannot truly blame her, for the humiliations, torments, and frights to be endured in this situation are in fact indescribable."[19] The reading-room of the British Museum served a dual purpose: there Marx piled up the excerpts from books that were to become the underpinning of the grand theoretical structure of *Das Kapital;* and the library was a place of refuge from the tearfulness of his wife, of which he was not always tolerant—indeed, he acknowledged the limitations of his own empathy.

In their shabby quarters, Marx held sway over his five women; though he was no spellbinding public orator, at close range his presence was hypnotic. His daughters not only embraced his ideas but so identified themselves psychically with his person that living outside his orbit was painful to them. Two of them married men who became minor figures in the French socialist movement: Laura was wed to Paul Lafargue and Jenny to Charles Longuet, both of whom had been subjected to Marx's scrutiny in tests they invariably failed, for who could measure up to the standards of the Moor, the monarch who ruled over his tiny kingdom? The Marx parents, despite their misgivings, finally allowed the marriages of Laura and Jenny. "My heart is as it ever was chained to the spot where my Papa is, and elsewhere life would not be life to me," Jenny wrote not long after her marriage to Charles Longuet.[20]

The fate of Eleanor, the third sister, was tragic. Her passionate love for the Basque Prosper Olivier Lissagaray, a dashing and courageous fighter on the barricades of the Commune and the brilliant author of its history, led to their "engagement," but Marx adamantly opposed the union and for years they had to meet in stealth. (There are indications that, in defiance of her husband, Jenny Marx had countenanced the liaison.) Eleanor led a chaotic existence, and ultimately entered into a relationship with a Dr. Edward Aveling, who was married. Aveling, involved in English radical politics, was accused of embezzling party funds. His escapades and peccadilloes made Eleanor miserable. The meticulous investigations of her recent biographer have not dispelled the doubts about the circumstances of her suicide. Laura and Paul Lafargue also took their own lives. By all accounts Marx's daughters were bright and at considerable sacrifice they had received some education in schools for ladies; but they never became free persons emancipated from their father's benign dominion. The men they chose had idiosyncrasies of their own, and the relationships were doomed from the outset.

In 1866, when Marx's health improved for a while and Engels sent a hamper of Rhenish wine for the family Christmas in London, Mrs. Marx remained dejected. In one of her letters to "my dear Mr. Engels," she permitted herself a rare expression of intimacy to the friend who had sustained them through so many years. For a moment she dropped the mask. "I wish I could see everything *couleur de rose* as much as others do," she wrote just before Christmas 1866, "but the long years with their many anxieties have made me nervous, and the future often looks black to me when it all looks rosy to a more cheerful spirit. *Cela entre nous.*"[21]

A year later, on Christmas Eve 1867, when Mrs. Marx wrote to their friend the Hanover gynecologist Ludwig Kugelmann, her worries were far from over. After a period during which Marx and Engels had played out their private daydream about the many happy events that would follow the publication of *Das Kapital*, Christmas festivities in the Marx household were overshadowed by the sight of her "poor husband," laid low with carbuncles. There was something absurd in the arrival of Dr. Kugelmann's Christmas present, a bust of *Jupiter tonans*, while the Germans reacted to the publication of *Das Kapital* with their preferred form of applause—Mrs. Marx's phrase—utter and complete silence. In her note of thanks to Dr. Kugelmann Jenny Marx gave vent to her pentup feelings about Marx's trials during the composition of his master work: "You can believe me when I tell you there can be few books that have been written in more difficult circumstances, and I am sure I could write a secret history of it which would tell of many, extremely many, unspoken troubles and anxieties and torments. If the workers had an inkling of the sacrifices that were necessary for this work, which was written only for them and for their sakes, to be completed they would perhaps show a little more interest."[22] Even in adversity a trace of aristocratic paternalism survived in her attitude toward the proletariat.

At fifty-three Mrs. Marx confessed that of late her faith, her courage in facing life, had waned. But despite another year of illness she managed to summon up enough humor to tease Dr. Kugelmann for his formality in addressing her as "gracious lady." After all, she was an old campaigner, a hoary head in the movement, an honest fellow-traveler and fellow-tramp—her self-portrait.

The next years would offer no recompense for her dedication to the cause to which a fiery young philosophy student and journalist had once committed her. The proletariat, instead of following her husband, had traipsed after the pied-piper Lassalle. Although she attended party congresses, she was never comfortable with those workingmen and women whose prophet Marx had chosen to be. As they aged, Jenny and Karl continued to work together for the movement, to nurse each other in periods of ill health, to bring up three daughters without falling into the abyss of proletarianization. The bequests from relatives were quickly spent, and not until Engels sold his share in the Manchester firm, settled an annuity of three hundred and fifty pounds on Marx, and moved to London in 1870, did Marx's economic situation improve, allowing the family to live a middle-class existence. By then both Marx and Engels had become patriarchs of the revolution, revered or detested by one faction or another, but too old to lead a new generation into battle.

Late in life Jenny achieved a certain calm, the calm of resignation. She worried about her husband's ill health and disdain for the medical profession, but acknowledged that any effort on her part to persuade him to follow doctor's orders would only have an adverse effect. She begged Engels to use his influence: "For me it was a great solace to pour out my heart to you because I am powerless to alter anything in his way of living."[23] After the defeat of the Communards, she lost confidence in the triumph of the revolutionary cause during her lifetime. Her despondency seeped into letters to old comrades like Wilhelm Liebknecht, in which she bemoaned the impotence of women, who had the harder part to bear in the contemporary world because it was the lesser one. The political debacle in France deepened a depression that had become her normal state. There are passages in which the "our" of her despair appears to include Old Mohr, but often the "we" in her letter refers to women with revolutionary convictions: "A man draws strength from his struggle with the world outside, and is invigorated by the sight of the enemy, be their number legion. We remain sitting at home, darning socks. That does nothing to dispel our fears and the gnawing day-to-day petty worries slowly but surely sap our spirit."

Jenny's complaint about the fate of women virtually repeats a wistful sentiment she had voiced three decades earlier in a letter to Karl on the eve of their marriage, a strange foreboding: "We have been condemned to passivity by the fall of man, by Madame Eve's sin; our lot lies in waiting, hoping, enduring, suffering. At the most we are entrusted with knitting stockings, with needles, keys . . ."[24] Jenny was not very adept at domestic management, and with a vital role in the movement denied her, she was largely bereft of a means of expression, outside her family, for her lively intellect and passionate temperament. Her attempt during her last years to do some writing on her own is rather touching: a few articles on Henry Irving and the London theater and on the political situation in Russia were published anonymously in German newspapers.

Though bitter at the lot of women, Jenny was still principally absorbed with the trials of her husband. Her letter of May 1872 to Liebknecht continues:

> Now I have grown too old to hope for much and the recent terrible events have completely shattered my peace of mind. I fear that we ourselves, we old ones will not live to experience much good any more and my only hope is that our children will have an easier time of it . . . As long as Moor had all the work and just managed, thanks to his diplomacy and tactical skill, to keep the various unruly elements together in the face of the world and the cohorts of enemies, as long as he succeeded in sparing the Association *ridicule,* inspired the trembling crew with fear and terror, attended no Congress and never claimed the limelight, had all the labour and none of the credit—as long as that was the case, the rabble remained silent. But now that his enemies have dragged him into the light of day, have put his name in the forefront of attention, the whole pack have joined forces, and police and democrats alike all bay the same refrain about his "despotic nature, his craving for authority and his ambition"! How much better it would have been, and how much happier he would be, if he had just gone on working quietly and developed the theory of struggle for those in the fight. But he has no peace by day or by night. And what deprivation, what *gêne* [straits] in our private lives! And at the very time when our girls need our help.[25]

In a parlor game Marx played with his daughters, he announced that strength was the quality he most admired in a man, weakness in a woman. Neither Jenny nor her Karl were patterned after these ideal images. During four decades of marriage Jenny was subjected to the tensions of living with a man who was not quite so brave as he imagined when confronted by the bourgeois counterparts of the gods hated and defied by his hero Prometheus. When Jenny collapsed under her burdens, Karl was not always either understanding or capable of dealing with her anguish. Though Louise Freyberger's report that at one point Jenny fled to Germany has not been corroborated, there is a touch of irony in her dubbing Marx her "lord and master." She defended him against his enemies, and commiserated with him over his physical torments during intermittent onslaughts of the carbuncles. When she was fatally ill, she showed a fortitude that her husband often lacked, though she wrote to Dr. Ferdinand Fleckles in Carlsbad: "I should so like to live a little longer. How strange it is that the nearer the whole thing draws to an end, the more one clings to this 'vale of tears.'"[26] Jenny's letters to her old friends, the moving revelations of her thoughts and emotions, are at moments the voice of a submissive Victorian wife, and perhaps an echo of the protestations of her sex through the ages; but she wrote no feminist manifestoes. For his part, her husband often seemed oblivious to the needs of half the human race, allowing their pain to be swallowed up in his abstractions.

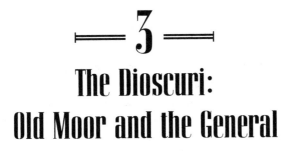

3

The Dioscuri:
Old Moor and the General

Engels . . . is my most intimate friend. I have no secrets from him.

—Marx to Dr. Ludwig Kugelmann, October 25, 1866

What juvenile enthusiasts we were twenty-five years ago when we boasted that by this time we would long have been beheaded.

—Engels to Marx, May 6, 1868

When Karl and Jenny Marx landed in Paris in October 1843 they found a city teeming with intellectuals who periodically invented new paper systems of society, a potpourri of doctrinaires who fought with one another as vociferously as with the bourgeois they denounced—and from whom they were often undifferentiated in education and class status. All of them looked toward the end of the state in its political-bureaucratic format and its outworn economic system; but there was no further consensus among them, and the rival doctrines took off in diverse directions. The Saint-Simonians outlined a hierarchy of capacities and needs; the Fourierists discovered a multiplicity of passions in man that could be satisfied only by an intricate system of psychological combinations; the Blanquists stuck to the old French Revolutionary Manifesto of the Equals, to be implemented on the morrow of a political coup d'état.

How could a recent German émigré, former editor of a liberal democratic newspaper in Cologne, and his wife, of an aristocratic German family, fall in with these noisy antagonists, or join the motley followers of the autodidact printer Proudhon, with his uto-pian fixation on free voluntary cooperatives? Marx had easier access to German expatriates such as Heinrich Heine and Moses Hess, who had preceded him and already formed ties with radicals of every stripe awaiting the collapse of the monarchy of Louis Philippe. They were Marx's intimate friends for a time.

In his essay on the Jewish question, *Zur Judenfrage* (1844), Marx had approximated his theory of the chasm separating a political from a social revolution. Soon he abandoned the idea of a political revolution as a solution to the miseries of the human condition. He ridiculed the purveyors of democratic political shibboleths in France, as he would in Germany during the uprisings of 1848–1849, when as editor of the *New Rhenish Times* he was once more an active participant in politics for a while and stood trial for insulting officials and inciting rebellion. Expelled from Germany, he spent a brief period in Paris again in the summer of 1849, before moving to London, his final place of refuge.

At the time of his first emigration to Paris, Marx had begun to outline his philosophy in a series of manuscripts that enjoyed a great vogue when they were published in the next century. Underlying these writings, which were drenched in Hegelian and other German philosophical terminologies, was the same basic premise accepted by critics of the age, philosophers and novelists alike, that mankind had become dehumanized. Many who were once Marx's friends cher-ished the belief that if only men were enlightened about this degrad-ing process, the mere revelation would restore them to their human-ity. But Marx eventually came to regard such verbiage as idealistic twaddle. A new system of production relations was the only way to return man to himself, and this ultimately involved the abolition of private property and the creation of a social species-being, man-kind's true destiny.

Marx later recollected that, during his extended stay in Paris in 1844–1845, before his expulsion to Brussels, he became familiar with leaders of the *Bund der Gerechten* (League of the Just) and other clandestine workers' groups, but did not actually belong to any of them. That he kept a certain distance is implied in a letter of Arnold Ruge's in July of 1844: "Marx has thrown himself into the

German communist movement here, by that I mean to say that he frequents the communists, though I do not think that he can attach the slightest importance to their lamentable political activity."[1] Any aloofness on the part of Marx apparently did not diminish the admiration of Dr. Hermann Ewerbeck, a follower of Cabet and luminary of the *Bund der Gerechten,* who later eulogized him in *L'Allemagne et les Allemands* as a man endowed with extraordinary intelligence, vast erudition, an iron will, and great perspicacity—in sum, a critical genius equal, if not superior, to Lessing.

Ruge, to whom Marx had revealed himself with youthful candor and who once admired Marx's intellect, was nevertheless not altogether pleased with his ebullient young friend's disorganized work habits, and complained to the philosopher Ludwig Feuerbach in May of 1844 that though Marx read profusely and worked with great intensity and a sharply critical intellect, he finished nothing, interrupting every project he undertook to drown himself in a sea of books. Ruge commented on Marx's increasing violence and excitability, especially when overwork and prolonged sleeplessness had made him ill. As the months passed, Ruge grew even more impatient with Marx's failure to bring to fruition his interminable investigations. A letter written in August, at the moment when Marx was forging his bond with Engels, portends another of the many fractures in personal friendships that punctuated Marx's career and led to unrelenting animosities. Ruge grumbled about Marx's incessant reading and excerpting, though he did not exclude the possibility that this prodigy would produce a huge book, swollen with all the information he had gathered.

The year 1844 was a fateful one for Marx: it saw the initiation of his friendship with Friedrich Engels, a comrade-in-arms who would sustain him through four decades of war against the capitalist system of exploitation and its ideologies, a field of combat onto which he had previously ventured only as a journalist, obsessed as he was in his inner being with an abstruse philosophical quest for the way to spiritual justification. After joining with Engels, the son of a textile manufacturer with factories in Barmen and Manchester, who had undergone a religious crisis and arrived at a tenuous accommodation with his domineering father, Marx no longer lived in intellectual isolation. Engels became the Jonathan to his David, and he lifted responsibilities from Marx's shoulders. From the time of their pact, Engels was the boon companion, a lively embodiment of what the dark Moor perhaps would have wished to be: tall, blond, learned but not pedantic, a man who easily resolved his conflicts, could lead a double life in two separate residences, and was unburdened by conventional marital ties. Without the moral and economic support of Engels, a self-educated man who, while performing his military service, had hung around academic groups in Berlin but was not formally enrolled in the university, it is doubtful whether the mighty warrior could have endured the fiascoes of failed revolutions and the endless quarrels with rivals competing for the allegiance of handfuls of believers dispersed throughout the Continent.

In the narration of events political, economic, and military that constitutes the substance of correspondence between Marx and Engels there are no happenings that are indifferent, however trivial they may be. Viewed as commentary and immediate reactions to daily occurrences, their preoccupation with intra-party intrigues, with the misconduct (by their lights) of one or another partisan—considered the crimes of enemies—appears to be unworthy of the lofty mission they had set for themselves. The very first letters of Engels in 1844, reporting from Paris to Marx, who had been driven into a Brussels exile by the French authorities, on the bickering among the few score German tailors who formed the nucleus of the Communist League's membership, established a tone for the future behavior of these two bourgeois gentlemen who would lead a communist revolution.

Marx and Engels were in agreement with each other from their earliest serious exchange of ideas in Paris during ten days of August 1844—a prior meeting in the Cologne offices of the *Rhenish Times* had not left a deep impression on either of them. It was ideological identity at first sight, and with the rarest exceptions they spontaneously found themselves in accord on all matters of policy. When there were momentary differences in their evaluation of a member of their communist group or the worth of a contemporary writing on religious or social questions, after a second look one of the dioscuri reconsidered his position and unanimity was restored. They checked with each other on the rumors that coursed through the émigré societies in which they lived, mostly to verify their judgments. There were consultations when necessary; usually they arrived independently at the same conclusions.

The social and psychological experiences of their upbringings hardly forecast their future harmony. The father with whom Engels warred was a manufacturer who never questioned the justice of the society in which he prospered or the Lutheran religious tenets that supported his world outlook. Within the confines of his large family his word was law, and he took for granted that he would determine his son's choice of a career and acceptance of a belief system. The elder Engels was given to verbal tirades that still terrified his son when he was in his early twenties, though what got under his skin even more than the threat of being kicked out of the house was the atmosphere of constant disapproval, the "long faces." His mother was the parent to whom he was bound by ties of love, though her muted misgivings were more difficult to bear than his father's choleric attacks, for Engels was reluctant to cause her pain. The obstinate, hidebound father made no distinctions among the political orientations of the young people in the town of Barmen who in the early 1840s attended meetings of communists or liberals, circles where abstract principles were debated. After Engels stayed out late one night his father questioned him about where he had spent his time, and the young man admitted that he had been visiting Moses Hess, a Jew and a preacher of utopian communism. Such conduct was too outrageous for his father to stomach and he sharply rebuked his son for the company he kept. Engels defied his father in secret, but never mustered the courage to remain estranged from the family for long.

During the Revolution of 1848, when a warrant was issued for her son's arrest, Engels' mother begged him to break away from the friends who had embroiled him in the uprising, and joined his father in a plea that Friedrich migrate to America for a while, assuring him a place at their hearth after the storm blew over. "Believe me when I say that your father no less than I will bless the day when you return to us again and once more consent to be our child and walk the same path with us. Then we shall forget all the worry and distress we have endured on account of you. May God soon grant us that joy."[2] Though their emigration proposal was rejected, Engels returned to the fold and accepted a post in the Manchester branch of the family business, a safe haven from which, though he was under supervision, he could become a mainstay of the Marx family. Not that all was smooth sailing in the relations of Engels and his father. When the old man made one of his inspection tours Engels reported to Marx that had he prolonged his stay by a few more days they would have been at each other's throats, mostly over Prussian politics. Fortunately, in between the annual visits Engels could arrange to use his expense allowance for "other purposes," which included postal money orders to Marx. Unlike Engels, Marx had no home to fall back upon after the 1848–1849 debacle and the liquidation of the *New Rhenish Times,* which had brought him notoriety.

Engels was aware of his bondage to the overeating, overdrinking society into which he was born, and he spent most of his life expiating his bourgeois sins. His moving book on the condition of the working classes in England had been written under his father's roof. Since he was not ready to share the lot of the impecunious émigrés, socialists, and communists of various denominations, he devised a way of living in two worlds, participating in the management of his father's companies, while coordinating business trips with attendance at meetings of the embryonic communist organizations and directing the collection of funds for persecuted political dissidents. This complex existence has left its record in the correspondence with Marx; before the family moved to England and the security of the local postal system could be relied upon, Engels arranged multiple maildrops for the two of them. Usually his business address in Manchester was sufficient cover, but the dioscuri were always wary of police intrusions and they took precautions. As late as 1870 Engels was still proffering advice to his friend on how to seal an envelope properly so that any tampering on the part of the Home Office would be disclosed.

For two decades, from the 1850s to 1870, Marx and Engels were separated by about five hours, the train time from Manchester to London, near enough to feel each other's presence, but too far for frequent eye-to-eye meetings. The exemplary British mails filled the gap and facilitated a constant flow of letters, books, and periodicals between them. Their correspondence has been preserved (with the exception of letters destroyed by Engels or the Marx daughters), a unique record of a friendship whose emotive nature heightens rather than diminishes the worth of this obbligato to mid-nineteenth-century European history. There were no forbidden subjects; the diseases of Marx's most intimate bodily parts and the turbulence of his family life were spelled out in minute detail. The letters were also, for many years, the life line of Marx's economic existence, as English pounds that escaped the vigilant bookkeepers of Engels' business partnership were transmitted to succor his hard-pressed friend.

It is possible to define the Marx-Engels relationship, at least to the point where all such close bonds recede into the shadows. They themselves used analogies to heroes of the ancient world in describing their friendship. Or, as Engels is said to have remarked often to their comrades: "In Marx's lifetime I played second fiddle, and I think I have attained virtuosity in it and I am damned glad that I had such a good first fiddle as Marx."[3] Both exhibited a tender solicitude for each other. After the debacle of the revolution in Baden in the summer of 1849, Engels, along with a few other stragglers, had made his way into Switzerland. At the first opportunity he appealed to Mrs. Marx from Vevey for information about her husband's fate during the defeat of the revolutionaries in Paris. Somewhere along the route he had heard that Marx had been arrested, and his letter of July 25th voiced deep anxiety about his friend. He begged Mrs. Marx to free him of his apprehensions. Marx himself replied directly to the letter, in turn expressing his uneasiness about Engels and his joy on receipt of the news from Vevey. The French government had ordered Marx's exile to Morbihan, the Pontine marshes of Brittany, but he was busy trying to stave off the execution of the decree—his wife was pregnant and he could not leave Paris.

At an early date it was established that Marx was the superior intellect whose genius had to be protected, not only for its own sake but because its preservation was bound up with the hastening of the revolution that would bring about the metamorphosis of man from a necessitous to a free being. One of the major instrumentalities in effecting this revolution in human consciousness was the writing and publication of the book ultimately called *Das Kapital,* which analyzed the contemporary process of production in the industrial nations, how it came into being, and what inevitable transformations of this process, now brutal and ineffective by its own previous standards of achievement, were about to take place.

Marx and Engels also shared a fantasy of man living in a "realm of freedom" that belongs to the long history of utopian thought. It was a conception that had been nurtured for more than twenty-five hundred years by a series of imaginative moralists, secular and religious. An ultimate source for the utopian propensity in human nature—a prior question—is as unknowable as that of the religious propensity it resembles. Discover the enigma of one and the secret of the other cannot long remain hidden. But Marx and Engels had formally repudiated both of these propensities as illusory and had chosen to anchor their own dream of freedom in the rock bed of science as they understood it—knowledge that was subject to laws as mathematically demonstrable as Newton's. Only in the light of this belief does the central significance of their three-volume historical-analytical work make any sense. The tomes had to be thick since they were writing for Germans, they joked in private. Engels was the Halley who would cajole his Newton-Marx to formulate in a single impregnable, intellectual masterpiece the ultimate truth about the development of society. Marx had the requisite philosophical acumen and dialectical skill to assume this historic burden, and it was Engels' calling—the secret fire of a pietist was inherited from his mother—to shelter him in his bosom so that he might complete the task. He early recognized that Marx was a man of sorrows whose cross he could help bear and whose wounds he would wash.

In all things great and small Engels would serve his chosen man. Whenever possible he would take upon himself disagreeable writing chores, conduct tiresome party business, console his friend in moments of tribulation in his domestic life. The movement to redeem mankind needed a scientific equivalent of the Bible—at one point Engels used the word—and he would act as a propagator of the new dispensation. The religious analogy would have been distasteful to both Marx and Engels, but for all their rejection of the example, they had no other way to follow but the path laid out by Christianity. Preaching a New Christianity had been proposed by Saint-Simon in the 1820s, and there were scores of other European writers and scribblers and men possessed who were concocting systems of redemption. Many of them were even aware that they were fighting for supremacy like adepts of the rival mystery cults at the time of Christ. In 1894, a year before his death, Engels wrote an essay that appeared in *Die Neue Zeit* (The New Age) in which he elaborated on the similarity between the disputations of the early Christian Church and the wranglings of the multifarious doctrines of socialism and communism in which he had participated for nearly half a century and which he now viewed with a measure of detachment.

Engels was imbued with the faith that his Marx had the only true doctrine; but since they were atheists, there was no reason for them to behave like ascetics or Christian angels, despite the resonance of Engels' name (which German punsters turned to jests). Sensuous gratification was part of the new dispensation, and Engels could abandon himself to the enjoyment of drink and sexual converse, more at ease with these pleasures than was his colleague, in whose nature there lurked a grim, puritanical streak. Marx was possessed by his magnum opus. "The thing *[Zeug]* weighs upon me like an Alp." In despair he once cried out to his friend that he was ready to croak if only he were given a chance to complete it. And when the first volume appeared he burst forth with a shower of gratitude to the "dear, dear friend" without whose aid he would never have finished it.

Whereas Marx lived only for the culmination of the long-term historical process in a revolution, Engels had plans for the immediate solution of personal problems. The revolution was always in his mind's eye, but if the revolution did not intervene and make all financial schemes supernumerary, he had projects for temporary deliverance, such as writing a light-hearted book on the "Woes and Joys of the English Bourgeoisie." What he would do about Marx if the income from his business should be sharply reduced was an element in his calculations, and he provided for that eventuality. Marx and the revolution were the guiding lights of Engels' existence, but he somehow managed to keep them in sight without surrendering the enjoyments of a bourgeois businessman, for which he was prepared to pay the price with long hours of drudgery in his company office. Marx never succeeded in making similar compromises, and he allowed his personal affairs to fall into chaos, perhaps relying upon his friend to save him *in extremis*. Incapable of compartmentalizing his existence, Marx would not perform the basic tasks of earning his daily bread. On the altar of the revolution he sacrificed his wife, his children, his own elementary well-being. He mumbled *mea culpa* when the disasters he brought on himself impeded the completion of *Das Kapital,* the great work on which the revolution depended.

The meeting of Karl Marx with Friedrich Engels was a fortunate moment in both their lives, creating a couple that is rare in the history of social thought. Estranged from the families into which they had been born and from the society that surrounded them, they found each other. Now they would be alienated together. At no moment was there recognizable rivalry between them, since from the very beginning they settled into their respective roles without the hint of a contest: Marx, the senior by a mere two and a half years, became the elder brother to young Engels, a friend who was no toady but a trusted aide-de-camp in the battle against the capitalist mode of production, the historical enemy of mankind whom they had not yet formally named. There was a quiet understanding, an unspoken sympathy in their relationship that Marx evinced to no other man. As if acting out in their personal lives the dialectic that became the logical foundation of their philosophy, they represented opposites that had achieved a conciliation.

The warmth of their union was fortified during occasional alcoholic binges in London, especially around Christmas, when they disappeared for days at a time; Marx bragged about his drinking capacity and his knowledge of wines, quoting Martin Luther to support his contention that a man who did not drink would never amount to anything. In his advanced years Engels in a light-hearted mood confessed to Eleanor, the youngest Marx daughter, that Château Margaux 1848 was his idea of happiness. Marx was a *Doktor* of philosophy, and Engels never formally attended the university, but both had a hostility to official learning that fed their penchant for sarcasm and ridicule. As their bonds became firm, one discerns a division of labor, with Marx developing a theory of political economy and Engels acting as authority on military affairs, nicknamed the "General" because he had served as a military aide to the revolutionists during the abortive 1848 uprising in Baden. Both men were journalists of unusual skill, and when Marx could not or would not fulfill his commitments to editors, Engels did the chores over the elder's signature, as if Marx's energies had to be conserved for the holy work, completion of *Das Kapital.*

Their political activities were coordinated behind the scenes before council meetings of the International in London; together they could outmanoeuvre the minions of the fiery orators, rabble-rousers like the revolutionary heresiarch Bakunin. Although much of the First International's correspondence went out in Marx's name, it was often Engels who kept business affairs on a relatively even keel. Virtually everyone, including the police spies of many nations, testifies to the disorder of Marx's papers and his work habits. He was easily seduced into digressions as he researched materials for *Das Kapital* in the British Museum. When he smelled blood, a chance to embark on a polemic with a theorist who contradicted him, he spent himself in folios of vituperation and Engels had to call him back gently to his primary mission.

Engels continued to serve the interests of his family's textile manufacturing, which he loathed and which brought on brief crises of conscience when he recalled the sufferings of the working class of Manchester from whom his wealth was derived. He longed to be emancipated from vile commerce, which demoralized and depressed him; he felt that he was wasting his time. But after rare periods of gloom his essential serenity reasserted itself; the man would rebound, fortified by an innate self-confidence, one might say optimism, in his character. The love he bore his mother, who cushioned him against his father's wrath, comforted without smothering him, helped to make his relations with women easy and appreciative, and fostered emotional attachments.

On trips to Paris Engels was pleased with his conquests among the grisettes, and he openly frequented brothels. For many years he lived in Manchester with two Irish working-class girls, the Burns sisters, occasioning some clucking of tongues among the émigrés, who disapproved of this radical rich man's exploitation of the disinherited of the earth. In sexual behavior Engels was free of the hypocrisy and prudery of Marx, who was repelled by Charles Fourier's depiction of multifaceted love among the sexes in his ideal society and what good bourgeois called perversities. Although both Marx and Engels inveighed against the enslavement of women and exposed the hollowness of bourgeois marriage (after the manner of Fourier and Balzac), their conduct did not always conform to the ideal images they painted. There were events in their lives that flawed their portraits, blemishes that loyal members of prim and proper socialist and communist parties sought to hide from posterity. Sometimes their peccadilloes were innocent enough. Marx, who enjoyed playing the Victorian gentleman, once chaperoned Bismarck's young niece when she landed at the wrong London railway station and sought his aid—they had met on a boat from the Continent. The hours of waiting before her train departure were spent in London parks and in shops that dispensed ice cream. The young lady, initially startled when her companion identified himself as Karl Marx, quickly regained her composure, and Marx later recounted the adventure with relish.

Engels adopted the whole Marx family as his own and became their chief provider, though he did not have unlimited access to the till of his Manchester company and had to use discretion in withdrawing funds for Marx. On October 5, 1860, he wrote Marx almost apologetically: "Enclosed £5 note E/L 33688 Manchester, 12 January, 1860. I would have sent it sooner, but Gumpert [a physician friend] pumped me for £10, after which I had to wait a couple of days in order not to call attention to myself by drawing out a lot of money at one time."[4]

Marx was jubilant over the death of any relative who bequeathed money to him and Jenny, but he depended heavily on supplements from Engels that were sent in response to urgent pleas. This wearisome and repetitive note in their correspondence did not interrupt the steady exchange of information on war and peace, revolutionary politics, the periodic oscillations of the world economy, bits of gossip about the émigrés, salacious French verses, and anecdotes about medieval Welsh sexual customs. Even after Engels moved to London in 1870 and arranged for an annuity to be paid to Marx, the requests for money continued: there were illnesses that required journeys to the English coast, German spas, or refuges from winter as remote as Algiers.

Marx entertained all sorts of scatterbrained notions for relieving his financial duress. Perhaps with strict economy he could live on the few pounds a week that he earned as a newspaper correspondent; perhaps his mother would relent and send him some money; and when these possibilities proved illusory, he resorted to the most fanciful of his daydreams, the financial success of *Das Kapital,* in whose composition he was mired. Marx deceived himself not only about the impending revolution, even when the rational political analyst knew better, but about a succession of schemes for earning a living. When there were proposals for employing his journalistic capacities, he managed to put obstacles in his own path. He raised impossible conditions of editorial control; or he suddenly could not stomach the political tenor of a bourgeois newspaper to which he had agreed to contribute. When the American Civil War cut off his connection with the *New York Herald Tribune,* which was forced to drop its foreign correspondents, he imagined that another paper would clamor for his services.

An episode that occurred in January of 1863 was the one incident that threatened to mar the Marx-Engels friendship. Marx dismissed the news of Mary Burns's sudden death with a brief, almost casual remark: "I was surprised and overwhelmed. She was sweet-tempered, witty, and clung affectionately to you." He then launched into an extended lament on his finances and futile attempts to raise a loan; but he was vaguely aware of the inadequacy of his response: "It is terribly egotistical of me to tell you of all these horrors at such a time. But the method is homeopathic: one misfortune drowns out another. And *au bout du compte,* what should I do? In the whole of London there is not a single human being to whom I can speak freely, and in my own house I play the silent stoic in order to balance the outbursts from the other side. But to work under such conditions is utterly impossible." In passing, Marx committed to paper a shocking wish: "Instead of Mary, wouldn't it have been better if it were my mother, who in any event is now beset with physical complaints and has lived out her fair number of years?" A step back that followed only highlighted the monstrosity of the sinful sentiment: "You see what strange ideas come into the minds of 'civilized men' under the stress of circumstance."[5]

The infelicitous letter led to a crisis. Engels waited five days to reply to his friend's offhand notice of Mary Burns's death, a frosty, laconic sentence, when even philistine acquaintances had deluged him with their condolences. His condemnation was sharp: "You found the moment suitable to display the superiority of your cool way of thinking. Soit!"[6] Marx soon realized the enormity of his offense, and eleven days later made a further attempt to exonerate himself by dwelling on the desperation of his family:

> It was very wrong to send you the letter and I regretted it as soon as it went off. I did not act out of heartlessness. My wife and children will bear witness that upon the arrival of your letter (which came early in the morning) I was shaken as if it were the death of someone very close to me. But when I wrote to you in the evening I was extremely hard-pressed. I had a broker in the house put there by the landlord, a note was protested by Metzger, there was no coal or food in the house, and Jennychen lay sick in bed. The only way I can cope with such a situation is to resort to cynicism. What especially maddened me was my wife's belief that I failed to communicate to you in full detail the real state of affairs.

In a fit of self-castigation Marx resolved to put an end to "false appearances," to declare himself bankrupt, to send out his two eldest girls as governesses, to have Lenchen seek a place in someone else's service, while he and his wife and Eleanor sought refuge in a City Model Lodging House. To highlight the family's misery Marx concluded his letter with a curious "by the way" which may be a cover for a plea to Engels for aid: "My wife, without my knowlege, turned to Lupus [Wilhelm Wolff], begging one pound for immediate necessities. He sent her two. The matter is for me unpleasant, but a fact is a fact."[7]

On the twenty-sixth Engels wrote to "Dear Mohr" (his early, angry letter had been addressed simply to "Marx"): "I thank you for your forthrightness. You yourself understand what an impression your earlier letter had made on me. One cannot live with a woman for so many years without keenly feeling her death. I sensed that with her I buried the last fragment of my youth. When I received your letter she had not yet been buried. I must tell you that your letter lodged in my head for a whole week; I could not forget it. Never mind; your last letter smooths things over, and I am happy that I did not lose my oldest and best friend, along with Mary."[8]

By the twenty-eighth of the month, after receiving a small remittance from Engels, an obvious token of forgiveness, Marx managed to place a major share of the blame for the whole incident on Jenny. It is doubtful that he appreciated how stilted his new explanation would sound:

> I can tell you now, too, without further ado, that despite the straits I've been in during the past few weeks, nothing oppressed me so much as the fear that there might be a rift in our friendship. Repeatedly, I told my wife that nothing bothered me in all this filthy mess as much as the fact that at such a moment bourgeois nasty tricks and her exacerbated nervousness had made me capable of bothering you with my private needs instead of consoling you. Consequently, domestic peace was disrupted, and the poor woman had to suffer for something of which she was in fact innocent, since women are accustomed to demanding the impossible. Naturally, she did not have any clue as to what I had written, but a little reflection should have made her understand something of the outcome. Women are odd creatures, even those equipped with high intelligence. In the morning my wife wept over Marie and your loss, thus becoming quite oblivious to her own troubles, which came to a head that very day, while in the evening she felt that, except for us, no one in the world could suffer who didn't have a broker in the house and children to care for.[9]

The apologia having been disposed of, Marx embarked directly on a long overview of the technology that had led to the Industrial Revolution and concluded with a tirade against Ferdinand Lassalle's grandiose self-defense in his trial before the Berlin court, an oration that Lassalle considered a scientific achievement and that Marx called a rank plagiarism of the *Communist Manifesto*.

In the spring of 1863 a liver attack halted all creative work: "You will at once understand my long silence if you can imagine a very swollen liver with all its 'appurtenances.' For about twelve weeks now I have been enduring more of this nonsense than ever before. You can hardly believe how it affects someone's morale, especially the feeling of a heavy head and paralysis in the limbs. In particular, one can't bring oneself to do anything, not even, *inter alia,* to write letters. For the past two weeks things have again become bearable."[10] Since total idleness was impossible, he took to amassing diplomatic and historical materials for a book on the Polish uprising of 1863 that he and Engels were planning to write—another project that never materialized. And he was strong enough to start copying for his compendium of excerpts from early writers on political economy—again a piece that was left unfinished and was not published until 1910 in a version by Karl Kautsky that may be considered a fourth part of *Das Kapital.*

As soon as the juices began to flow again Marx gleefully reported on a ridiculous episode in Ferdinand Lassalle's life—his futile attempt to persuade the poet Freiligrath to write verses in praise of the new movement of the German proletariat and its founder, Lassalle. When Marx could strike out against his megalomaniac rival "Itzig" he was on the way to recovery. What he found preposterous was Lassalle's reference to "*my* proletarians," when Marx knew that they were *his* proletarians.

Marx's wish for the death of his hated mother was speedily fulfilled. On November 30, 1863, Henriette Marx died in Trier, and Engels provided her son with money for a trip to Holland to see what he could salvage of his inheritance. There he fell ill and remained at his uncle's house for two months. (The relationship of Lion Philips with both Marx and Engels goes back to the 1840s and figures in their correspondence of that period.) When Marx returned to London he was still covered with carbuncles, making work painful. Perhaps he was paying retribution for the exercise of his occult powers. Apparently his black magic was operating in full swing that year: on May 9, Wilhelm Wolff, the friend who was often the butt of his bitter wit, had died, leaving him about £800; and on August 31, Lassalle had been killed in a duel—one enemy less to contend with in the General Association of German Workers.

When Marx was ashamed of the constant need to send his friend requests for money, he assuaged his conscience by recalling their pact to serve the revolutionary cause together. Descriptions of the carbuncles on his penis and detailed accounts of his debts were staples of his letters to Engels. "I assure you that I would rather have had my thumb cut off than write this letter to you," he moaned on July 31, 1865, after having moved into more spacious quarters the previous year, made possible by a legacy from his mother.

> It is really self-destructive to remain dependent for half one's life. The only thought that keeps me going is that the two of us form a partnership . . . It is true the house is beyond my means, and moreover we have lived better this year than before. But it is the only way for the children to establish themselves socially with the prospect of a secure future, apart from their sufferings in the past for which they have at least been compensated for a brief period. I believe you yourself will agree that even from a merely business-like viewpoint, to run a purely proletarian household would not be appropriate under the circumstances, although that would be quite all right, if my wife and I lived by ourselves or if the girls were boys.[11]

Most of the regular money requests were more terse, and Engels would reply with a bank note or an apology explaining that at the moment he was strapped. The humiliation Marx felt was often concealed, but occasionally a long-winded justification of his condition allows us to witness his embarrassment. The image of self-castration, cutting off his thumb, might afford some analyst a peep-hole into an unexplored aspect of his character.

Almost two decades earlier, back in 1844, in his first letter to Marx, then in self-imposed exile in Paris, Engels had reported from Barmen that in his region one could stumble upon individual communists everywhere among professionals, but not among the workers, who had reached the last stage of degradation in the old civilization, venting their anger in individual criminal acts instead of voicing collective protest by a commitment to communism. At this point in their relationship Engels lapsed into momentary despair. "If one could only show the fellows the way! But that is impossible."[12] Yet despite such outcries of frustration Engels was always wracking his brain for means of gaining access to the minds of ordinary people. He thought of publishing a series of French and English utopias that depicted the future state of communism, a project that came to naught and later would not have enjoyed Marx's approval.

In other early letters to Marx, Engels chronicled his machinations among the communist artisans of Paris to ward off the attempts of followers of Proudhon, Weitling, and Karl Grün to dominate the rhetoric and practice of a movement whose active membership was confined to a small number of half-literate workers. The working-class response to the educated intruders Marx and Engels was at best ambivalent. The jealousy—the word is Engels'—felt by other radical writers and workers because the outsiders were learned did not escape him. Engels was frequently exasperated with the dumb fellows who changed sides without knowing it when momentous guidelines for the communist organization were being formulated. In these tiny assemblies, organisms with a long future history were emerging from a primordial slime. After nights of argumentation in the Paris committees, Engels ultimately prevailed upon the artisans to adopt his three-pronged definition of communist goals, which he dispatched to the Communist Correspondence Committee in Brussels, dominated by his friend Marx, on October 23, 1846: "1. To promote the interests of the proletarians in opposition to those of the bourgeois; 2. to achieve this through the abolition of private property and its replacement by the community of property; 3. to recognize no means for reaching these goals other than a violent democratic revolution."[13]

Despite apparent deviations, Marx and Engels remained steadfast in these principles throughout their lives. Tactics changed, but not the fundamentals. Over the succeeding decades they would refine their communist goals and introduce the idea of historical stages into their statement of objectives; but they never moved far from these three elementary propositions, which distinguished them from an array of socialist, "true socialist," democratic, and other communist pretenders to the leadership of the world revolution, all of them constantly concocting new abstract schemes and systems. The preposterous spectacle of cliques of adherents belaboring one another with scatological epithets continued so long as the German influence was preponderant in these assemblies. As the radical movement became international, a more varied vocabulary of name-calling evolved.

Marx and Engels were skilled manipulators of small committees. Their talents had been exemplified early in the Communist League, 1847–1848, which was engaged in formulating a statement of principles that became the *Communist Manifesto,* and they used the same stratagems decades later in defeating their formidable enemy Bakunin, as cunning and ruthless a combatant as they were. Along the way many an opponent was liquidated. In his *Critique of the Gotha Program* (1875) Marx was still wielding a bludgeon against the followers of the deceased Ferdinand Lassalle in the German Social Democratic Party. The wars of Karl Marx with his enemies in the revolutionary movement are a prefiguration of the struggles, with far more lethal weapons, in communist parties for more than a century after his death. His methods may have been derived from the age-old annals of cabals and conspiracies, the heritage of an unregenerate man; in turn, his refined techniques of underhanded party politics were passed on to communists in the pursuit and exercise of power. If such devices have become the political equipment of revolutionary factions that came after him, the meat of Marx's theory may be less important than its shell.

Marx and Engels created the *Communist Manifesto* after shoving aside those who differed from them through intrigues that modern politicians would recognize as part and parcel of their trade. During this period of their lives, they gave every sign of enjoying the game immensely. The *Manifesto* did not spring full-grown from their two-headed brain. Engels was composing drafts for a catechism or a confession of faith behind the backs of the general membership of the communist conventicle in Paris, in preparation for a congress of revolutionaries that was to take place in London. "This congress must be a decisive one," Engels wrote triumphantly to Marx, "as this time we shall have it all our own way."[14] As in all revolutionary parties, secrecy was of paramount importance in keeping the police spies at bay, but it was even more imperative that revolutionary rivals remain in the dark about their tactics. The founding fathers of communism had learned their lessons from extensive reading in the history of the French Revolution, and they would hand on to future generations the art of altering party documents and plotting decisions behind closed doors.

In the beginning there was something boyish about the efforts of

Marx and Engels to control their "party"—they knew that they were being naughty and were delighted with themselves when they pulled a fast one on opponents. "Confidentially," Engels in Paris wrote to Marx who was in Brussels, unable to afford the expense of the Channel crossing,

> I've played a hellish trick on Mosi [Moses Hess, who had introduced Marx to the French communists and earned the epithet "communist rabbi" for his pains]. He had actually put through a God-inspired improved confession of faith. Last Friday at the district [committee of the Communist League] I took the matter up question by question and had not got halfway through when they declared themselves satisfied. Without any opposition I had myself charged with drafting a new one, which will be discussed in the committee next Friday and will be sent to London behind the backs of the [communist] communities. Naturally not a devil must know about this, or we shall all be unseated and there'll be a dreadful scandal.[15]

Their foreplay now looks innocent enough, an accompaniment to the sort of factional quarrels that beset all human collectives—the virtuous organizers of the American Revolution put on similar skits. When the men of thirty—Marx and Engels in 1848–1849—grew older, disingenuousness assumed a grim mask. In later generations such petty disputes became tribal battles and minor differences ballooned into wars of principle over which men slaughtered one another. The lackadaisical Prussian and Austrian police who submitted reports on the conduct of Karl Marx were a puny cohort in the annals of world revolution; in the twentieth century such functions devolved upon agents of the mammoth Soviet security system, who were far more zealous. Police techniques are readily passed across geographic and ideological boundaries and are transmitted to posterity. They know no fatherland, as victims and punishers learn from each other. Marx was not an innovator in revolutionary cruelty, nor was he a martyr of capitalist agents; but after the appearance of Darwin he came to consider violence an ineradicable aspect of the human condition, the struggle for existence. Social Darwinism thus had its Marxist cloak.

Neither Marx nor Engels ever assumed direct titular leadership in the communist leagues and correspondence committees with which they were involved in the two decades that elapsed between their meeting in 1844 and the founding of the first International Working Men's Association in St. Martin's Hall, London, in 1864, a heterogeneous assembly during which Marx sat on the platform, mute. And at no time in the period that followed was Marx the president or chairman of the international organization that faded away in New York in the early 1870s. Neither of them was a popular orator, with the capacity to bring an audience to its feet in tumultuous applause or to direct action in a demonstration of mass power. They might be chosen as honorary chairmen at a banquet, a meeting, a closed session of a congress, but they could not harangue multitudes. Engels never quite lost his slight stammer and Marx never rid himself of his Rhenish-German accent, which made it difficult for German émigrés from other provinces to understand him.

The dioscuri possessed extraordinary linguistic talents, though they were not necessarily conducive to mass revolutionary leadership. Engels learned at least the rudiments of twenty languages, and both men were quite fluent in English and French, breezily peppering their German letters with colloquial phrases from these languages and from the gymnasium-taught Latin classics that they had never forgotten. Their skills made it possible for them to detect errors in botched translations of crucial International documents printed by rival factions. Marx was a purist who chided his most devoted admirers for even trivial mistakes in diction. The facility of Marx and Engels with words made them ideal draftsmen of addresses, proclamations, manifestoes, and circular letters. Like St. Paul, they could speak to each nation in its own tongue. However odious a resolution might be to Marx as it was first presented to a small revolutionary committee on which he sat, when the text finally emerged from the hands of the master draftsman it was miraculously cleansed of ideological heresies; and when he was constrained to accept rhetorical flourishes that nauseated him, he managed to cover over the scum so adroitly that only when he was ill and absent did the repugnant phrases surface again.

Marx and Engels rarely if ever differed over nuances of language. Engels was the more spontaneous writer. His elegant businessman's script was far more legible than the cramped handwriting of his friend; and after Marx's death, Engels had to give Eduard Bernstein, the German Social Democrat who planned to print the hoard of papers left behind, lessons in Marxist paleography. The decipherment of Marx's unpublished manuscripts ranks among the major intellectual achievements of the Moscow Marx-Engels Institute under the tutelage of its first director, David Rjazanov (later exiled to Siberia for crimes unrelated to his historical work). The Marxian gospel according to Rjazanov remains a monument of meticulous erudition that puts to shame the earlier, bowdlerized publications of Marx's manuscripts by members of the socialist Second International. Since Marx did not write with ease, his frequent deletions, insertions, and corrections turned pretenders to the true text into editors who, in the tradition of Judaic and German biblical scholarship, sweated over *errata* and *dubiosa*. Translators in many languages have been confronted by equally daunting problems, and interpreters have been saddled with the task of guessing when Marx was in deadly earnest, when he was giving voice to black humor, and when he was indulging in private jokes to which only Engels held the key.

As the member of a revolutionary committee, Marx immediately assumed control, and he could be relentless in beating down opponents. Though he usually won in a showdown, there were murmurings in the wings about his autocratic ways. He knew that some called him a tyrant. The front men Marx chose for titular leadership in the International were half-educated workers, a small group of loyalists overawed by the learning of the doctor of philosophy. For years, men like the tailor Georg Eccarius, who became general secretary of the International, did his bidding, and Wilhelm Liebknecht, a veteran of 1848 who later was a backer of the German Social Democratic Party, ran errands for Marx, though they had some differences of opinion. In the 1840s in Paris and the 1850s in London, Marx had access to colonies of German artisans who had migrated partly for political reasons and, just as often, because of the demand in England for skilled German tailors and shoemakers. He had no contact with French textile workers in centers such as Lodève, where new machinery was being introduced that provoked riots, nor did he understand the rebellious miners of Rive-de-Gier, or the Paris construction workers who had organized a strike in the 1840s. The only French worker with whom he had a brief connection was Pierre-Joseph Proudhon, the autodidact philosophical printer, but their exchanges were futile exercises with no meeting of minds.

For a while Marx had found for himself a German proletarian hero, Wilhelm Weitling, the author of an autobiography entitled *Gerechtigkeit* (Justice), who had depicted the trials of an ordinary worker and had pleaded for righteousness after detailing the rough treatment he had endured at the hands of the police, digressing to paint a picture of a utopia in which possession of a watch became a symbol of independence. At first Marx had hailed the book as an example of the potentialities buried in the soul of the simple German worker that might be realized if he were emancipated from bourgeois servitude. But when Marx and Weitling were members of the same committee in one of the many radical leagues that sprouted like mushrooms on the eve of the Revolution of 1848, there was a flare-up of mutual hostility. Marx lost his temper and banged on the table, while Weitling bragged about the roster of his followers among workers throughout Germany and scoffed at the influence of the "learned ones," who could not feel a worker's deep longing for justice. To this Marx retorted: "Ignorance never yet helped anybody."[16] Thereupon, it is reported by a Russian who chanced to be present at the meeting, Weitling turned pale and there was a parting of the ways. Moses Hess was outraged at the manner in which Weitling was treated by the dioscuri: having driven him to distraction, why were they surprised when he actually went mad?

In dealing with intellectual inferiors Marx betrayed a streak of brutality. He and Engels in their private letters constantly deplored the obtuseness of the *Kerle* (fellows) to whom they were preaching, and when Marx deigned to lecture to a workingmen's institute in London he referred to his audience as yokels. Marx and Engels found more sympathy for their sophisticated historical-philosophical doctrine among professionals—a doctor here and there, a radical publisher willing to risk his money on an abstruse economic treatise.

Marx's relations with the English workers were restricted to a few Chartist leaders or an old Owenite or a dissident Positivist, all of whom he ridiculed at one time or another.

Engels in Manchester knew far more at first hand about the condition of industrial workers than did Marx, whose descriptions of their living conditions were drawn primarily from testimony delivered before parliamentary commissions. Marx was the Moses leading the proletariat, the new Israel, out of capitalist bondage, and, as was the fate of his ancient predecessor, when he turned his back the workers lapsed into worshiping false gods, corrupt word-mongers like Lassalle or Bakunin. Belief in his vision made Marx impatient with those who differed with him. He founded no school of prophets, and young upstarts like Lassalle embittered his middle years. In the end, he became enmeshed in political tactics, where the purity of his ideal was always contaminated by enemies. At his side stood brother Engels, who beat the drums for the true doctrine, ever the devoted publicist, empathetic with Marx's pain, never—or hardly ever—uttering a word of reproach that might wound his friend.

The dioscuri had early recognized the need for performing simultaneously two functions in the revolutionary arena, formulating theory and directing practice, and they established a precedent that the communist leaders in Russia and China later honored. Marx in his utopian mode looked toward a time when there would no longer be a separation of mental and manual labor. He and Engels translated this hope into personal terms, concentrating both practical political and philosophic activities in their own hands. In their prime they relinquished direct control of any national radical section only with great reluctance. Putting into practice their theory and their theory alone precluded a division of powers or a division of labor.

Lenin combined the two powers in accordance with the original model Marx and Engels had established for revolutionary leadership. Once Stalin was in control he too had theoretical works published under his name, and he became in a Russian version a continuator—and a travesty—of the dioscuri in the 1840s. Mao, who molded his image after the same pattern, vested spiritual and temporal powers in his own person, a formula that enjoyed the added advantage of being in harmony with the traditional role of a Chinese emperor. The amalgamation of political and philosophical leadership was a key provision of the Marxist legacy, a characteristic of the old concept of kingship that made it difficult to differentiate a communist dictatorship of the proletariat from the brutal tyrannies of the old system. Not much of the intricate British political heritage—so profusely documented in the British Museum, which nurtured both Marx and Lenin—rubbed off on either their theory or their practice. After decades of living in England, Marx and Engels remained continentals partial to the art of ruling broad land masses and suspicious of local or loose federal authority.

Marx's temperament followed a curve that in his mature years moved from depression to deeper depression. Engels was well aware of his friend's gloomy side; he could not cure him, but he made every effort to alleviate his suffering. Marx had a singular notion of Engels' sunny disposition. On the boat trip from London to Hamburg to deliver the manuscript of the first volume of *Das Kapital* to his publisher, Otto Meissner, he thought he recognized his friend's features in the good-natured ship's captain, and in a letter to Engels he drew an idealized portrait that was a composite of his shipmate and his friend.

The correspondence of Marx and Engels is one of the richest repositories of Marx's thought. In a spirited private conversation, the brothers let themselves go, uninhibited by public considerations of revolutionary tactics. Marx was the more venomous of the commentators on the performance of the actors in the political dramas taking place in Europe and America, in which they were mainly spectators. On paper he exploded in impotent rage, charged into enemies and rivals who were thrown onto the same stage with him, rarely letting a character cross it without at least a pinprick. Though he tried to don a Stoic's mantle, he did not conceal his pain from his friend; even in the direst circumstances, however, he was on rare occasions capable of self-mockery, a saving grace.

Though Engels appears to be the milder man, he was not all sweetness and light; he could be a merciless tale-bearer about the marriages of their acquaintances. When his countryman Carl Siebel of Barmen, who helped propagandize *Das Kapital,* sent Engels a portrait of his betrothed he provoked malicious jests: "Very pretty. Marie Antoinette with just a suggestion of the virtuous Eugénie, but very mannish all the same—she will wear the pants. His 'sensible creature' will give him a few surprises. *Madame la baronne*, her mother, was a milliner-cum-shop assistant in Düsseldorf and is still supposed to frequent Küpper's beer garden, where she downs three or four pints in an afternoon. So says the philisterium."[17]

The literary and political collaboration of Marx and Engels has become legendary. But on a deeper, psychic level Engels played a role in Marx's life of which neither may have been wholly conscious. Engels was the nurturing parent whom Marx could never accept in his natural mother. Engels not only provided him with sustenance—the bank notes sent through the British postal system—but constantly worried about Marx's health, especially the accursed carbuncles whose spread Marx would report upon with the intimate detail of a child talking to its mother. And Engels' responses were maternal and caring, as he repeatedly admonished his friend not to neglect taking his arsenic, the latest treatment recommended by Dr. Edward Gumpert. Unfortunately, the bacteria that brought forth the carbuncles never disappeared for long after the first major eruption in the early 1860s.

In addition to carbuncles, Marx suffered the normal illnesses recognized in his times, at least those his doctors identified. When he was a young man, heart irregularities excused him from military service. (His claim was supported by a medical certificate and a bribe—his mother had advised him to offer a modest sum, since those on the take would perform the service for a small as well as an inflated amount.) Liver trouble, headaches, tearing eyes, and sundry respiratory diseases were among the long list of ailments that plagued him. In the summer of 1870 he was afflicted with insomnia brought on by attacks of rheumatism, and he whiled away the hours with fantasies of Paris. From a spa in the Ahr Valley, Marx in August 1877 reported on the state of his bowels. "I would have written to you before now, but when the whole person is stuffed up for days—in my case *a posteriori* always the immediate effect of the journey, and which taking the waters the first weeks only consolidates—it makes him totally incapable of action."[18]

For two decades the virulent carbuncles that kept breaking out despite the ministrations of Marx's physicians occupied a position of primacy among his illnesses. The boils recurred intermittently in the parts of the body they usually assail—the armpit, the back of the neck, below the breast, the area of the groin extending back to the buttocks and forward along the penis. Untreated, the eruptions were extremely painful and kept Marx awake for nights on end; he could neither sit nor lie without agony. When an attack lasted for weeks, he lost the equanimity on which he prided himself. The doctors to whom he had recourse offered diverse potions, and he refrained from letting one know of another's prescription. The local physician, Dr. Allen, probably saw the carbuncles in their most aggravated state, and lanced them in Marx's rooms. After the surgical intervention, the doctor, his assistant, and the patient refreshed themselves with wine that Engels had sent from Manchester. Advice that the victim lead an orderly life, not stay awake all night, suspend his intellectual labors, and eat a normal diet went largely unheeded.

The doctor in whom Marx may have had at least tentative confidence was Gumpert, the German émigré practicing in Manchester who was Engels' physician. The consultations from afar were supplemented by examinations when Marx visited his friend. Gumpert was committed to Fowler's Solution, a medicine administered orally that was supposed to take effect after a number of months—he had the testimonials of two worthy ladies who had been cured by this regimen. Marx in desperation accepted the drug, which had an arsenic base, but would periodically abandon it, to Engels' dismay. The arsenic stupefied Marx, a complaint that Gumpert dismissed lightly, observing with professional dogmatism that it was supposed to have the opposite effect. Though Marx often denounced all doctors, a severe attack would return him to their remedies.

During an outbreak of furuncles and carbuncles Marx would take refuge in forced black humor that could not veil his anguish. In 1864 he regularly dispatched clinical reports to Engels from Zalt-Bommel, where he was tended with care by his uncle and cousins.

This is a perfidious Christian sickness. When I received your letter, I congratulated myself on the healing of old wounds, but the same evening a big furuncle broke out on the left side of my chest under the neck and an antipodal one on my back . . . A few days later, another carbuncle erupted on my right leg, right under the place to which Goethe refers: And when he has no posterior, how can the nobleman sit? This is now the most painful of the known abscesses that I have ever had, and I hope it will finally be the end of the series. In the meantime I can neither walk, nor stand, nor sit, and even lying down is damned difficult. You see, mon cher, how the wisdom of nature has targeted me. Would it not have been more rational if it had visited this trial of patience on a good Christian, a person, for instance, such as Silvio Pellico? Besides the carbuncle on the posterior, you should be informed that a new furuncle has broken out on my back, and the one on my chest is only beginning to mend, so that like a true Lazarus (alias Lassalle), I am attacked simultaneously on all sides.[19]

In checking the proof sheets of *Das Kapital*, Engels tactfully imputed infelicities and faults of organization to the attacks of carbuncles in inconvenient places; he made his subtle criticisms of the presentation of the argument with an almost maternal solicitude, convinced that in a revised edition the book would be more comprehensible. Marx agreed with the criticisms and replied sardonically that the bourgeoisie, if it lasted long enough, would be held responsible for the carbuncles and their consequences. The carbuncles pursued him like furies, erupting at unpredictable moments, in times of stress and on the eve of a triumph. In early January 1866 he was making rapid progress copying the manuscript of the first volume of *Das Kapital* and appeared to be in the best of spirits, when three carbuncles developed in rapid succession in the area of the groin, preventing him from walking, sometimes from moving about at all. Bleeding afforded temporary relief, but in the end he had to resort to arsenic.

Jenny Marx reported that in a nocturnal delirium her afflicted husband talked on and on about the chapters of his book that were whirling through his head. What aggravated his condition was his dismay over the goings-on in the Council of the International, where there were interminable debates about preparations for the congress scheduled for February, about a new weekly, *The Commonwealth*, envisaged as the authentic voice of his party, about the policy of the

Reform League and the cooperative societies. In his mind, he alone could settle these nettlesome questions, and there he lay, incapacitated by carbuncles. Amid the torment of his ailments the *Communist Manifesto*, which had been virtually ignored when first published in 1848, was being reprinted, and Marx doggedly insisted that it be reproduced in its original form without alteration of an iota since it was a historical document, proof of his prophetic vision. As illness brought on mild attacks of paranoia, the usual concern over the security of his confidential letters was exacerbated, and he hid behind conspiratorial pseudonyms.

Dr. Gumpert dispatched his patient to Margate when the most dangerous abscess began to heal, sea air being the British cure-all equivalent of the waters of the German spas, while Mrs. Marx took over his correspondence. She was shaken by the pain her husband was suffering just when the completion of his great work was in sight. Perhaps the prospect of success caused him to visit punishment upon himself—a theory that he would have rejected with disdain.

The descriptions of his illness Marx sent his friend in Manchester—meticulous, uninhibited, objective, like everything else he wrote to Engels—sometimes sound as though he is reporting on the operations of a machine in which his person is not involved, or that he loathes his body for having taken over and thwarted his will. Analysis of the capitalist system was the mission to which he had dedicated his life, but the oozing carbuncles impeded its fulfillment. Letters exchanged during the last years of composition of *Das Kapital*, volume I, bear witness to the birth pangs of creation. Marx's clinical accounts are followed by Engels' motherly pleading that he take his medicine. On February 20, 1866, in a show of bravado, Marx reported to Engels that he had attacked two of the vicious beasts with his own weapon:

> Concerning the upper one, from my long practical experience I was able to tell you that it really needed lancing. Today (Tuesday), after receiving your letter, I took a sharp razor, a relict of dear Lupus [Wilhelm Wolff], and lanced the cur myself. (I cannot abide doctors meddling with my private parts or in their vicinity.) . . . The bad blood, as Mrs. Lormier [a friend of the Marx family] says, spurted, or rather

leapt, right up into the air, and I now consider this carbuncle buried, although it still wants some nursing.

As far as the lower cur is concerned, it is becoming malignant and is beyond my control and kept me from sleeping the whole night through. If this diabolical business advances, I shall have to send for Allen, of course, as owing to the locus of the cur, I am unable to watch and cure it myself. And in general it is clear that on the whole I know more about carbuncular complaints than most doctors.

And by the by, I still hold to the view that I suggested to Gumpert during my last stay in Manchester: that is, that the itching and scratching between my testis and posterior over the past 2 1/2 years and the consequent peeling of the skin have been more aggravating to my constitution than anything else. The business started 6 months before the first monster carbuncle which I had on my back, and it has persisted ever since.[20]

The separation of self from the ailing parts of his body penetrates Marx's reports to Engels. When he calls the carbuncles "curs," he regards them as autonomous entities. When he lances one with a sharp razor he is assailing a foe. His eyes start tearing without the permission of their host. Emotions he could not repress were forces external to his real being and he was ashamed of their power over him. He admitted to his confessor in Manchester that he had chosen to avoid confrontations in the International lest they bring on ungovernable rage, a resolve often violated. The illusion that he was a man with mastery over himself died hard. With obvious pride he quoted his London doctor to the effect that he was one of the most uncomplaining patients on whom he had ever operated; he simply endured what had to be done.

On February 22, 1866, Engels replied to Marx's story of the lancing of the cur: "He [Dr. Gumpert] favors your starting the arsenic at once. In any case, it can do you no harm, only good. He thinks [Dr.] Allen's opinion that it does not agree with you is idiotic. He also considers treatment with poultices to be nonsense; it only promotes inflammation of the skin, which is exactly what ought to be inhibited, while it does not encourage suppuration." Engels joined his entreaties with predictions of the dire consequences that might ensue if Marx failed to follow the medical prescription. Engels was the anxious mother threatening a difficult child. "With this eternal delay you are simply destroying yourself; no one can endure such a history of carbuncles in the long run, apart from the fact that eventually you may get one in such a form that you'll go right to the devil. And what will then become of your book and your family? . . . What would become of the whole movement if anything were to happen to you, and the way you are operating, it must come to that."[21]

By midsummer 1866 Marx was in a quandary about how to cope with ailments requiring drugs that might be antithetical to each other. He appealed to Engels on July 7: "In any case I must continue with Gumpert's liver medicine every day, as otherwise I would immediately be laid low. Question: is the arsenic (neglected for many weeks now) compatible with it? I ask because for four days another carbuncle again has begun to appear above my right breastbone. I thank the Bordeaux more than any medicine. For the rest, I work only by day, since a sporadic attempt to work at night (once or twice) immediately had very unfortunate consequences."[22]

The aggravation and alleviation of Marx's carbuncles dominated his moods, which swung from dejection to euphoria and back again. Sometimes frenetic activity served as a distraction from his suffering. When in a crisis he was reduced to immobility, misery wholly possessed him. He could not conceal his agitation from either his wife or his friend Engels. The doctors frightened him with the possible sequelae of frequently recurring carbuncles, and *in extremis* he accepted their treatments though he often doubted their efficacy. In later years, when Engels could afford it, the prescribed rest in the sea air of Margate was shifted to Austrian spas, as liver disease assumed pride of place among his maladies.

When Marx was assailed by physical attacks, he sometimes looked for the genesis of disease in his mental condition (he implied not insanity, but an amorphous and ill-defined state of nerves). "My liver no longer shows any sign of further enlargement; the digestive apparatus is somewhat disordered, but the real trouble is of a nervous character."[23] In correspondence with adherents who were far less intimate than Engels, Marx nevertheless openly used his nervous condition as a reason for failure to fulfill his obligations. To the Russian revolutionary Vera Zasulich he explained on March 8,

1881, that a "nervous disease" from which he had been suffering periodically for the past decade had delayed his reply to her letter.[24] That one or another outbreak of his many physical ailments had its origin in his mental state had been a self-diagnosis for many years. He had written to Engels on October 19, 1867: "My illness always comes from my head."[25]

In Marx's day the attribution of a physical ailment in males to psychic causes was rather uncommon. When Marx delved into the contradictions of the capitalist system, he discovered formulas for their resolution; his own mind-body connection was not subjected to so thorough an analysis. An orthodox Hegelian idealist might pass over the inquiry; but a materialist who probed his own consciousness as deeply as Marx did and often concluded that his diseases, let alone his frequent periods of insomnia, had psychic origins, was faced with serious intellectual problems that Marx was prone to evade. The power of the irrational among civilized men was not alien to him and analogies between primitive beliefs and the contemporary behavior of classes were frequent; but a complete theory for personal psychological diagnosis was beyond his ken, despite his curiosity about works on medical physiology.

Marx could understand the actions of classes such as workers in the Paris luxury trades, who "without realizing it" were easy prey to Proudhonian platitudes because they were involved with the garbage of the past, but the psyche of individuals was not part of the general theory. When he sketched the personality and motivation of individuals, he fell back on conventional explanations such as greed, ambition, envy, and sexual passion, drawing upon his storehouse of Shakespeare and Balzac. By the time of Marx's death, the role of the unconscious, formally baptized with the appearance of Eduard von Hartmann's *Psychology of the Unconscious* (1869), was being explored by psychologists and novelists of many lands. But though Marx on some level of consciousness was aware of the buried sources of his self-loathing, he did not reflect on the manner in which the psychic denial of his Jewish origins and his constant caricaturing of Jews might have ravaged his physical health. The Marx household was regularly convulsed by crises, and it would be presumptuous to fix on any single psychological source for the dreaded carbuncles, now called *hidradenitis suppurativa.*

Some twentieth-century observers have raised aggression against the self to the status of a primary instinct. In turning that aggression outward against others the torment of self-inflicted psychological pain may be alleviated for a while; and when there is an outlet in action, building a system or organizing a world movement, the respite may be prolonged. But the palliatives do not provide a permanent checkrein on the administration of pain to the self.

Both Marx and Engels accepted the military nicknames bestowed upon them in the family circle—Marx was Mohr, the Moor of Venice, the alien captain of a great fleet, and Engels was the General. One need not be so tightly locked into the aggressive military metaphor that one forgets the mythic image of Prometheus the firebringer, with whom Marx identified himself from his youth on. There is a print of Marx published in 1842 during his crusade for freedom of the press when he was editor of the Cologne *Rhenish Times:* a powerful, bearded figure, respectably dressed in a pair of drawers and tied to a printing machine, is gnawed by a royal eagle. Aeschylus was the other poet, with Shakespeare, whom Marx had chosen as a model. In *Prometheus Unbound* the firebringer does not suffer silently in the flesh; he cries out, "I hate the pack of Gods."

Marx and Engels were fighting not for an illusory utopia but for a reality that enjoyed the blessing of the god of the new age, Science. In the myth of the class struggle, re-created by Marx and Engels and clad in the vestments of science, aggression was sublimated into a philosophical-historical world view that became one of the most potent political instruments in the twentieth century; but like the battles with enemies in which Marx was so often engaged, the myth afforded him only temporary relief from his sufferings.

4

Émigré Cannibalism

If anyone had conceived the idea of writing from the outside the inner history of the political *émigrés* and exiles from the year 1848 in London, what a melancholy page he would have added to the records of contemporary man. What sufferings, what privations, what tears . . . and what triviality, what narrowness, what poverty of intellectual powers, of resources, of understanding, what obstinacy in wrangling, what pettiness of wounded vanity! . . .

Meeting the same men, the same groups, in five or six months, in two or three years, one becomes frightened: the same arguments are still going on, the same personalities and recriminations: only the furrows drawn by poverty and privation are deeper; jackets and overcoats are shabbier; there are more grey hairs, and they are all older together and bonier and more gloomy . . . and still the same things are being said over and over again.

—Alexander Herzen, *My Past and Thoughts*

An element of paranoid behavior is often intermixed with the loving passions of those who set out to be the saviors of humanity. Leaders of small clandestine societies, the self-chosen ones, have a natural tendency to believe themselves the targets of hostile conspiracies, and they are. Spies and squealers abound in organizations that are pushed out of respectable society, and an illusion of being persecuted that lurks in the secret recesses of everyman can among revolutionaries be unleashed and strengthened by the reality principle. The embryonic working-class movements of Western Europe were breeding grounds of cabals and intrigues that were regularly nourished by personal animosities and ideological differences.

Marx and Engels held fast to the conviction that they and they alone were the repository of both the correct theory and the tactical principles that would guide the proletariat to victory in the class war. But the mid-nineteenth century was thronged with other revolutionary chieftains, each of whom was driven by the certainty that he embodied the true principles for the redemption of mankind. They attracted to themselves cohorts of adherents whose numbers they inflated and who took on the trappings of political parties; they were usually labeled with the name of their founder, even when in public print they adopted more grandiose appellations such as leagues, alliances, associations. Partisans of one or another leader frequently shifted allegiances, though a small core of loyalists generally remained to attack the defectors as traitors. Since no leader was secure in the command of his foot-soldiers and recruits were dispersed throughout the Continent and in the United States, the spectacle of the radical and revolutionary parties seen from afar is one of tohubohu. To compound the confusion, the wary governments of the Continent infiltrated the little groups with spies and special agents whose psychological stability was dubious and whose livelihood came to depend upon exaggerating the strength of the revolutionaries.

Exposing spies, agents of provocation, and journalists who enjoyed subventions from secret government funds was a steady occupation of radical party heads, who often saw conspiracies, plots, and betrayals even where none existed. They lived on rumors, gossip, tidbits in party newspapers that led to accusations of treachery. During outbreaks such as the revolutions of 1848–1849 and upheavals like the Paris Commune, there were temporary alliances and alignments, but in the intervals the revolutionaries devoured one another.

From the early 1850s on neither Marx nor Engels treated sympathetically the mixed bag of refugees from failed Continental revolutions who turned up in London. With the exception of a few loyal adherents to their party line, they regarded the exiles with contempt, marking them with the stigma of their ethnic origins. Engels complained to Marx on February 5, 1851:

> From a stupid Hungarian refugee whom I came upon today, I heard that this noble ilk are once again prattling about murder conspiracies

and revolts on the occasion of the Great Exhibition. Amidst the din I almost thought I heard the heroic voices of those London hotspurs, Willich and Barthélemy. There's really no way to avoid this gang; recently a fellow approached me on the street and behold, it was a Great Windmill Street [The London German Workers' Educational Society] refugee who now had a job in Liverpool. "If I take the wings of the morning, and dwell in the uttermost parts of the sea," I shall not escape that band.[1]

Emigrés from defeated revolutionary coups had huddled together in the only European country that tolerated them. They formed a society of wretched outcasts, dividing into cliques and subcliques, envious of anyone who found a job, accusing one another of betrayal, a swarm of anonymous former fighters, some of whom were all too ready to collaborate with the police spies who hovered on their fringes. Engels in his Manchester office and Marx in his London rented rooms acted as though they were the rulers of a colony of ants. They had guards who kept tabs on the goings-on among the defeated refugees of many nations. With recourse to both mental and written archives of the revolutionary past and present of the exiles, they chose their favorites after due deliberation. They were especially vigilant in thwarting the activities of nationalists like Mazzini, who in an admixture of religious and ethnic verbiage were casting doubts on the primacy of the proletariat in the world revolution.

On joint committees Marx, the frequent draftsman of the final declarations, was assiduous in excising nationalistic phraseology and high-flown moralistic sentiments, though he had to make some compromise with working-class adherents of Weitling in Germany and Proudhon in France, among whom vapid phrase mongering had become ingrained. Perhaps even more threatening to Marx and Engels were the hotheads who kept hawking the advantages of the seizure of power through secret organizations and sudden coups d'état, without careful consideration of objective and subjective circumstances in the country where the uprising was being plotted.

When the personal emissaries Marx used in communicating his policy to workingmen's associations and communist leagues erred in the interpretation of his directives, delivered orally, they brought down upon themselves the full fury of his wrath. Marx berated them as stupid and incompetent, while he bewailed his need to rely on half-educated workers incapable of understanding his straightforward instructions. His letters are dotted with contemptuous remarks about his stand-ins—Georg Eccarius, Wilhelm Liebknecht, and Wilhelm Wolff. When Wolff, the hapless émigré who eked out a frugal living as a tutor in Manchester, bequeathed to Marx seven or eight hundred pounds, he became more tender in his recollections of the little man to whom he had often referred with disdain, and he dedicated to his memory the first volume of *Das Kapital*. A thorough search of the Marx correspondence turns up a few words of praise for minor disciples—usually the young ones—on whom he bestowed the accolade of "good fellows." Scanning the list of his friends, one finds almost no one with whom he maintained consistently amicable relations; with the notable exception of Engels, all of them felt the sting of his sharp tongue at one time or another. Marx broke with Dr. Ludwig Kugelmann at a spa they frequented because he objected to the gynecologist's noisy maltreatment of his wife; Marx insisted that the standards of a Victorian gentleman be upheld in public conduct.

Marx's scorn for most human beings can be related either to an inborn arrogance or, more charitably, to the historical conditions of this stage of capitalism, in which, in his view, virtually every creature, master and proletarian slave alike, was corrupted by the circumstances of his status. All men were dehumanized by the production relations in the age of capital, which made of them either exploiters or exploited. In that sense, all were contemptible. His own secret self-loathing was pervasive, hidden from the émigrés who could observe only his sneers turned outward.

When Marx had first arrived in London late in 1849 he was prepared for, even pleased with, a respite from communist revolutionary action while the "1848 democracy," meaning the liberal bourgeois, had a chance to molder away. For lack of anything vital to absorb him he vented his spleen against the group around August Willich and Karl Schapper, accusing them of betraying their friends to government agents. In troubled times for the refugees, Marx teetered on the edge of clinical suspiciousness. He was "morally" convinced of treachery and heeded his "reliable sources," not all of them credible. When during the Cologne trial of communists accused of treason the Prussian police tried to invent a network of connections between the accused and those émigrés Marx and Engels denigrated, no ties were discovered despite persistent house searches and arrests, demonstrating that the London émigrés were four-flushers when they claimed close relationships with Continental revolutionaries. By the spring of 1852 the dossiers the dioscuri assembled on the émigrés were fat enough for them to prepare a long, wordy pamphlet, with the aid of Mrs. Marx and Ernst Dronke, a member of the Communist League, that was sarcastically entitled *Die grossen Männer des Exils* (The Great Men of the Exile) and was submitted to a Hungarian refugee for publication. He promptly sold the manuscript to the Prussian police.

When Marx let loose on the windbags among the former forty-eighters and forty-niners who were hanging around London pubs, he did not spare the adjectives. August Willich, the former Prussian officer whom Engels had served as adjutant in the Baden-Palatinate uprising, was Marx's *bête noire* among the émigrés.

Willich is a thoroughly common, mark well, thoroughly common *chevalier d'industrie, pillier d'estaminet* [swindler, bluffer]—and—or so I am told by a respectable philistine, though I cannot myself vouch for it—also cardsharper. The lad lopes around all day at the pub, a democratic pub, naturally, where he drinks *gratis,* bringing customers in lieu of payment and entertaining them with his stereotyped phrases about a future revolution in which the chevalier himself no longer believes, so often has he reiterated them under such widely disparate circumstances, and always with the same result. The fellow is a parasite of the basest kind—invariably of course, under patriotic pretenses.

All this individual's communism amounts to is a determination to tread the primrose path, always at the public expense, in communion with other footloose chevaliers. This man's activities consist solely in gossiping and lying about us in pubs, and boasting of connections in Germany which, though non-existent, are nevertheless taken for gospel by the Central clown A. Ruge, the ideological boor Heinzen and by the stagey, coquettish, theologising belletrist Kinkel, connections of which he also boasts to the French.[2]

Joseph Weydemeyer, a forty-eighter to whom Marx wrote this explosive letter on June 27, 1851, ultimately made his way to America, where he remained in friendly correspondence with Marx, avoiding the fetid atmosphere of émigré society in London.

Engels took the opportunity presented by the Cologne treason trial to deflate the pretensions of the Willich gang, and exulted over getting rid of the whole noisy, confused, ineffectual émigré rabble in London. At long last he and Marx would be able to work again, unhampered. His report of July 9, 1851, to Ernst Dronke, the friendly editor from the *New Rhenish Times* days who had emigrated to Geneva, was hardly animated by good feeling or optimism; chattiness and self-mockery only partially temper its spiteful tone.

> They say you are a husband and a father, and that you are also on friendly terms with Moses [Hess]—with an eye to Mrs. Moses [Sibylle Hess]. Others have it that all this is sheer calumny but—at a distance of 10 degrees of latitude—that would be difficult to judge. Freiligrath, too, is in London and is bringing out a new volume of poetry. Weerth is in Hamburg and, like myself, is writing business letters pending the next set-to. He brought nothing back from his travels in Spain, not even the clap. He is, by the way, coming to London this month. Red Wolff [Ferdinand Wolff, another *New Rhenish Times* veteran] has gone through various phases of being an Irishman, a worthy bourgeois, a madman and other interesting states, and has completely abandoned *Schnaps* in favour of half-and-half. *Père* Marx goes daily to the library and is adding amazingly to his knowledge—but also to his family. Finally, as to myself, I drink rum and water, swot and spend my time 'twixt Twist and Tedium.[3]

Despite the ennui and the acrimony, however, neither Engels nor Marx had abandoned his dedication to the cause. In the 1850s they were busy re-establishing contacts with their stray partisans in different parts of Europe and were re-examining the events since 1848, awaiting a new round. This time they would have the advantage of well-defined goals, in contrast with their democratic rivals and the swashbuckling members of the Willich school, all of whom were looking forward to some sort of government post on the morrow of the revolution. The émigré cliques invariably developed internal fissures, which Marx and Engels greeted with malevolent glee.

In the stifling atmosphere of nineteenth-century émigré society, insignificant incidents, like the rumpus over Marx's neglecting to return a Spanish grammar he had borrowed from Wolff, could lead to temporary breaks in relationships. Emigré *entremangerie* is universal. That Marx on one level of consciousness was aware of the nature of the disease may account in part for his studied attempt to distance himself whenever possible from German and French refugees in London; but at the same time that he reviled his fellow émigrés, he resented their neglect. On June 18, 1862, he whined to Engels: "No one visits me, and I'm glad, for I don't give a . . . for the humankind we have here. A fine bunch!"[4] It was Marx protesting too much. Total isolation, even from the despised exiles, would have been unbearable. Often they were his only audience; and in a crisis he was instrumental in collecting funds for them. He was trusted by the contributors to the charitable organizations that doled out small sums to the stranded foreigners who had escaped from their native countries after the failure of the revolutions and uprisings that periodically broke out on the Continent.

Political émigrés' vilifying of one another—that is the almost invariable practice of defeated exiles obsessed with rehearsing their former triumphs, blaming one another for failures, and spinning fantasies of a victorious return. Marx and Engels escaped the fate of other émigrés by remaining steadfast in their friendship to each other and in their commitment to the doctrine they were forging—though they, too, in spite of themselves, got entangled in the web of intrigues and partisan squabbles. In time they managed to secure a measure of authority over a phalanx of loyalists, though it was achieved at greater cost to Marx's fragile psyche than to Engels, whose temperament and material comfort allowed him to find consolation in wine, women, and, despite his slight stammer, song.

Marx was a master of vituperative prose when assailed, even if his only audience was Engels and the victim was a man whose identity has been lost in the émigré crowd. The outpouring could be a long, intricate spewing of bile, as in his rampage of August 1, 1856, against *Aus dem Exil,* the two-volume jeremiad of émigré Ludwig Simon, who had been a deputy in the Frankfurt National Assembly: "Diluted twaddle, every other word a solecism, a puerile hodgepodge, wobbly artifices, foppish naive pretension, a mess of Grünian Jew's ears in beggar's broth, a long platitude—nothing like it has ever been printed. What was still lacking to give the 'German Parliament' the last kick in the arse was this exhibitionism on the part of one of its heroes. Naturally, I only thumbed through it. I'd as well drink soapsuds or fraternize with the great Zoroaster over hot cow's piss than read through the whole thing."[5] Denouncing to each other the stupidities of their reformist or putsch-prone rivals buoyed the spirits of the dioscuri, a therapeutic tonic that had to be replenished at regular intervals.

In gossiping about the weaknesses of those who had sought refuge in London from failed European revolutions, Marx often adopted the stereotypes of middle-class Victorian moralism. Empathy with their hardships in an alien land was infrequent, irritation with the boredom of their presence the norm. A letter of September 22, 1856, from Marx to Engels was packed with malicious tattling about the sex lives of the émigrés, prurient asides to discredit former friends. The prostitute with whom Heinrich Heine had been living was fetched away by her pimp on the day of Heine's death. Moses Hess—who had some money of his own—was exploited by Nikolai Sazanov, a Russian adventurer who played the revolutionary, extolled Hess as a great literary light, and bedded his wife Sibylle, a former trollop, until Sazanov married a rich old Jewess, when he changed his opinions and called Hess a common fellow. Marx wallowed in tales of the "grandeur et décadence de la Maison Hess." The ex-sweetheart of Freiligrath, the once radical poet, had settled in Australia, where she married, turned religious, and drove her new man into the madhouse, literally.[6] Such scandalmongering was interspersed with information about French and English thievery on the various exchanges and speculation about an impending crash in 1857—a prophecy that proved to be reasonably accurate.

Marx boasted to Engels on November 4, 1864, that he had skillfully changed the draft of the *Inaugural Address of the International Working Men's Association,* entrusted to him for completion by a sub-committee. Prometheus was proud of his capacity to play Mercury the trickster. "I changed the whole preamble, chucked away the *déclaration des principes,* and finally replaced the forty rules by ten.

When International Politics occurs in the 'Address,' I speak of countries and not nationalities, and I denounce Russia, not the *minores gentium*. The sub-committee accepted all my proposals. I was only obliged to include in the preamble of the statutes two phrases about 'Duty' and 'Right' and ditto about 'Truth, Morality and Justice,' but they are so placed that no harm can be done."[7] Marx the manipulator, capable of compromising with the "idealist" verbiage he associated with the socialists of the Weitling, Hess, or Karl Grün orientations, established a Machiavellian precedent in the International for hoodwinking ignorant worker representatives on committees; but in open assemblies his tactics were hardly effective when the tribunes Lassalle or Bakunin let loose an oratorical barrage. One might look with greater indulgence on Marx's duplicities had he been less absolutist and puritanical in flagellating his opponents for their contradictions and inconsistencies.

During the short life of the First International, Marx occasionally intervened in strike movements by keeping its sections informed of events in various countries and hindering artisans of one land from scabbing in another. Such trade-union aid by the International enjoyed the approval of Marx and Engels since it contributed to the heightening of world proletarian consciousness, an area of sharp disagreement with the anarchists, who were intent upon aiming directly at the jugular vein of the state and regarded industrial actions like strikes as diversionary.

When squabbling among sections of the International intensified in the late 1860s and early 1870s, the shakiness of the whole structure, buttressed only by elaborate paper regulations that Marx had composed, was obvious to any observer, as Proudhonists, Bakuninists, Lassalleans, and proper followers of Marx jockeyed for position and intrigued against one another, resorting to contradictory interpretations of the rules adopted by the General Council in London and approved by international congresses. Rumors of dissension in the International were either denied or resolved by ousting the deviationists. Under Marx's authority, new sections were refused admission into the International, old ones were threatened with excommunication for their contumely, for their failure to respect solemn decisions of the London Council, which Marx and Engels dominated by manipulating votes as astutely as any local politician in twenti-eth-century advanced democracies. An overriding issue was the autonomy of individual sections in opposition to the centralizing authority of the Council in London, which often was itself divided. This internecine strife led to the accusation that Marx was exercising dictatorial powers and was an authoritarian who illegally sup-pressed sections that showed any Bakuninist or Proudhonian lean-ings.

Charges and counter-charges eventuated in secret trials and the preparation of long-winded disquisitions, often drafted by Engels, on the nature of governance. To newcomers in a section he argued that no body or enterprise or factory or ship could function without a central authority legally chosen in conformity with approved regu-lations. Any worker knew this from his own experience, even if the doctors and petty bourgeois who sided with Bakunin did not. As an erstwhile military man, Engels pontificated that to conduct an or-ganized struggle against the bourgeoisie—the mission of the working class—required a central command. Once the battle for emancipa-tion was won, the proletariat, all the people, in unison, would then decide upon the forms of organization appropriate for the new communist society. Drawing upon his archive, Engels recalled that originally members of the Bakuninist faction, the anarchists who espoused absolute liberty of action, had proposed many of the rules against which they now inveighed.

By November 1871 Marx was on the defensive for the unpardon-able fact that he was born a German and by his own admission exercised a decisive intellectual influence on the General Council of the International. Ethnic rivalries among the French, the Germans, and the English were fed by complaints that the Council was domi-nated by Pan-Germanism. However much Marx and Engels sought to underplay the role of nationalist movements of emancipation in achieving the world revolution, they could not prevent national loyalties from tearing apart the Council itself.

When Marx, then in his early fifties, issued instructions to Wil-helm Liebknecht, he expected to be obeyed blindly because he was better informed about the intrigues in the International. "[Y]ou have simply to make up your mind whether you wish to act *against* us or *with* us" were the stark alternatives he presented to his waffling adherent on November 17, 1871.[8] (The Joshua test—are you for us or against us?—had already been applied by the young man Marx.) Angered by the ingratitude of the French refugees in London on whose behalf he had labored and whom he had vindicated in *The Civil War in France,* he had poured out his bitterness in a message of November 9 to Friedrich Adolph Sorge in Hoboken, New Jersey. The object of the émigrés' attack "is not the governments and ruling classes of Europe, allied against us, but the General Council of London, and particularly my humble self."[9] In times of trouble the hangouts of the exiles turned into snake pits.

In the aftermath of the Commune and the Bakuninist attack on Marx, Engels finally undertook to clarify their position on the nature of authority and centralization in the world revolutionary movement in language that their far-flung if sparse adherents could understand. The extensive military researches of the "General" indelibly marked his thought, leaving behind an authoritarian heritage for leaders of future generations. A draft of a January 14–15, 1872, letter to Carlo Terzaghi, an Italian lawyer and journalist, secretary of the Federazione Operaia in Turin (who became a police agent that year), affords an insight into Engels' thinking that was shared with friend and foe alike.

> It seems to me that the phrases "authority" and "centralisation" are much abused. I know of nothing more authoritarian than a revolution, and when one imposes one's will on others with bombs and rifle bullets, as in every revolution, it seems to me one performs an authoritarian act. It was the lack of centralisation and authority that cost the life of the Paris Commune. After the victory make what you like of authority, etc., but for the struggle we need to gather all our forces into a single band and concentrate them on the same point of attack. And when people speak to me about authority and centralisation as if they were two things to be condemned in all possible circumstances, it seems to me that those who talk like this either do not know what a revolution is, or are revolutionaries in name only.[10]

In the voluminous corpus of the writings of Marx and Engels there are many variant formulations of the nature of the final struggle, some even accepting the feasibility of a seizure of power through the exercise of the franchise, but in attempts to homogenize their works the frequent shifts of position have been neglected. Among the portrayals of Marx and Engels that have been hawked in the marketplace for a century, the presentation of the dioscuri as genteel reformers is the least credible. Violence was inherent in the process of historical revolutions.

Engels' letter of the same period to Wilhelm Liebknecht in Leipzig about the "funny goings-on" in the German Workers' Educational Society in London depicts in detail a fracas typical of the tempests that raged in the isolated enclaves of the émigrés. The names of the combatants and the bones of their contentions have long since been forgotten, but the spirit that animated the pitched battles between the partisans of Marx and their antagonists lingered on for decades, a harbinger of the manoeuvres of democratic and not so democratic politics in modern times. The tactics adopted in the making of the new man imitated the behavior of the old man.

> Schneider [Karl Schneider, the lawyer who defended the communists in the Cologne trial] and that asinine old scoundrel, [Andreas] Scherzer, thought they had got a majority, and together with [Louis] Weber, who acted as intermediary, they made common cause with the dissident French and then proposed that the Society should *resign from the International*. Our people had become lax, had squandered their advantage and admitted far too much riff-raff. But this time things had gone too far. They were called out in force and the proposal was defeated by 27 votes to 20. A motion to expel the 20 was then tabled. The disorder made a vote impossible. Whereupon our people immediately salvaged all the Society's property, moved to another pub and expelled the 20. The rebels are now out in the cold and don't know what to do, but they had the impertinence to send Scherzer as *their delegate* to the General Council on Tuesday! Naturally, he was not admitted.[11]

Communist and socialist ideologists who appeared to be kindred were the most dangerous interlopers, for they could become replacements. The major religions have reserved their bloodiest reprisals in this world and threats of the cruelest torments in the next for doctrinal deviationists from the messianic leader's well-marked course, though their differences may be hardly discernible or seem trivial in other periods. The little deceptions that Marx might pull when he was engrossed in the intrigues of the First International were inflated into life-and-death struggles when enacted on the expanded Muscovite stage after the Bolshevik Revolution. His vehemence against opponents endured in the political speech of communist leaders, dressed up in ideological wrappers, after they became heads of state. There is an unbroken continuum between the émigré cannibalism of the 1850s in London and the triumphant Muscovite revolution devouring its children seventy years later.

The Albatross: Das Kapital

Well, why didn't I answer you? Because I was constantly hovering at the edge of the grave. Hence I had to make use of every moment when I was able to work to complete my book, to which I have sacrificed health, happiness, and family. I trust that this explanation needs no supplementation. I laugh at the so-called practical men with their wisdom. If one chose to be an ox, one could of course turn one's back on the sufferings of mankind and look after one's own skin. But I should have really regarded myself as impractical if I had pegged out without completely finishing my book, at least in manuscript.

—Marx to Siegfried Meyer, April 30, 1867

In a few days I shall be fifty. As that Prussian lieutenant said to you: "Twenty years of service and still lieutenant," I can say: half a century on my shoulders, and still a pauper. How right my mother was: "If only Karell had made Capital instead of writing about it."

—Marx to Engels, April 30, 1868

Das Kapital was the supreme achievement of the Marx-Engels collaboration. Marx prepared a text, Engels popularized its major principles, and they defined it a science that would supersede the achievements of English political economy. The pretension of the system to being scientific was its greatest attraction for scientists and autodidacts alike in their quest for certitude. But the identification of socialism with science was not achieved overnight, nor was it self-evident to ordinary men, who were more prone to forge a bond between socialism and a new religion or a natural right that had been usurped.

Though Marx's education in the Trier gymnasium was primarily literary, philosophical, and theological, he had acquired from one of his professors an abiding curiosity about geology and the history of the earth. Engels had received a far better general grounding in the sciences in the secondary school he attended, and throughout his life he kept abreast of the new discoveries. Without having studied any science in detail, Marx was alert to the philosophical and social implications of the novel scientific conceptions about which Engels sent him regular reports. Marx was struck by the underlying thesis of Darwin's *The Origin of Species,* though he was put off by the "vulgar" English manner of its presentation, by which he meant its philosophical superficiality, and he did not swallow everything Darwin wrote without submitting it to his critical scalpel:

> I'm amused that Darwin, at whom I've been taking another look, says that he also applies the "Malthusian" theory to plants and animals, as if with Malthus the whole point wasn't its *not* being applied to plants and animals, but only to people—with its geometric progression—as opposed to plants and animals. It is noteworthy how Darwin recognizes again, among the beasts and plants, his English society with its division of labor, competition, opening up of new markets, "inventions," and Malthusian "struggle for existence." It is Hobbes's bellum omnium contra omnes and reminds one of Hegel in the *Phenomenology,* where civil society figures as a "spiritual animal kingdom," while in Darwin the animal kingdom figures as civil society.[1]

The story that Marx intended to dedicate one or another volume of *Das Kapital* to Darwin has long since been exploded.

Engels had read Darwin's work as soon as it appeared in 1859, Marx in 1860, following a pattern Marx commented upon to his friend: in scientific matters he always walked in Engels' footsteps. When Marx was unable to proceed with his own work during periods of illness, he caught up with the scientific readings that had been recommended to him. In a recumbent position, he became fairly conversant with the advances in mid-nineteenth-century science and technology, compensating for the deficiencies of his early education.

In *The Origin of Species* Marx and Engels found proof that in nature itself there was a dialectical process of advancement, of improvement, that could serve as an underpinning of their system. In 1873 Marx sent copies of the first volume of *Das Kapital,* second edition, to Darwin and Spencer, eminent Victorians who were willing to risk subverting the spiritual foundations of their society, though not the society itself. Too much has been made of Darwin's polite letter of acknowledgment of the volume, most of whose pages remained uncut. But even when Marx, while praising Darwin, made a point of distinguishing human development from evolution in plants and animals, and he missed the philosophical profundity to which the German school had accustomed him, he could not reject the crown of science. The Darwin-Marx analogy was used by radical political parties when the theory of evolution conquered the scientific world.

The absorption with Darwin was accompanied by a renewed examination of Hegel. Neither Marx nor Engels had forgotten their previous attacks on Hegelian idealism; now they were prepared to reverse themselves and accept the "old man" back into the philosophical fold, adapting the logic of his dialectic to their own purposes and defending him against recent detractors. Plain materialism, which by that time had become quite modish, was by itself insufficient as a philosophy of science. As Marx and Engels read Darwin, nature proceeded along a dialectical path; having resurrected Hegel, they adorned old-fashioned materialism with his dialectic, the conflict of opposites ever generating new forms. Social evolution was part of natural evolution, and their theory of the development of economic systems was in harmony with the Darwinian depiction of the origin of species in a struggle for existence. Hegel's triad of thesis, antithesis, and synthesis could readily be integrated with this natural history, and isolated passages from Hegel could be cited as philosophical prefigurations of the transformations that scientists were recognizing in many fields. The turning of quantitative change into qualitative novelty was later illustrated in Engels' *Dialectics of Nature,* with homely examples that the average man could comprehend, though they often repelled the educated.

Marx may or may not have planned initially to apply Hegelian dialectic to his analysis of the process of capitalist production.

Suffice it that Rjazanov, the first director of the Marx-Engels Institute in Moscow, placed the dialectic at the core of the thinking of the men who founded the system of scientific socialism, which any true believer had to distinguish carefully from utopian communism and ordinary materialism. Lenin thoroughly appreciated the philosophical theory of Marx and Engels, which alone among a welter of radical doctrines put communism on a solid scientific foundation.

Unrelenting criticism of everything that exists is a precept formulated as far back as September 1843 in a letter Marx wrote to his friend Arnold Ruge setting forth the spirit, if not the detailed program, of the German-French Yearbooks they were planning to publish in Paris. Arnold Ruge, no longer young, was not an original thinker, but he had married well and his editorial ventures provided employment to some of the Young Hegelians, with whom he did not always agree. They were juvenile Mephistoes, eager to negate, analyze, criticize everything. At times their proclamations sound like a Cartesian vow to the goddess of absolute doubt or a continuation of the Voltairean crusade against the infamous one; yet echoes of their philosophical and religious past reverberate. Critical philosophy was to them a matter of confession: mankind had only to declare its sins as they really were to have them forgiven. Marx quickly enough abandoned such platitudes; Ruge did not, and soon became one of the first inmates in the crowded zoo of Marx's *bêtes noires*. Eventually, Ruge found Marx's early attraction to communism intolerable, and after their rupture he labeled his former protégé indigestible, accusing him of duplicity in their relationship.

Professor Hegel had been torn from his young disciples by the cholera epidemic of 1831. With the master gone, the struggle among his would-be heirs was a free-for-all unbecoming the aspirants to the philosophical guidance of Europe. The battle of the Young Hegelians, in which Marx participated, has been chronicled *ad nauseam* by modern Marxologists. The dioscuri escaped relatively unscathed from the paradoxes of Hegel and his pupils, though no one plunged into the boiling cauldron of his philosophy has ever recuperated completely. Idealism might be replaced by materialism, but the historical dialectic survived to envelop Marxism in its coils.

Like many unbelievers in Christian Europe, Marx early delighted in verbal play with religious symbols, turning them topsy-turvy to heighten and advertise his blasphemy. The first offspring of his collaboration with Friedrich Engels, written in the fall of 1844 and published in Frankfurt the next year, was perversely called *The Holy Family*. It announced their break with the remains of Hegel by attacking in turn Saint Bruno (Bruno Bauer), Saint Max (Max Stirner), and other sainted philosophers. The two young revolutionaries—Marx twenty-six, Engels twenty-four—recently united in the friendship that was to last four decades, early sensed the need to sever all ties with the old spiritual man of bourgeois Christian Europe, irrespective of whether he was enveloped in a religious habit or decked out in a professorial gown. Only after the disappearance of this specter could the new universal man, whom they were creating out of the common clay of economic reality, emerge.

The turning point in the intellectual development of Marx and Engels came when they realized that their socialism was scientific in contradistinction to all other socialisms, which were either utopian or metaphysical. What distinguished the discoveries of Marx from previous theological teachings and philosophical logomachies was the assumption that their truth had a unique quality which mankind had only recently begun to appreciate: "scientific" was the magic word that Marx and Engels extended to embrace social and revolutionary thought. They knew that there had been many social thinkers before, but they had been predecessors, *prodromoi*, foretelling the coming of the final savior of mankind. In his funeral oration at his friend's grave Engels later compared Marx to Darwin, as the utopian forerunners Saint-Simon and Fourier had paraded their identification with Newton. Since Marx was not a skilled mathematician, the intricacies of Newton's proofs in the *Principia* were beyond his comprehension, but the reduction of the universe to a few basic laws remained the epitome of scientific truth both for him and for Engels, as it was for most scientifically autodidact system-builders in the nineteenth century. The dynamic element in Darwin, however, made him the analogue preferred by Marx even when he invoked the imagery of Newton's immutable laws of motion.

Some years had elapsed before Marx, urged on by Engels, came to accept as his primary philosophical-social mission the drafting of a basic work on political economy. Early in their relationship Engels had begun to prod Marx in that direction, though both were at first unaware of the magnitude of the task they had undertaken. In a letter written around October 8–10, 1844, after a visit to Cologne during which, in a burst of naive optimism, Engels expressed amazement at the success of their communist propaganda, he broached the movement's need for an in-depth study: "As long as the principles [of communism] are not developed logically and historically in a few works out of the previous world outlook and out of previous history and as its necessary continuation, everything is still in half-doses, and for the most part we are thrashing about blindly."[2]

The work turned out to have an inordinately long gestation, if one includes the preliminary drafts of *A Contribution to a Critique of Political Economy* (1859), the first volume of *Das Kapital* (1867), Engels' assembly of volumes II (1885) and III (1894) after Marx's death, and Kautsky's 1905–1910 collection of manuscripts on theories of surplus value that belonged to an earlier period. As far back as 1845 a critique of politics and political economy had been promised to a Darmstadt publisher. Capitalism slid into imperialism, economic crises went through their predestined cycles, abortive uprisings took place in 1848, the massacre of the Paris Commune was memorialized, native workingmen's parties sprouted; but *Das Kapital* kept on growing by accretion.

Although in June 1851 Marx had not yet decided what dimensions his study of political economy would assume, it was first conceived in finite terms. Within another six to eight weeks he would complete the book. The materials were "damnably involved," and he spent his days in the British Museum from nine in the morning until seven in the evening. Little did he reckon that another fifteen years would elapse before the first volume of *Das Kapital* appeared. In the author's preface, dated July 25, 1867, he explained the long hiatus between his 1859 *Contribution to a Critique of Political Economy* and the publication of the first volume of *Das Kapital* with a medical report that is not customarily offered as a justification for an author's delinquency in following through with his work plan. "The long pause between the first part and the continuation is due to an illness of many years' duration that again and again interrupted my work."[3] If he is referring to the frequent outbreak of carbuncles it is probably the first time in the history of political economy that this particular bacterium has figured so prominently.

Reviewing the body of writings attributed to Marx, one is struck by the incapacity of this man, who had a superb mind and was immersed in the literary and philosophical culture of Western society, to finish his major work. At his death he left behind piles of notebooks and drafts to be combed by disciples and institutes for excerpts that exerted unusual fascination on European and American intellectuals. With the aid of Engels he wrote a *Communist Manifesto* that has been studied by revolutionary leaders as sophisticated as Chou En-lai, who took a copy with him on the Long March of the Chinese Communist Party, as well as by half-literate workers and peasants. Later pamphlets analyzing crises in French nineteenth-century politics were adapted by members of communist parties and quoted in and out of context for decades. The *Critique of the Gotha Program of the German Social Democratic Party* was a treasury of slogans on the dictatorship of the proletariat and the higher stage of communism. *The German Ideology*, not published until the twentieth century, was laboriously put together and remains a sourcebook for a not very original philosophical anthropology.

But without exception, the writings that Marx brought to completion were slashing polemics. From the days of amity with the Young Hegelians, he was a virtuoso at refutation and at composing critiques. Twenty pages by Engels against a few of their philosophical opponents in the 1840s had been expanded by Marx into a volume more than ten times as long, the mordant *Holy Family*, which now holds chiefly antiquarian interest. The inflated diatribe against Herr Vogt, whom no one has heard of since, troubled some of Marx's adherents, who opposed its publication. The attack on Proudhon's *Philosophie de la misère* is noteworthy only for a mocking inversion of the title into *Misère de la philosophie* and a repetitive denigration of the Frenchman's ignorance of German philosophy and English economic thought. A long-winded tirade against

Bakunin that enjoyed the sponsorship of the International is no more worthy of Marx than any number of his unpublished denunciations of deviant rival leaders.

Since Marx in exile always operated on two levels simultaneously, the lofty theoretical and the down-to-earth propagandist, the quest for a newspaper that would be the organ for popularizing his ideas was a constant preoccupation. It ended in failure, even when he was willing to compromise and accept participation in a liberal bourgeois journal; the halcyon days of the radical *New Rhenish Times* during the Revolution of 1848–1849 when he was in complete control as editor-in-chief could not be revived. Articles in the *New York Herald Tribune*, most of which Engels prepared, were justifiable as a way of earning a few pounds; other journalistic activities in which Marx engaged with a view to making some money or sneaking his ideas into the press, bourgeois or revolutionary sectarian, served only to distract him from his grand undertaking.

By contrast with the ephemera that consumed so much time and energy, Marx thought of *Das Kapital* as a formidable weapon in the class war that would outweigh in importance the party congresses, most of which he did not attend. It was destined to deal the bourgeoisie a theoretical blow from which it would never recover, he boasted on October 4, 1864, to Carl Klings, a German metal-worker in Solingen who was one of his agents in the hostile Lassalle camp. Marx had to master this monster of a book or perish in the attempt. But the creature often escaped his grasp, as he stockpiled the paper armaments to subdue it, constantly apprehensive lest he had omitted some detail in planning the assault. A monomaniacal belief in his own chosen role as the prophet capable of delivering society from bondage and leading it into the promised land of communist plenty alternated with seizures of self-doubt that could be temporarily quieted only by pouring on more and more factual evidence from the seemingly inexhaustible arsenal of the British Museum. The self-doubt, the obverse of his intellectual arrogance, could reach such colossal proportions that it sometimes paralyzed him, and he took refuge in one of the many illnesses to which he was susceptible.

The capitalist system not only had created the proletariat, a class that would be the instrument of its destruction, but had forged canon balls, in the shape of British parliamentary commission reports, that would be used against it. The bourgeoisie had turned the globe into one world in which no event or development was irrelevant, from the organization of primitive Russian agriculture through the rapid fluctuations in the price of cotton on the exchange, affecting the capacity of an Indian peasant to buy the British manufactured goods that were inundating the market. And every economic happening on earth had to be fitted into Marx's schema. The patient, capitalism, was sick, and only Doctor Marx could prognosticate its future by analyzing the periodic crises that shook the system.

"I hope to win a scientific victory for our party" was Marx's encapsulation of the purpose of his economic studies to his former comrade-in-arms Joseph Weydemeyer on February 1, 1859.[4] The idea that a scientific exposition of the capitalist process would be the jewel in the crown of the revolution had finally taken full possession of the former student of jurisprudence, who had once vacillated between building a new philosophical system and becoming a literary luminary. But to middle-class adherents to the cause of the revolution, let alone the workers who were members of communist leagues, the technicalities of economics were incomprehensible. They could understand a summons to strike, a call to arms, tearing up cobblestones to raise street barricades, attending mass meetings at which numbers infused them with a momentary sense of power, reading a manifesto, seizing weapons from military barracks. These were time-honored heroic actions that had become hallowed memories passed down from one generation to another since the great French Revolution. Workers were schooled in the ways of secret societies—in France the craft organizations of *compagnons* had never completely disappeared—and appropriate conspiratorial behavior had traditional origins. But what had the recondite researches of a German intellectual to do with an insurrection of workingmen?

Marx and Engels were forever arguing with their most loyal followers, who were puzzled that their leader was spending his efforts and energies on an abstruse work instead of devoting himself to recruiting members, to propaganda, to planning the revolution. The pamphlets Marx and Engels wrote, their newspaper articles, could be read by middle-class subscribers, but what was the immediate use of a treatise that was becoming ever more bloated? And yet among some literate sympathizers with the cause, especially among those incapable of understanding *Das Kapital,* an aura enveloped the massive head of the doctor of philosophy.

The very title of the fragment *A Contribution to a Critique of Political Economy* betrays the hesitancy, the tentativeness, with which the prophet approached his sheaves of paper. Although Marx saw his masterpiece as a revelation that would finally destroy the theories of the bourgeois economists who had been explaining the capitalist process in terms of profit, he was himself not a confident seer. The taint of being a neophyte, a newcomer to political economy, never altogether faded. He mounted his shaky structure in a constant state of insecurity, and he was consumed with self-doubt as he loudly proclaimed his triumph over the economists and gloated over how backward the science of political economy really was. Marx could be impudent when he pummeled the French autodidact printer Proudhon into a pulp, but when writing for professors, the stars in his hoped-for audience, Marx was not at ease. He alternated technical pedantry with sarcasm and, here and there, he introduced a note of pathos into his chronicle of human suffering, the price mankind paid to keep the capitalist mechanism grinding.

In 1857, as a world economic crisis re-opened for a moment the prospect that Europe was on the eve of revolution, a fantasy that had been suppressed by the fiasco of 1848–1849, Marx tackled his economic researches with renewed vigor. On December 8, 1857, he sent a message to Engels: "I am working like mad through every night pulling together my economic studies so that I at least get the fundamentals straight before the deluge."[5] And by mid-January 1858 he was euphoric over having completely demolished the theory of profit. As the apocalypse kept being postponed, *Das Kapital* assumed different forms. By 1857–1858 the whole work had been outlined, but Marx continued to gather his excerpts. Each visit to the British Museum took its toll, as there were new books and pamphlets to be read. A schema of 1858–1859 envisaged six books, of which *A Contribution to a Critique of Political Economy, Part One,* was merely a sample. When the first volume of *Das Kapital* finally did appear, Marx immediately embarked on revisions to be incorporated in a second edition. The swelling of *Das Kapital* over the decades turned the enterprise into a *folie à deux*. When Marx and Engels allowed others, such as Lassalle or Bakunin, to peer into the arcana, their comments were sneered at and they were summarily brushed aside as either fools or plagiarists.

The movement, the revolution, the livelihood of Marx depended on *Das Kapital,* and Engels from Manchester and Lassalle from Berlin repeatedly urged him to finish it. But there was no end to the vital detail that had to be incorporated if he was to substantiate his boast that he knew more about the capitalist process in all its parts than the renowned British economists and if he was to demonstrate conclusively that his proletariat had been despoiled of their birthright by the bourgeoisie. He was not a member of their professoriat and he dared not open himself to criticism. The theory of surplus value had to be the foundation on which the proletariat would build its inalienable right to become the ruling class and stamp its philosophical signature on the next phase of world history. Marx's monumental work would set forth the whole past of capitalism and the dynamics of its operations; portray its contemporary depredations through excerpts from official British blue books; demonstrate the inevitability of a declining rate of profit, elimination of the landed interest in the classical triad of land, capital, and labor, and reduction of labor's share to a bare subsistence level; explain the periodic paroxysms known as economic crises; and foretell the doom of the capitalist system.

But instead of sticking to his last, Marx allowed himself to be diverted by the composition of manifestoes, political pamphlets, wordy attacks on opponents. These efforts could have been regarded as useful for the movement he was directing, if they had left him some freedom for his primary task. But the violence of his aggression against enemies and misleaders of the chosen nation of the proletariat was all-absorbing. It wasted his strength as he tore the scribbling of opponents to shreds line by line. Perhaps the growling attacks projected outward at least some of the destructive drive that, if contained within the confines of his body, might have wrought even greater havoc than he sustained in a life of illness that made work a torment.

= III =

To be the herald of mankind's redemption and to be scorned is often the fate of those possessed by the illusion of their omnipotence. They are not wholly secure in their election. Although Marx's theory was sketched sometime in the 1840s, he did not yet have the proofs; and when he began to accumulate the data, the gathering of materials was without end because he could never rest assured that there was not another mound of facts to be examined that would buttress his conclusions. Engels could write with facility; he was not persecuted by the need to have everything that occurred in the material world fit into the mold. If there were additional books on the Russian land system, Marx had to learn the language to read them. A new economic crisis—even transitory changes in the world textile markets—had to be examined as corroborating evidence. When would the anxiety of incompleteness and fear of exposure be allayed? Since the hunger for new facts was insatiable virtually nothing could be declared finished.

But when rival prophets in the ranks of revolutionaries raised their heads, Marx's doubt vanished overnight. They had committed themselves in writing and thus their ignorance was easy to lay bare. Undermining their error-ridden structures was child's play. His demolition missions were numerous, and he had no difficulty in polishing off his competitors—Bauer, Weitling, Stirner, Proudhon, Blanqui, Grün, Hess, Bakunin, Vogt, Lassalle, Dühring (here Engels served as agent). The victims could be great or small, important or insignificant; whatever their status, Marx purposefully and quickly brought to completion his tirades against them. When the polemical writings failed to see the light during his lifetime it was usually because a publisher was not available. There was an immediacy of satisfaction in aggression against living enemies that work on *Das Kapital* could not afford him.

The authoritarian streak in Marx's character was communicated to those who accepted *Das Kapital* as a secular Koran even when they never read it, as was frequently the case. He fought mortal battles with socialists or communists who differed with him in the slightest on any theoretical point once the main lines of his system had been established. Rabbinic insistence upon the right interpretation of each letter in the Torah was his heritage, though there is no evidence that he could spell a Hebrew word. He was a close reader, and after detailed analysis of a hostile work marginal commentaries served him well in the withering of an opponent. Lenin adopted this method, and in the process of preparing meticulous glosses on Marx's texts he sanctified them. Like most Judaic and Christian commentators, Marx and his true followers recognized only one interpretation as correct.

Marx was possessed by analogies to the physical sciences. In his preface to the first volume of *Das Kapital* he warned the reader of the difficulties that lay ahead in assimilating the opening theoretical section into which he would directly be plunged, while assuring him that the peculiar terminology was unavoidable in a new science. Marx unabashedly presented himself as its founder, explaining that every science encountered impediments at the outset. Though he had made strenuous efforts to get to the bottom of the nature of value in a popularized form, he had not always succeeded—the secret evaded the human mind for two thousand years because it was the basic cell of economic existence and less accessible than the body as an organic whole. The reader prepared for something new was not to be frightened off. That this caveat would immediately drive away potential readers was evident to Engels, but Marx expected his audience to make the effort necessary to understand his text. Though Newton was not called upon to bear witness, Marx compared himself to the scientist who observes physical phenomena in their most typical form, and he thus excused in advance his almost exclusive reliance upon English illustrations. England was the classic ground for examination of the capitalist mode of production, and Germans who believed that conditions in their country were not so bad as those depicted in his work were self-deceived. *De te fabula narratur.* Indeed, realities in Germany were worse than in England because of the absence of any counterpoise such as the Factory Acts. As an exercise in theory *Das Kapital* ranks among the masterpieces of a nineteenth-century economic science that purported to describe an ongoing historical phenomenon. But in fact Marx was time-bound, rooted in the British model, the smokestack landscape from which he saw no escape until the morrow of the revolution.

In the preface to *Das Kapital,* Marx appeared in the protective armor of the laws of science. There he distilled the essence of the law of revolution. Though it was an iron law, it could be bent, adapted to circumstance.

> Intrinsically, it is not a question of the higher or lower degree of development of the social antagonisms that result from the natural laws of capitalist production. It is a question of these laws themselves, of these tendencies working with iron necessity toward inevitable results. The country that is more developed industrially only shows, to the less developed, the image of its own future . . . One nation can and should learn from others. And even when a society has got upon the right track for the discovery of the natural laws of its movement— and it is the ultimate aim of this work to lay bare the economic law of motion of modern society—it can neither clear by bold leaps, nor remove by legal enactments, the obstacles offered by the successive phases of its normal development. But it can shorten and lessen the birth-pangs.[6]

Despite the clear-cut formulation, a disciple who stressed the iron law in this affirmation might be led to one course of action, and an adherent who discovered the malleability of the metal might follow another.

The preface depicted Marx as a scientist who adopted an objective attitude toward the phenomena he was describing. He viewed the evolution of the economic formation of society as a process of natural history, and freed the individual from responsibility for relationships whose creature he essentially remained. Such proclamations of scientific neutrality are of course belied by the pages of polemics and letters written to brother Engels, in which nearly every utterance about individual behavior is charged with violent affects. There is a flagrant contradiction between Marx's self-image as a detached scientist who analyzes phenomena like a chemist or a physicist and Marx the man of rage, and the inner tension between the two is evident. He is aware that free scientific inquiry in the realm of political economy must do battle with its foes, the "most violent, mean and malignant passions of the human breast, the Furies of private interest,"[7] but he lives with the illusion that he himself is unsullied by such baseness and is leading the charge against it. At rare moments he appears to become aware of his own "uncivilized" passions, but most of his recorded words weigh far more heavily than the mea culpas intended to disarm his critics.

During Marx's lifetime, Russia did not fit neatly into the system of capitalist development. The Russian professors early appreciated his critique of bourgeois political economy and were profusely thanked for their approval in the introduction to the first volume of *Das Kapital.* Unfortunately, in the revolutionary arena it was the Russian bear Bakunin, incapable of comprehending elementary economic laws, who threatened the very existence of the First International with his putschist propaganda. Russian radicals sought Marx's counsel on how their unique economic evolution could fit into the pattern of *Das Kapital,* which had been cut to the frame of British historical experience. His response to the nettlesome question whether the existence of the primitive communal Russian *mir* might favor a leap over the period of bourgeois industrialization, which had not occurred in the east, to modern communism, proved to be oracular, though ambiguous enough to support the discordant interpretations of Russian intellectuals for generations. Their protracted debates centered on the universal applicability of the fundamental law of economic development, which Engels singled out in his funeral oration as Marx's greatest discovery. Marx bridled at the idea that interpreters of the first volume of *Das Kapital,* especially in Russia, would read it to mean that whenever a peasantry was turning into an urban proletariat, a capitalist system of production, with all its revolutionary consequences, would inevitably evolve. There was no such overriding historical-philosophical rule unaffected by the particularities of time and place. Although he was flattered by the attentions of the aristocratic Russian intellectuals, he deplored their penchant for extreme and modish theories. Russian émigrés like Herzen had never enjoyed his confidence, and they in turn were suspicious of him.

On the eve of the publication of volume I of *Das Kapital* Marx suddenly experienced a feeling of elation and his ailments vanished. Engels caught the new tone in Marx's letters and agreed that the future looked brighter. *En passant* he took the opportunity to offer his friend an astute analysis of the psychic havoc for which the damn book Marx had been carrying for so long was to blame. It was at the root of the misfortunes from which he could not extricate himself until he had gotten it off his back. Forever resisting completion, it had been driving him physically, mentally, and financially into the ground. Having shaken off the nightmare, he could now feel like a new man. Applying balsam to Marx's wounds, Engels assured him that the book would create a stir as soon as it appeared.

The weeks in 1867 that Marx spent in Hamburg waiting around with his publisher for page proofs of volume I of *Das Kapital* were a period of unwonted euphoria in the life of the middle-aged man. At forty-nine, he was suddenly basking in the approval of Prussian officials who, without having read a line of his work, feted him as an eminent German intellectual. Marx remarked wryly to Engels, to whom he sent full accounts of his stay in Hamburg, that he was garnering more praise from leading members of the civil service than he had ever received from the workers. Engels, caught up in Marx's elation, began to paint a rosy picture of their future when the financial success of *Das Kapital* would extricate Marx from his entanglement in debt and allow Engels to throw off the shackles of his business commitments. The letters conjure up the prospect of a private utopia in which the comrades-in-arms would be at liberty calmly to prepare for the emancipation of the world proletariat, a revolution that was again showing signs of an imminent outbreak.

When the proofs of *Das Kapital* were long delayed, Marx could not continue to accept the hospitality of Dr. Ludwig Kugelmann, the friendly gynecologist who welcomed him to Hanover when he was in the area, and he returned to London to confront his domestic troubles. The daydream quickly evaporated, and Marx and Engels settled back into their old routine: Marx lamenting his misfortunes, Engels bustling around to gather a few extra pounds to send to London, all to the accompaniment of a running commentary on current events, the manipulations of Bismarck and Louis Napoleon, the prospects of war, the course of the economic crisis, and, what was reported with the same minutiae, the bickering in the International and in the German working-class movement. Still, there were moments of rapture as the date of publication drew near. On the night Marx finished correcting the proofs, August 16, 1867, he wrote his cherished friend: "And so this volume is done. To you alone I give thanks for making it possible! Without your sacrifice for me I could not possibly have performed the monumental tasks required for the three volumes. Full of thanks, I embrace you!"[8]

Engels was ill-prepared for the wall of stony silence that faced *Das Kapital,* but he moved into action with a battle plan. Determined to get the book discussed, whether favorably or not, he enlisted Dr. Kugelmann in the crusade. Since Marx himself was not a free agent and was as bashful as a young girl—Engels' analogy—he plotted to compel the vulgar economists to criticize it by flooding the newspapers with articles, regular features, and unsolicited pieces in the correspondence section. It was their moral duty, he wrote Kugelmann, to follow their old friend Jesus Christ, to be as innocent as doves and as wise as serpents. Engels was prepared to compose attacks on the book himself, reviews that would then be distributed by third persons, anything to tease a response out of the bourgeois press. His exertions produced a few stray notices; for the rest, the book was ignored.

After weeks passed without any attention to one of the revolutionary creations of the age, on a par with *The Origin of Species,* Marx succumbed to an attack of nerves. He realized that the large book would weigh heavily on the stomachs of ordinary German readers, but he hoped against hope that they would ultimately be able to digest it. Although the heart of the volume was a dense, abstract economic argument and the illustrations were so profuse that an average reader lost the main strand of the reasoning—a flaw Engels pointed out when examining the proof sheets after it was too late to recast the work—every so often a graphic metaphor highlighted the barbaric nature of the capitalist system: if money came into the world with a congenital blood-stain on one cheek, then capital came dripping from head to foot, with blood and dirt oozing from every pore. But revolutionaries were accustomed to a diet of brief vituperative pamphlets that sustained their interest. In the guidelines he sent to friends who were preparing notices for *Das Kapital* Marx made a valiant effort to bypass intricacies and simplify his argument. In the end, those who entered the lists against him were mostly German professors of political economy. Neither in England nor in France did *Das Kapital* surmount the handicap of its format.

Only in the twentieth century have commentators begun to examine the wealth of literary analogies that were an intrinsic part of the argument in *Das Kapital*. Most contemporary readers concentrated on the rational thesis to accept or to refute it. In vain had Engels, in his publicity for the work, made an effort to highlight its ironic style in order to attract a wider audience. The scoffing tone of Marx's first book—the heavy-handed satire of *The Holy Family*—pervades *Das Kapital*, though mockery of the capitalist system and the jargon of the economists who defended it had with time become more subtle, even covert. In any event, a reader had to be well educated and acquainted with the principal characters of German, English, and French literature to grasp the full meaning and content of many snide remarks, or savor the erudition crammed into the footnotes. Workers were by definition excluded from this select audience.

There is something wondrously innocent, almost pathetic, in Engels' persuading Marx to introduce subheadings and outlines into the more abstruse parts of the text, in the forlorn hope that it would become more palatable to workers and ordinary followers. *Das Kapital*, like other arcane gospels, required a generation of intermediaries, church fathers of the new faith who would translate the work into more popular language and derive from it guides for action. In discharging this responsibility Engels, who outlived his friend by twelve years, became a zealous apostle, though by all odds the pivotal figure in reinvigorating the doctrine was Lenin, who discovered the works of Marx in 1889, six years after his death. When *Das Kapital* came into the hands of Lenin, who studied it line by line, as his wife, Krupskaya, bore witness, the text, which had been talked about and perused more than read, was granted a new life. Engels had nurtured the work in progress for decades and had expected it to become the canon of the revolutionary movement; in fact, it was only through the mediation of Lenin that the hope was fulfilled.

On the eve of his death, in making his way north through France from Algiers, where he had sought to recover his health, Marx became aware that his presence was not particularly welcome to either "Marxists" or "Anti-Marxists." He imputed the attitude of run-of-the-mill Frenchmen to their ignorance and primitive reasoning: Marx was a German, alias a Prussian, hence French Marxists were traitors to their country. But there were exceptions, as Marx sardonically reported: when in his radical days Georges Clemenceau was recuperating from a serious illness, he took *Das Kapital* to bed with him, from which Marx whimsically surmised that the work was becoming fashionable among actual or would-be forward-looking leaders.[9]

A French translation of *Das Kapital* did not please Marx; he knew the language well enough to discover innumerable flaws in a text that was supposed to convey his precise meaning. The Russian translation that Marx received from Nikolai Danielson in April 1872 was subject to less meticulous supervision, but Marx's promise to provide an introduction more popular than the ponderous theory with which the work opened was not fulfilled. The English translation by Sam Moore, Engels' friend, and Dr. Edward Aveling, Eleanor Marx's common-law husband, was too late for scrutiny by the author; it would have hastened his demise had he lived to see the mutilation of his work.

Members of socialist and communist parties found in Marx a champion who could worst the major English economists. He seemed to defeat outstanding bourgeois theorists with his union of the labor theory of value and the idea of surplus value, economic constructs that bolstered the faith of nineteenth-century believers, though they have lost their significance among the sophisticated modern economists of Europe and America who deal with models and the techniques of higher mathematics. Rather late in life Marx made a half-hearted attempt to learn its language by attending courses in mechanics institutes, and in a letter to Engels he tried to explain calculus, a parallel to Engels' attempt to elucidate the intricacies of bookkeeping to Marx. His education had been literary and philosophical; in the world of mathematical science he remained a novice, as evidenced in his published mathematical papers, assembled with piety by twentieth-century admirers.

As a dream of reason *Das Kapital* is the most comprehensive summation of Marx's thought, testimony to his analytic capacity. The history of its composition documents his perfectionism, his continual postponement of the end, and suggests the insecurity that underlay his bluster. In the mighty struggle to complete the work as he had originally contemplated it, he succumbed to psychic and physical illness. *Das Kapital* was the albatross that hung about his neck until his death.

Karl Marx as Prometheus, flysheet on the banning of the
Rheinische Zeitung, 1843

Karl Marx in 1866

Karl Marx in the late 1870s

Friedrich Engels in the late 1870s

Jenny Marx, née von Westphalen, during her last years

Moses Hess, after a portrait by an unknown artist

Ferdinand Lassalle, after a portrait by an unknown artist

Mikhail Aleksandrovich Bakunin

═ 6 ═
The Arena of Class War

Dies irae, dies illa
Solvet saeculum in favilla
Teste David cum Sibylla.

—Latin Requiem Mass

The festering wounds of Marx's self-loathing might have destroyed him had he not found salvation in the fantasy of an arena of combat in which he would lead the forces of the proletariat to victory. The transformation of world history into an age-long war of classes was based upon a view of reality that had predecessors and contemporary believers. His was not a solipsist's dream, though it liberated the aggressive drive that was embedded in his personality and constantly sought release. From the very beginning his preoccupation with the class struggle involved the composition of critiques and the invention of philosophical language for the fray. A structure was erected, a fortress defended against all comers, a stronghold from which forays could be launched in any direction. The theory of class struggle, presented in different rhetorics attuned to particular audiences, became the center of a world view to which he clung tenaciously throughout his life. The grandiose edifice was defended by weapons that had not been known before in the social conflicts of European societies, most portentous among them the book *Das Kapital,* the obsession of Marx and his faithful lieutenant Engels.

Marx's class war differed from battles for territory and power, goals of the Shakespearean heroes from whom he borrowed much of his violent language. There was an ideal city that he promised his proletarian forces after their triumph, and a new man who would rise from the debris of bourgeois civilization. Others, too, had conjured up visions of the peace that would descend upon the world on the morrow of Armageddon. But theirs were utopian, paper plans, hollow promises, and, most treacherous of all, they were diversions, distractions, wasteful of the efforts that had to be concentrated on the enemy. Old utopians from the past might sometimes be tolerated, even appreciated with a pat on their ghostly heads as prescient forerunners; contemporary utopians were dangerous fools. With zest Marx ripped apart the speculative systems spawned by utopian and demagogic misleaders of the proletariat—Proudhonists, Blanquists, Lassalleans, Bakuninists—who promised an instant millennium if only their tactics were adopted.

If pretensions to the mantle of science were among the seductions of Marxism, the mythology of class and class warfare became the driving force leading to the "final struggle"—that stirring climax to the hymn of the International. It was an idea far easier to comprehend than the theory of surplus value that was the cornerstone of *Das Kapital;* it was, moreover, a fluid concept that could be put to many uses, even as it defied precise definition.

The third volume of *Das Kapital,* put together by Engels from Marx's manuscripts after his death, ends abruptly with a section provocatively headed "What is a Class?". One would have supposed that the query had been answered early in the *Communist Manifesto,* in one of the most commonly cited passages of the Marxist canon: "The history of all hitherto existing society is the history of class struggles.

"Free man and slave, patrician and plebeian, lord and serf, guildmaster and journeyman, in a word, oppressor and oppressed, stood in constant opposition to one another, carried on an uninterrupted, now hidden, now open fight, a fight that each time ended, either in a revolutionary reconstitution of society at large, or in the common ruin of the contending classes."[1] Actually, neither this resounding salvo of the *Manifesto* nor the truncated concluding section of volume three of *Das Kapital* adequately covers the bewildering variety of contexts to which the concepts of class and class conflict were adapted in the Marxist corpus. In making the workers aware that they were members of one world proletariat Marx and Engels believed they were hastening the coming of the revolution. Only by examining their writings closely can one discern the different shades of meaning with which at one time or another they endowed the concepts, even when they presumed to devise exact definitions in the scientific manner.

Class was a relatively new term in the vocabulary of political and social thought, an alternative to "estate." Eighteenth-century and French Revolutionary usage was loose and flabby; following the pattern set by the Abbé Sieyès' famous pamphlet "What is the Third Estate?" journalists on occasion referred to workers as the Fourth Estate and presented grievances on its behalf. Only in the nineteenth century, when the Owenites, the Saint-Simonians, and the Fourierists attached the idea of class to "workers," did "les classes ouvrières" and "working classes" become a common part of popular speech. By the 1840s in France and England class terminology had been assimilated by state institutions and learned academies, where inquiries into the plight of the working classes were frequent subjects of discussion among officials and philanthropic citizens. Friedrich Engels' *Condition of the Working Class in England in 1844* is one of the most moving surveys among a host of *enquêtes* produced during this period on both sides of the Channel.

The coupling of class with conflict and war also had eighteenth-century origins; but elevating the idea to a position of centrality in a social world view was a task Marx and Engels reserved for themselves. In his *Working Class in England* Engels wrote: "The enemies are dividing gradually into two great camps—the bourgeoisie on the one hand, the workers on the other. This war of each against all, of the bourgeoisie against the proletariat . . . is only the logical sequel of the principle involved in free competition."[2] As early as 1852, Marx had weighed the significance of his discovery against the achievements of predecessors; a seemingly modest evaluation that he may have modified in later years appears in a letter of March 5 to Joseph Weydemeyer: "As for myself, I do not claim to have discovered either the existence of classes in modern society or the struggle between them. Long before me bourgeois historians had described the historical development of this struggle between the classes, as had bourgeois economists their economic anatomy. My own contribution was 1. to show that the existence of classes is merely bound up with certain historical phases in the development of production; 2. that the class struggle necessarily leads to the dictatorship of the proletariat; 3. that this dictatorship itself constitutes no more than a transition to the abolition of all classes and to a classless society."[3]

Klassenkampf not only became the critical element in the theory but also served as a vital stimulus in raising the consciousness of workingmen. And writing about the phenomenon on an abstract level allowed Marx to release aggressive passions seeking a philosophical object. In his cramped study he lived vicariously through the emotions of leaders of class struggles over the ages. Spartacus was his contemporary; Pompey was a *Scheisskerl*. Ironically, the inevitability of a *Klassenkampf* was one of the first concepts to be dropped by the wayside when European Social Democratic parties recast their revolutionary slogans in the period following World War II, though the idea hovered in the background and periodically an idiosyncratic Marxist theoretician raised the prickly question of whether under a communist regime class conflicts could persist.

Marx was heir to an ancient dichotomic tradition, that throughout Western history men were divided into opposing camps. Among some theorists the bifurcation had a neutral tone; it was a mere description of a social reality, with the implication that this condition was in the nature of things, and it was devoid of any hidden suggestion that the order should be overturned. In fact, there was often an inference that if this natural arrangement were disturbed, the fabric of society would be rent asunder and chaos would ensue. But during grave social crises the affirmation was quickly transformed into a summons to rebellion. In the 1830s and 1840s, in popular Chartist literature and in the scores of books by members of French Revolutionary and communist groups who decried "la misère des classes ouvrières," the dichotomy was invoked as a call to arms or a militant demand for social reform.

In many respects the division mirrored social reality in the first half of the century: workers dressed differently, were smaller in stature (if conscription records are to be credited), lived on restricted diets, inhabited segregated localities, often talked an argot that was peculiar to themselves, and had their own sexual mores. A novelist like Balzac, who specialized in the physiology of social classes and whom Marx admired, etched the subtle distinctions among the various upper-class sub-groups with whom he had converse; but in his human comedy the gap between the proletariat and the rest of the population was too wide for him to bridge—he had no direct access to industrial workers. Neither had Marx. Without Engels, who had rubbed shoulders with the proletariat exploited by his family business, Marx's class war might have remained a bloodless literary performance.

Many passages in Marx are proclamations of armed revolt against oppressors. Even when his intent was not so blatant, one branch of the social revolutionary movement that he founded and that acknowledged his leadership generally interpreted his words in this sense. When he invoked the dichotomy in its starkest form it became the basis for a declaration that class divisions, being unnatural, should be abolished and communist equality in the primitive sense of Babeuf's *Manifesto of the Equals* should ultimately be established among men—in due time, not in a putsch or a coup d'état, but in a revolution representing the vast majority of citizens.

In many of Marx's works, even when the fundamentally simple duality is retained, it is rendered more complex by the introduction of historical considerations. Duality in the patriarchal, the ancient, and the medieval societies was complicated by the action of spiritual and moral forces of cohesion that swayed men on the conscious level of their existence—loyalty to a lord or to fellow members of an artisan guild, faithful adherence to religious symbols and their priestly guardians. Although class conflicts were omnipresent in the ancient and medieval worlds, they did not always cleave the social order into two sharply defined segments; there was multiplicity in human relationships as traditional allegiances mitigated the intensity of the underlying antagonism.

The modern capitalist period was in this respect a *novum* in the history of mankind. Though it may have originated among the manifold corporate entities of the Middle Ages arranged in a semblance of hierarchy, the inevitable historical drive was to split society into the proletariat and the bourgeoisie. In Engels' "catechism" for proletarians, the draft that preceded the *Communist Manifesto*, and in the *Manifesto* itself, Marx and Engels emphasized the distinction between the proletariat, a noun they would reserve for the laborers of nineteenth-century capitalism, and all previous working classes. Marx shied away from asserting that the proletariat-bourgeoisie separation was already complete and ubiquitous in mid-century. Rather, it was about to become so, and as political events altered the social alignments within the system, he modified his schedule for the eventual maturation of the struggle, the coming of the final stage of the crisis. In his Victorian old age, full of good burgundy, Engels at times may have questioned the notion of a "final struggle"; but transitory wavering aside, he stood by the principle that the capitalist process in its fullest development, on the eve of an apocalyptic revolution, would bring forth the first society in world history in which the confrontation of the inveterate class enemies would be absolute, as all intermediary social groups sank into the ranks of the proletariat.

There is another, more technical use of the concept of class war in Marx's works. In *Das Kapital* and economic writings that analyze the functioning of the capitalist mode of production and its history since the later Middle Ages, Marx tended to become triadic. Both in his analysis and in his prognosis of future development he continued to rely upon the categories of classical economics set forth by Adam Smith and perfected by Ricardo. Marx viewed the process of capitalist evolution as a clashing interplay of three social collectives: the men of the land; the men of capital; and the men of labor. In his analysis of their internecine conflicts a moral argument intrudes: the men of labor receive in return for their work an unfair share, a pittance so small that it hardly provides for their bare subsistence. Their wages are determined by an iron law that keeps them forever on the verge of starvation.

The three classes are defined exclusively in terms of their relations to the capitalist mode of production and the social-economic system that allocates the profits. Marx was well aware that historically interests sharply divided landlords and men of capital—their war raged in the politics of industrial countries in the nineteenth century—but the triumph of capitalism spelled the predominance of the moneyed over the landed class. The capitalist system, operating through inexorable laws, had determined the outcome, and the three

classes had to behave in accordance with their position in the productive process. Individuals might alter their status; classes had to
act as elements in the triad.

Marx's economic history of Europe detailed the movement from
the triad toward the elimination of one element, the landlords,
through their assimilation with the moneyed interest, the capitalists.
The history he envisioned inverted the value system attached to the
eighteenth-century physiocratic division between the productive agricultural and the unproductive classes: instead of remaining the
propelling force of the economic process, the landed interest was
absorbed by the capitalist. Marx introduced subordinate economic
groups, particularly in tracing the early history of capitalism; he
differentiated between the manufacturers, which in his language
meant the organizers of the putting-out system, and the more advanced proprietors of factories, those who owned the large indus-
tries concentrated under one roof. Underlying the whole economic
process was a theoretical separation between those who controlled
or owned the instruments of production and those who did not.
Temporarily, capitalism might still allow for complexities in the
distribution of industrial property, but in the end the simple dichotomy would prevail; the economic history in *Das Kapital* included a
chronicle of the progressive obliteration of relatively independent
sharecroppers and small craft masters. The last volume of *Das
Kapital* was a *tour de force* devoted to the functioning of the banking system; it was of dubious relevance to raising working-class
consciousness, but Marx had committed himself to delineating the
operations of the system in all its major institutions.

The proletariat were Marx's chosen people, and the destiny of the
whole of mankind was bound up with their victory. His admiration
for the proletariat had come early in the apprenticeship of his French
exile, and was expressed in intimate letters to his friend the philosopher Ludwig Feuerbach. In the first months of his Paris sojourn
Marx was a dazed suitor not quite certain which among the various
national working classes he should embrace with the greatest fervor.
On August 11, 1844, he wrote in glowing terms about the workers
who gathered in groups of twenty or thirty in small meeting halls
on the outskirts of Paris. He was inspired by their enthusiasm:

You would have to attend one of the meetings of the French workers to appreciate the pure freshness, the nobility which burst forth from these toil-worn men. The English proletarian is also advancing with giant strides but he lacks the cultural background of the French. But I must not forget to emphasize the theoretical merits of the German artisans in Switzerland, London and Paris. The German artisan, however, is still too much of an artisan.

But in any case it is among these "barbarians" of our civilized society that history is preparing the practical element for the emancipation of mankind.[4]

Later in life he permitted himself less dithyrambic asides on proletariats that failed to live up to his expectations. But when he found fault with a proletariat he managed to exonerate them—they were set on the wrong path by leaders who acted out of vanity, stupidity, or pusillanimity.

All proletariats had their faults, which Marx quickly identified, fashioning national prototypes that possessed him for the four remaining decades of his life: the English were too phlegmatic, the French too political or addicted to utopian visions, the Germans too much given to abstraction. As for the Russians, he was suspicious of their wild plots, especially when the madman Bakunin reappeared on the European scene, after escaping from exile in Siberia and making his way around the world back to London. Sometimes Marx's attempts to explain why the proletariats embraced false doctrines and adopted incorrect tactics emphasized the stereotypes of national character he had coined; but more often it was convenient to blame their mentors Proudhon, Bakunin, Lassalle, and the supine English trade union officials. Marx died without having fixed on an ideal proletariat, free of an antiquated artisan spirit, immune to Bismarck's political blandishments, averse to Mazzinian religio-nationalist slogans and to conspiratorial putsches, a proletariat that would fulfill its true destiny as spelled out in *Das Kapital* and in tactical analyses of French political defeats.

Despite the fact that for periods in the 1850s Marx shared the grinding poverty of many of his London neighbors, that he visited his friend Engels in industrial Manchester on numerous occasions, he did not experience in the flesh the wretchedness of the English textile workers about whom Engels wrote the classical report. In Paris Marx had lived among artisans rather than factory workers, and in his last years his circumstances were middle class. Yet digressions on the sufferings of the proletariat entangled in the class war introduced a passionate note into what otherwise would have been a dry economic treatise. The cruelty of the process overwhelms even the callous reader of *Das Kapital* absorbed in following the intricacies of a disquisition in the scientific mode.

Capitalism had come to full fruition only in England and communism existed nowhere on earth; thus a central problem of Marx's thought was how to effect the transition from one to the other. There was room for dispute about what stage a nation-state had reached at a given moment, and how national character could modify the historical timetable of economic and revolutionary development. Despite what he knew about the phlegmatic Englishmen from living among them, Marx was on the lookout for the emergence of signs of political militancy in this most industrialized of all countries. If only the English were as passionate as the French, there would be no question about their proletariat seizing the reins of the world revolution. But the apparent passivity of the English trade unions, a body of proletarians who should have been in the forefront of revolutionary activity, yet were not, discouraged him from identifying them as the vanguard. Though their practicality would preserve them from adventures in the French Revolutionary temper, Marx in his soliloquies deplored their lack of spirit. Even in the final decades of his life he never imagined that parliamentary democracy in the English manner or in a Bismarckian Reichstag might conceivably effect the transition to the first phase of communism. A well-prepared revolution under appropriate objective circumstances was the most probable course of history. (All the same, the impatient, irritable Marx wished he did not have to listen to the revolutionary phrasemongering of the long-winded émigrés on the Council of the First International.)

In political pamphlets written for the express purpose of prescribing action and devoted primarily to a theoretical diagnosis of the situation in France, the bellwether nation of the nineteenth-century social revolution, the society is portrayed as stratified into diverse units, but the connection of a political unit to its economic base is often tenuous. In one section of *The Eighteenth Brumaire* (1852) it is possible to count on the side of the triumphant bourgeois republic after the June insurrection nine separate groups that are loosely called "classes": the aristocracy of finance; the industrial bourgeoisie; the middle class; the petty bourgeoisie; the army; the *lumpenproletariat* organized as the Mobile Guard; the intellectual luminaries; the clergy; and the rural population. In other passages of this lively polemical work, the bourgeoisie, which Marx still retained as an over-all term, was not fragmented into quite so many subordinate entities. Often he restricted himself to presenting the political viewpoints of three: the Bourbon landed aristocracy, the Orleanist capitalist interest, and the social democratic petty bourgeoisie. In the fluid political situation Marx recognized that rival constituent elements of the bourgeoisie might pull in different directions; each had distinct ideal images for the superstructure of society, and by no means did they share common fantasies of the good social order—society was still in a period of transition. But once the revolutionary crisis erupted, as expected, the subordinate groups of the bourgeoisie would close ranks against the proletariat.

When analyzing the actions of men in concrete political situations, Marx could slip into loose phraseology and write about the masses, the upper classes, the aristocracy, the peasants, the old powers of society; or he might fall back on purely political designations such as revolutionary communists, republicans, and plain communists, names whose correspondence to specific social classes he failed to spell out. He even casually used "social strata" to alternate with "classes." In some countries there is what Marx calls a developed formation of classes, the prime example being mid-nineteenth-century France, which derived from a certain rigidity in the structure of society, as well as the existence of modern modes of production. The first fruit of the unique concatenation of circumstances required for a revolution was the emergence of an intellectual superstructure of new ideas and values. Marx pointedly contrasted the French situation with that of the United States of America, where, though classes indeed already existed, they had not yet become fixed, but changed and interchanged their components in a constant state of flux.

Marx left his followers examples of hard, tactical analysis in his political pamphleteering on events in France that followed major debacles like Napoleon's coup d'état and the defeat of the Commune. These writings became mandatory guides for the correct thought and action of a revolutionary party after it had met temporary defeat. In demolishing rival interpreters and tacticians Marx excelled in irony, wit, the astute dissection of class intentions and underlying motives. But after his death, as the generations of activists followed one another, perceptions on political behavior that were fresh and vibrant when they originally flowed from Marx's pen became desiccated and sclerotic formulas patently inapplicable to new situations. Nevertheless, Marx's method of political diagnosis, when internalized by men of Lenin's stature, was no mean weapon—though it required a Lenin to read Marx's articles in the *New Rhenish Times* of 1848 (the one period when he was a militant participant in a revolutionary struggle) and, in a feat of political translation, to derive from them analogies adaptable to twentieth-century Russia.

When Marx employed class terminology in a political context, he presupposed that a vital new ingredient, class consciousness, had been added to the social situation as it would be defined in purely structural economic terms. For him, the attainment of class consciousness was the crucial event in the modern history of classes; it was the form-imprinting moment when an inchoate mass of men, naturally destined to assume character and unity by their position in the productive process, actually achieved consciousness of their role. They became aware of their historical personality, and henceforth they were organized for political action. Such class consciousness, as presented in the *Eighteenth Brumaire,* is not normally born overnight.

The act of becoming conscious of one's condition usually involved the fabrication of ideological formulas about property, family, religion, order, and ultimately the creation of political parties and programs. If Marx had a tactical mission, it was to accelerate the maturation of the class consciousness of the proletariat through his philosophical work; the goal had already been forecast in his theses on Feuerbach. The completion of *Das Kapital* became the focus of Marx's existence because it was destined to be the basic instrument for the creation of class consciousness. When Marx was not assailed by self-doubt he cast himself in the role of the bearer of class consciousness to the proletariat, the modern counterpart of Prometheus the firebringer. This was the self-image that sustained him when all else failed.

The inevitable Hegelian distinction between the subjective and the objective was incorporated into the schema. The subjective, class consciousness, could not be born until the requisite objective conditions had come into being, a development clearly dependent upon the emergence of advanced modes of production. The factory system and capitalism were necessary conditions for the transformation of workers into a proletariat. Only then could the subjective act of becoming conscious of one's historical class role take place. When both objective and subjective conditions were fulfilled, the eve of the revolution would have arrived. The proletarian army with Marx at its head would be ready for battle.

There is in Marx an implicit physiology of social classes that he never elaborated, perhaps because it might have smacked too much of idealism in the Hegelian manner. Each class stands for a virtue— the aristocracy for honor, the bourgeoisie for liberty—almost in the same way that every historical culture as defined by Herder or Hegel is an embodiment of Spirit in time. A basic premise of Marx's theory of social classes was that a ruling class at the top of the economic, social, and political pyramid determined the character of the society and imposed its values, expressed in law, art, and literature. Fully fashioned classes spontaneously generated higher mental systems, ideologies, religions, works of artistic genius. Although Marxist texts vary on the importance of age-old inherited traditions in mankind's creative manifestations, Marx always related high culture to a particular ruling class.

The classes have an essential individuality: they are reified as bodies with psychological attributes. But at crucial moments in their history they may play parts that seem to be out of character: for example, the bourgeoisie struck heroic postures and even performed grand deeds when it was organizing the French Revolution. Such actions, however, are always conceived by Marx as factitious, temporary aberrations, for after the revolutionary apex has been reached, the class regresses to its authentic personality. Classes are subject to self-delusion and they concert to delude others. Their fate can be viewed as tragic in the same sense that Hegel applied the word to the decline of cultures, or it can be looked upon as comic. Since Marx's literary tastes favored Shakespeare, he mixed the genres: the same class could experience episodes of grandeur and periods of low comedy. Though Marx writes of the doom of classes with the same tonal effects that Hegel used in forecasting the downfall of civilizations and Shakespeare the destruction of heroes, the bourgeoisie in its death throes is denied a noble tragic end. This class is prone to spew forth absurd figures such as Napoleon III, the adventurer who hides his trivial, repulsive features under the iron death mask of Napoleon I.

All classes and the ideologies they imposed were judged by moral criteria that Marx was reluctant to spell out. Despite his mockery of the Saint-Simonians and the Fourierists and the rarity of passages in which he set forth a utopian plan for the future city of terrestrial happiness, he could not wholly avoid leaving behind traces of his moral outlook. The bourgeoisie is depicted as having a face with two sides, not always harmonious. The bourgeois is a hypocrite—here the spirit behind Marx's analysis is Balzacian and Fourierist. In a way, hypocrisy is an inevitable component in the rhetoric of a class that noisily espouses universal freedom while in reality restricting it to only one segment of society, its own. There is a flagrant contradiction between the "rights of man" ideology and the actuality of bourgeois exploitation, a deception Marx skillfully unmasked.

Marx frequently distinguishes between the bourgeois and the proletarian personalities. The performances of the two classes on the world-historical stage differ markedly from each other. The revolutions in which they are the protagonists do not have the same natures. Bourgeois revolutions like those of the eighteenth century are flashy, dramatic, and quickly consummated—"men and things seem set in sparkling brilliants; ecstasy is the everyday spirit"; but their vitality is soon spent, and in their wake "a long crapulent depression lays hold of society." On the other hand, proletarian revolutions—and here Marx was prophesying more than characterizing—do not take place all at once. The proletarians "criticize themselves constantly, interrupt themselves continually in their own course, come back to the apparently accomplished in order to begin it afresh, deride with unmerciful thoroughness the inadequacies, weaknesses, and paltrinesses of their first attempts . . . recoil ever and anon from the indefinite prodigiousness of their own aims, until a situation has been created which makes all turning back impossible."[5] Since Marx was the symbolic embodiment of the proletariat he had created, the idealized history of this class was also an autobiography of the hero he would have liked to be.

Although all social systems had hitherto been marked by exploitation and oppression, in Marx's contrast between the dominance of the bourgeoisie and feudalism, a residual romanticization of the Middle Ages seeped through, despite the attempt to take a matter-of-fact stance. The adjectives "patriarchal" and "idyllic" were applied to feudal relations. The rhetoric can be satirical—Marx pokes fun at ecstasies of religious fervor, at chivalrous enthusiasm, at philistine sentimentalism—but the exploitation that is tempered by religious and political illusion seems preferable to the naked, shameless, direct, brutal exploitation of the bourgeois age. The reduction to the cash nexus of every human relationship that was once honored is described with a soupçon of appreciation for what had been superseded.

Bourgeois society was in a constant state of turmoil. Since its very nature involved continually revolutionizing the instruments of production, it was unstable, ever changing. A grand society in its monuments and activities, it had provided the first real inkling of the human potential. The revolutionary character of bourgeois society was unparalleled in world history; all earlier classes that controlled the forces of labor had been conservative of the modes of production and partial to sameness. The bourgeois was the first to live by an inner necessity to reorganize ceaselessly the productive mechanisms of society, not merely in Europe but throughout the globe. Since nothing could be stabilized, no forms ossified, no illusions hardened.

As a result of the rapid transformations, men could not long be hoodwinked by ideologies that did not last, and they were driven to face soberly the real human condition and their relationships with one another. Bourgeois society was inevitably cosmopolitan, indifferent to national boundaries both in the economic and in the spiritual spheres. There was a world market and a world literature; all previous ruling classes had been local in character.

The European compelled bourgeoisification everywhere, imposing the character of his civilization over the whole surface of the earth. Marx looked upon the spread of this civilization as a good, for he had no appreciation of the uniqueness of native cultures or of the wisdom of the East. The cult of nature was a frequent subject for satire in his writings, and only in his last years did he describe with pleasure the walks in the woods around the spas that were prescribed for his health. He hailed urbanization because it rescued a considerable part of mankind from the idiocy of rural life. The force of capitalism had once burst asunder the social system in which it was born, the structure of the feudal world, and in Marx's day, as in the waning years of feudalism, there was a similar contradiction between the political-social system and the productive possibilities of society. The recent history of industry and commerce was essentially the history of modern productive forces in rebellion against the existing conditions of production (that is, the social system), against the property relations that were the underpinnings of the bourgeoisie and of its rule. There was an unprecedented economic disease afflicting bourgeois society—overproduction—and in crisis the bourgeois class had become hostile to new productive forces. Bourgeois organization had already created the instrumentality of its own destruction, the proletariat, the bearers of man's future emancipation. Marx's phraseology had preserved the overtones of Hegelian dialectic—a negation, a clash of opposites, and then a higher synthesis.

Often in the *Eighteenth Brumaire* Marx set up the petty bourgeoisie as an intermediate stratum between the bourgeoisie and the workers. Social democracy was its political superstructure and an ideological position that reflected its place in the spatial hierarchy. The petty bourgeoisie sought to establish some sort of viable political harmony between the bourgeoisie and the proletariat, softening the hard edges of class antagonism and hoping to end the conflict. For Marx, this petty bourgeoisie, which was ultimately doomed to disappear through the operation of the laws of capitalist development, was a victim of the same self-deception that had possessed the grand bourgeoisie in the eighteenth-century revolution. The petty bourgeoisie imagined that its special interests and the objective conditions necessary for its emancipation were identical with the well-being of the whole of society, including the upper bourgeoisie and the proletariat. What was good for the petty bourgeoisie was good for everybody, if only because their social-democratic ideology pretended to save modern society from the class struggle à outrance.

The *Eighteenth Brumaire* raised the question of the relationship between the political and literary representatives of the petty bourgeoisie and the class itself: "According to their education and their individual position they may be as far apart as heaven from earth. What makes them representatives of the petty bourgeoisie is the fact that in their minds they [the literary and political representatives] do not get beyond the limits which the latter [the petty bourgeoisie] do not get beyond in life, that they are driven, theoretically, to the same problems and solutions to which material interest and social position drive the latter practically."[6]

The ambiguous class position of the petty bourgeoisie made it impossible for them to follow through on any political policy, and Marx took mischievous delight in ridiculing them. They were the toadies of the capitalist order. All classes deceived themselves to some extent (except perhaps the proletariat), but the petty bourgeoisie were invariably the most self-deluded, the most pretentious, because their actual position was so weak and the fantasy image of their political capacities so grandiose. But whatever he may have said in making fun of the petty bourgeoisie Marx was unconsciously ridiculing himself.

The key to an understanding of the petty bourgeoisie lay in its transitional character—the term is Marx's. In fact, it was doubly transitional: spatially in the social pyramid, in between the proletariat and the great bourgeoisie, and temporally because it was destined to be drowned in the proletariat in accordance with the principle of increasing and intensified social polarization. At the same time, the spokesmen of this self-deluded class—Marx's inveterate enemies—pretended to set forth the prospect of a future society in which virtually everybody would be petty bourgeois, *peuple*. The petty bourgeois were the clowns of the social order. The great bourgeois would come to a catastrophic end, the proletariat would have a glorious triumph, while the petty bourgeois, inflated buffoons, would see their role collapse like a pricked balloon. When Louis Blanc, the Lilliputian leader of the French democrats, once paid a visit to Marx's London flat and was waiting alone in the parlor, Karl and Jenny Marx through a crack in the door that led from their bedroom watched him preening himself in a mirror before the anticipated interview; they could hardly refrain from bursting into laughter—he was their symbol of the vain, petty bourgeois intellectual.

All of Marx's political works were devoted to demonstrating that the intricacies of political manoeuvering in France since the Great Revolution were explicable only in terms of the alliances and alignments of the major classes and their minor sub-divisions. Ideologies were merely the façade of what the classes truly represented. In deflating the oratory of their protagonists, Marx became one of the great revealers of the hidden political intentions of the classes. Real motivation was covert, and public speech had little import. "As in private life one distinguishes between what a man thinks and says of himself and what he really is and does, so in historical struggles one must distinguish still more the phrases and fancies of parties from their real organism and their real interests, their conception of themselves from their reality."[7]

The vocabulary for labeling social classes has changed radically since Marx's death, particularly in advanced industrial societies. In the United States, middle class is the preferred self-designation of most Americans, proletariat has disappeared, and underclass is a newcomer, as are the tags "blue collar" and "white collar," dictated by the kind of shirts supposedly worn by different categories of workers. Professionals are still particularized as doctors, lawyers, officials, artists, writers, clergymen, the military, teachers, and professors; a category of executives and administrators is gaining ground, being admitted to the formal classificatory system of venerable learned societies such as the American Academy of Arts and Sciences. It is difficult to envisage a struggle among these classes or to imagine what alliances and alignments they might form. When it is granted that gender, age, religion, race, and ethnic divisions crisscross the patterns of occupation, income, and geography, the concept of a self-conscious class loses its cogency. Though virtually all of these defining attributes existed in Marx's lifetime, they were rendered less significant by the relative cohesiveness of the larger collectives, lending plausibility to his scenario of the class struggle, which seems now to have crumbled away.

The historical schema that Marx developed along with his class theory and that covered the period from the high Middle Ages through the nineteenth century has been readily assimilated by modern historians in the West. Viewed in retrospect, his tableau of world history has come to occupy a place alongside the Four Monarchies doctrine of medieval and early modern interpreters of Nebuchadnezzar's dream, and Condorcet's ten-stage outline of rational progress, as one of the three most influential frames within which Western man has attempted to encompass historical experience. Of all Marx's theories, this historical schema has been the most enthralling; the Western mind has hardly begun to awaken from its narcotic effects. Though Marx's name was rarely invoked, the elements of his sketch of eurocentric world history have so saturated the intellectual atmosphere that we have ended up speaking Marxist prose without knowing it or being aware that alternative idealist and purely political or tragic interpretations of modern history were being abandoned without a struggle. Psychological models of history, dependent upon the emergence of great men who shaped states and empires, were surrendered by professional historians in favor of the grand succession of reified class systems in which individual names were virtually submerged.

The pattern of feudalism, capitalism, communism as the successive historical forms was not invented by Marx out of whole cloth, as he was well aware; he inherited from Saint-Simon, Guizot, Sismondi, and earlier French Revolutionary thinkers, who had proposed triads with a different nomenclature. But Marx's outline was so detailed and persuasive in its presentation that his doctrine routed its rivals, and we have unconsciously fallen in with his pattern, Hegelian residues and all.

Since a theory of classes in struggle was the clue to understanding the stages of social-economic development, Marx's conceptions of a dominant class ideology, the overlapping of the systems and their internal conflicts, methods of determining the tempo and conditions of the disintegration of old classes and the birth of new ones, infiltrated our vocabulary to the point where a deliberate effort must be made if one is to think in other terms. Economists and sociologists are constantly improvising new classificatory models, introducing terminology that gives the appearance of being empirically more valid than the structure Marx built, albeit in social crises we tend to fall back into his rhetoric. The myth of the class struggle has been one of the most tenacious illusions Marxist thought has bequeathed to the twentieth century. And despite its excision from political manifestoes, its day is not yet done. Like the ancient gods, it is capable of many metamorphoses.

Marx constantly revised the strategy for the coming revolution because the event was contingent upon unpredictable circumstances. Precise outlines of the next moves in the class struggle and elaborate descriptions of future post-revolutionary society were anathema to him. The whole body of his work depicted a hell on earth for workers and foretold a paradisaical future; but though the emission of this revolutionary haze into the atmosphere was permissible, the specific instructions for immediate action imparted by utopia-bearing rivals were forbidden.

Revolutionary redemption was pushed into the indefinite future in Marx's reflections, as each outburst of rebellious energy in the countries of Europe dissipated into thin air and left behind nothing but another cohort of disgruntled émigrés, who spent themselves in orgies of backbiting in Paris and London. The disasters of 1848–1849 did not shake Marx's faith in the revolution. He returned to the documents once again, and blamed himself for having misread the economic and political oracles. He was convinced that a more profound examination of the signs would this time lead him to the true analysis of revolutionary potentialities, though he remained leery of detailed utopian predictions.

Marx understood the kind of conduct that would raise proletarian consciousness and ring the tocsin of revolution when the appropriate objective and subjective conditions were ripe; but he would not lay down the law in advance in particular instances and he was loath to specify an arrival date for the revolutionary train. This uncertainty did not prevent him from making sanguine pronouncements in private correspondence about how auspicious a situation was in a given country. Often he grasped at a straw—an isolated strike, a riot, a passing electoral victory—as a sign of the impending apocalypse. Usually his wishes outstripped his rigorous, disabused analysis. Engels sometimes joined Marx in his rosy forecasts, though not without a touch of humor, as in his letter of late September 1856: "This time there will be a dies irae such as never before; the whole of Europe's industry will be kaputt, all markets overstocked (already nothing more is being shipped to India), all the propertied classes in the soup, complete bankruptcy of the bourgeoisie, war and total disorder. I, too, believe that it will come to pass in 1857, and when I saw that you were once more buying furniture, I promptly declared the thing to be a certainty and was ready to make bets on it."[8]

Among the coteries of London émigrés, Marx was respected by some old comrades as the strategist of the world revolution, even when the bailiff in London sequestered his furniture for non-payment of rent and there was no armchair from which he could exercise his authority. His judgments were frequently incisive, but he could be dogmatic and wrong-headed, too. Perhaps the ultimate verdict on the performance of Marx and Engels as a pair of revolutionary strategists for the direction of the class war was handed down in 1907 by Lenin, the supreme practitioner in the field, in his preface to a collection of letters from Marx to his friend Sorge:

> Yes, Marx and Engels erred much and often in determining the proximity of revolution, in their hopes in the victory of revolution (e.g. in 1848 in Germany), in their faith in the imminence of a German Republic . . . They erred in 1871 when they were engaged in "raising revolt in Southern France" . . . But *such* errors—the errors of the giants of revolutionary thought who tried to raise and did raise the proletariat of the whole world above the level of petty, commonplace, and trifling tasks—are a thousand times more noble and magnificent

and *historically* more valuable and true, than the puerile wisdom of official liberalism, which sings, shouts, appeals and exhorts about the vanity of revolutionary vanities, the futility of the revolutionary struggle, and the charms of counter-revolutionary "constitutional" fantasies.[9]

With the appearance of Lenin, the Marxist doctrine of class struggle assumed a new dimension, but Old Mohr was not forgotten, though his role shrank from that of a savior to that of a forerunner.

=7=
The Ambiguities of Nationhood

Their own mode of representing things is the more deeply imprinted on every nation, because it is adapted to themselves, is suitable to their own earth and sky, springs from their mode of living and has been handed down to them from father to son . . . The most arbitrary national ideas and opinions are frequently such brain-drawn pictures, lines of the fancy most firmly interwoven with both body and mind.

—Herder, *Reflections on the Philosophy of the History of Mankind*

Even as Marx exalted the class struggle, the monomania of his life to which he sacrificed the well-being of his wife and children, so did he dismiss ethnicity and nationalism as militant forces in modern political consciousness. This was the fatal flaw in the Marxist vision of man that sapped the vitality of the doctrine in Central and Eastern Europe. Where Marxism survived, as in China, albeit in a much diluted potion, it was integrated with a revolutionary national movement that drew its strength from the image of the people as an extended family, the *minzhu*. The unifying force of Han ethnic origins—93 percent of the population—has stood China in good stead, as the revolutionary nation directed its rage against the foreign imperialists. Though the attempt to integrate an alien ethnic culture such as that of Tibet has been floundering, the nation as a whole assimilated a measure of Marxist rhetoric without being put off by its universalism.

Lenin's empire was not so fortunate. From its very foundation it failed to grapple successfully with ethnic residues that after seventy years have stubbornly refused to disappear. Where nationhood struck deep roots in the West, Marxist universalism may have made inroads, but it had no staying power. In Spain's civil war of 1936, the fervid oratory of La Pasionaria failed to dampen regional allegiances that in the end were disastrous to the Loyalist government.

Marxism in the West faced a challenge from ethnic and nationalist ideologies once believed to be mere vestiges from the past that had been superseded by universalism. In Marx's lifetime the First International was organized as a loose federation of delegates from nation-states who may or may not have been natives—he himself once represented a Swiss canton—and support for ethnic independence movements, above all in Poland and Ireland, was sometimes intermingled with dedication to the cause of world proletarian emancipation. But from the outset there was a certain fuzziness in Marx's conceptualization of the relationship between an ethnic unit and the universe of communism. He could hardly have foreseen that ethnicity would become the juggernaut crashing through the agglomeration of Soviet republics; the very existence of many of these exotic peoples was unknown to the dioscuri, who for all their encyclopedic knowledge concentrated on the European land mass west of the Urals and took for granted Russian domination of the vast Siberian territories.

The competition between two bodies of the oppressed of the earth, subjugated nations and downtrodden workers, plagued the First International from the moment of its foundation. Marx insisted on keeping the emancipation of the working classes as the vital core of its existence, while Mazzini's representatives tried to sidetrack the central mission by bestowing equal prominence on the struggles for national independence, introducing banal phraseology about liberty and justice into the statutes of the International. Marx avoided speaking at the grand public meetings of the International, where he would be eclipsed by the fiery orators of national independence movements. Though he reluctantly allowed some of the Mazzini verbiage to sneak into the propaganda of the International, the first formal proclamation of the organization was an *Address to the Workers* (1864), which he composed in accord with his own principles. Those who wanted to turn the International into an agency for sponsoring national uprisings lost out, temporarily.

The simmering conflict between the rival orientations continued throughout the life-span of the organization. Compromises affected the rhetoric, without touching the essence of the struggle. Support for the Polish cause became part of the program, but when the issue of Irish independence was raised, Marx was ambivalent despite the fervent commitment of the two Irish girls with whom Engels lived. Marx did not trust the Feinians, though he mourned their martyrs when the British executed them for political crimes. Mazzinian phrases like *Dio e popolo* threatened to divert attention from the elaborate proletarian theory on which Marx had been laboring for decades and which was receiving its definitive formulation in *Das Kapital*. Not that Marx and Engels were ill-informed about the existence of minor European national and local allegiances. Engels, journeying through Schleswig-Holstein, was learned and extraordinarily perceptive in identifying linguistic and character differences among borderline groups concentrated in a small area. But the very attractiveness of local loyalties made them dangerous.

Back in 1851 Engels had voiced his skepticism about the merits of the nationalist movements that were competing with the proletarian revolution. He had little sympathy for most of the aspiring nations in Central and Eastern Europe, recognizing only the Germans, the Magyars, and sometimes the Poles as historical nations in that part of the world. And even the Poles were for him a *nation foutue* whose existence could serve a purpose only until Russia itself underwent an agrarian revolution. "From that moment," he wrote to Marx on May 23rd,

> Poland will have absolutely no *raison d'être*. The Poles have done nothing else historically but play silly pranks both valiant and provocative. Nor does a single moment stand out when Poland, even if only by comparison with Russia, has contributed to progress or done something of historical significance. Russia, on the other hand, is truly progressive by comparison with the East. Russian rule, for all its baseness, all its Slavic dirtiness, is civilizing for the Black and Caspian Seas and Central Asia, for the Bashkirs and Tartars; and Russia has assimilated many more cultural, and especially industrial, elements, than Poland, which by nature is chivalrously indolent.[1]

Engels' denigration of small ethnic collectives was shared by Marx and reflected in the views of Lenin. Engels wrote in an article entitled "The Magyar Struggle": "There is no country in Europe which does not have in some corner or other one or several ruined fragments of peoples . . . These relics of a nation mercilessly trampled under foot in the course of history, as Hegel says, these *residual fragments of peoples,* always become fanatical standard-bearers of counter-revolution and remain so until their complete extirpation or loss of their national character, just as their whole existence in general is itself a protest against a great historical revolution."[2] In the Mexican War of 1846–1848, Engels admitted the injustice and inhumanity of the Yankee seizure of splendid California from the "lazy Mexicans," but such considerations had to bend before the world-historical significance of the industrial and commercial development that the conquest would inevitably bring in its wake.

Though the Marx children when they grew up were demonstratively sympathetic to the Poles—one of them even wore a cross in an expression of solidarity with their 1864 insurrection—and Engels ultimately married Lizzy Burns, a Sein Feiner, on her deathbed, both Marx and Engels always opted for the larger units of governance because they were more likely to foster industrialization, and that was the inevitable course of historical progress, the yardstick for the judgment of political events. Later in their lives they modified somewhat their criterion for the acceptance or rejection of a nationalist movement, but the underlying principle remained the same even when they made exceptions in specific cases for tactical reasons. Marx's weak defense of the Irish independence movement was involuted: Ireland had to be free in order to unite the workers living in England and put an end to the mutual hostility of Irish and English laborers, which hampered the rise of a revolutionary proletariat in the state that remained the herald of industrial change in the modern world.

The stigmatizing of national movements as retrograde, bourgeois, aristocratic, was a costly decision that was handed down to the Soviet empire with unfortunate consequences. Having adopted a position founded upon their analysis of history, Marx and Engels stubbornly clung to it, rarely re-examining the premises of their argument. They would not be like the waffling leaders of other ideological factions. The zeal and persistence with which they pursued their goals were at once sources of great strength and, at times, entrapments. With reluctance Marx surrendered on details, always confident that these were minor manoeuvres from which he could return to the original principle.

The spirit that Marx infused into the movement lasted for more than a century after his death, when the communist system collapsed. The resilience that he preserved for himself *in pectore* was not amenable to incorporation into mammoth structures. The wariness of Marx and Engels when confronted by nationalist agitators did not, however, persuade them to make common cause with utopians like the Fourierists, who denied the right of existence to nations only to favor still smaller units, the phalansteries. Bakunin's anarchist conventicles and Proudhon's cooperatives, along with other such fixations, were outlawed by Marx and Engels, who in public grudgingly accepted the validity of authentic historical nations, an intermediate position difficult to communicate to oratorical zealots. Marx reported to Engels that he had administered a reprimand to French members of the General Council of the International for considering nations "obsolete prejudices." He was as leery of breaking the world down into communes, Fourierist phalansteries, or other utopian groups as he was of Mazzinian nationalism. Although nations were recognized as units of organization, however, they were not to become the building blocks of revolutionary propaganda, eclipsing the international working-class movement.

When the two revolutionary ideals of the nation and proletarian universalism collided, Marx would always opt for the position that furthered the interests of what he believed to be the world revolution. German unification had to be supported because the large territory would facilitate proselytizing among its working class. Engels held fast to his early sharp distinction between recognized historical entities and mere ethnic enclaves. Yet acceptance of historical national traditions as the foundation of future societies always threatened denial of socio-economic classes as the solid elements in the conflicts leading to the revolution. Mazzini was an enemy because he represented a popular bourgeois, not a proletarian, solution to the crisis of the age. Sporadic national uprisings tended to be ill-prepared, much like the coups Bakunin would later plot or his fabrication of a Slav crusade; these were distractions from the role of a class-conscious proletariat.

Nineteenth-century utopian movements that in retrospect can be described as communist, socialist, or anarchist were preoccupied with the nature and size of the unit of living together once the ideal system of society would be put into place. Associations, cooperatives, communities, and phalansteries were by definition minuscule and for the most part self-sufficient entities, and no adequate provisions were made for their interrelationships. When experiments of the new order were established by Owenites and Fourierists, they sought out virgin territories where members could live in isolation, uncontaminated by the corrupt economic and political institutions that had condemned mankind to wretchedness. The Platonic model was still a living presence; in *The Laws* the optimum number of households was predetermined and tight eugenic controls kept the figure stable at 5,040. Communism in its twentieth-century form was condemned to triumph in vast empires; but long before Russian and Chinese communism became political realities, Marx and Engels had advocated extended societies as the ideal embodiments of communist civilization, fitting successors on a higher level to the international capitalist organizations.

The early statement of communism in Babeuf's *Manifesto of the Equals* was a plain declaration written with the presumption that it would be applicable to all human collectives without modification. A few years before this forthright, if naive, document was drafted in Paris, a long, complicated treatise composed in overheated German prose was published in Riga (1784–1791) by Johann Gottfried Herder, a German born in the Baltic region who had once been Immanuel Kant's student at the University of Königsberg. Herder's voluminous work, which bore the inflated title *Reflections on the Philosophy of the History of Mankind,* when vulgarized and condensed, was destined to become the romantic manifesto of ethnic or *Volk* identity in Eastern and Central Europe, the Bible of a nativist cultural rebellion against Frenchified cosmopolitanism and a political assault against the dynastic empires—Russian, Austrian, Prussian, and Turkish—that had emerged from the medieval world.

Thus two antagonistic revolutionary forces with their respective communist and nationalist doctrines, sprouting many different species, confronted each other at the opening of the nineteenth century. The perennial war between the socio-communist and the nationalist world outlooks has been an undercurrent of modern history down to the present. When this historical antagonism is complicated by the intrusion of world religions on crusade, monolithic secular doctrines are driven to embrace strange bedfellows and to spawn political hybrids that Marx never conceived of in his theory or practice.

What could be more remote and impersonal than an all-embracing Comintern, a communist international? What is more individual, specific, particular than an ethnic commitment, love of the land of one's birth, nostalgia for the smell and taste of mother's food, for the familiar turns and twists of a folk dance or a folk song, for the magical resonance of a native tongue? The former Soviet world, a union in name only, is today fragmented into more than a hundred groups speaking different languages. In the ethnic utopia, the individual fulfills his destiny in ethnic, not universal, emancipation. The core of his being is his *Volk* nature, as if he were present at the genesis of his tribe in an aboriginal landscape. His humanity is expressed in the specific *Volk* nature fashioned in the early years of his life, modifiable perhaps but in its essence stable. Its language is preserved in the intimacy of the kitchen and the bedchamber. If the siren call of the universalist future is muted even temporarily, the voice of the ethnic past wells up. Under communist hegemony and the doctrine of proletarian internationalism, ethnicity for years was concealed, relegated to obscure places beyond public view, while proclamations of future happiness for all mankind were being trumpeted in the marketplace.

A prepossession with ethnicity, that composite of past and present, fundamentally contradicted a Marxist philosophy based upon progressive phases of economic development culminating in a future golden age. The ethnic philosopher glorifies a mythic, heroic past, usually incarnated in a military chieftain who once expanded ethnic territories beyond their current boundaries. The lines between a clan, a tribe, and a nation are blurred as the dry institutions of the modern state system are infused with more primitive and emotively powerful attributes. The idealized past, fortified by traditional objects of consumption and entertainment, is enjoyed to the full in the present and holds the promise of continued sameness of pleasure in the foreseeable future. Ethnicity wants no new words or social forms.

The illusion that ethnic grievances would evaporate under a centralized system that gave paper recognition to minority rights was bequeathed to the Soviets by a man who had in his mind's eye the abstract communist species-being of the future, in which he was all too eager to dissolve his own ethnic identity. For Marx and for Lenin the allegiances of nationality were fundamentally reactionary leftovers of a primitive barbaric past destined to be wiped out by the benevolent advance of large-scale industrialization. The Second Party Congress of 1903 was the forum where Lenin, who had absorbed the Marxist demeaning of small ethnic units, first formulated a position on the question of nationality, which had become critical in the Russian and Austro-Hungarian Empires.

From the beginning, the role of the numerous Jews as a separate entity in that part of Europe brought to the surface a conflict within the revolutionary parties. The *Bund,* the Union of Jewish Socialists, claimed the right to be the exclusive representative of Jewish workers, a pretension steadfastly denied by Lenin, Struve, and Kautsky on many grounds. The Jews did not have a common language or territorial base that defined other nationalities, but a general theoretical principle was perhaps of greater import. Conceiving of the party of the revolution as a mere aggregate of autonomous national entities was anathema to Lenin; adherence to the revolution was not to be based on ethnic origin or education.

The same party spirit was to be infused equally into all individual members, and centralized policy was to eradicate any divisive tendencies. But though central control had manifest advantages in forging a common party consciousness before World War I, the policy was undermined by the growing national feeling among many peoples under Great Russian dominion. During the outbursts of ethnic consciousness against Tsarist oppression Lenin had been constrained to side with the rebels in order not to appear to be allied with the great Russian despot. When in 1901 the Russian government violated Finland's limited autonomy, the November 20th issue of Lenin's newspaper, *Iskra*, denounced the Tsarist regime in terms appropriate for revolutionaries, warning that those employed to reduce other peoples to slavery remained slaves themselves.

In the dual monarchy of Austria-Hungary the Marxist party was deeply divided between those who openly advocated ethnic self-determination and those who, though willing to grant cultural freedom to the numerous nationalities, balked at the prospect of political autonomy, which would have torn the party into a dozen separate nationalities intermingled territorially and with conflicting claims. Distinctions between historical and unhistorical nations were traced back to Marx and Engels in an effort to underplay ethnic ambitions, but in practice no position could be defended without allowing for a host of exceptions. From the early twentieth century on, national self-determination as proclaimed by Marxist parties often remained a hollow phrase.

Of late, the interpenetration of economic, military, linguistic, and personal elements has added to the complexity, rendering it virtually impossible in many areas to demarcate ethnic boundaries. Enclaves within enclaves have multiplied. Ethnic loyalties die hard, and the memory of outrages that small contiguous groups committed against each other in the recent or distant past is constantly reinforced by new bloody attacks and counterattacks.

Lenin had again set forth the Marxist position on national self-determination in a work published in August 1915, *Socialism and War*. Although the fundamental thrust of the book was a call to revolutionary Social Democratic parties to turn against their own governments, transforming the imperialist war into a series of civil wars, Lenin devoted a significant part of his diatribe to a plea addressed to the Social Democrats of the great nations, the dominating powers, to support the right of oppressed nations to self-determination. This he spelled out to mean the right to political separation, laying the foundation for a Leninist policy of anti-colonialism and proclaiming the doctrine of ethnic independence. But commitment to this position could be fraught with danger for the cause of world revolution, and Lenin hedged on his proclamation of ethnic separatism. Since in its very marrow Marxism was unsympathetic to small units of administration, never could they be sanctioned in the initial stages of the revolution. There was a profound and lasting conviction that many ethnic groups harbored reactionary bourgeois and aristocratic political allegiances. Hence Lenin's dictum, in the spirit of Marx, that defending the right of self-determination was not to be construed as in any way encouraging the formation of small states. On the contrary, it would lead to a freer, bolder, and more universal formation of larger governments and unions of governments—an outgrowth beneficial to the masses and in harmony with economic development.

Whenever demands for independence were being voiced during the breakup of empires, the orthodox Marxist-Leninist was confronted by dilemmas, and his responses were equivocal. Everything in the Marxist mentality militated against smallness, for great size, even gigantism, was inherent in the nature of modern economic development. Isolated unions of workers could be crushed more easily than broad cohesive units. But Lenin was aware that persecuted minorities could never be persuaded to join in common revolutionary action with proletariats that tolerated imperial hegemonies. Then the coin flipped to its obverse: the idea of the lawful separation of one nationality from another, "so-called national cultural autonomy," sheltered in its bosom a reactionary spirit, and the revolutionary struggle needed a broad-based organizational unity.

Weighing the thorny alternatives, even Lenin betrayed moments of indecision. He had little appreciation of the potency of ethnic cultural bonds; and in finally opting for centralism, as in virtually all other major choices, he was the true disciple of Marx and Engels. That Marx was born a Jew, that Lenin's maternal grandfather was a converted Jew, that many of the early Bolshevik leaders were Jews, should not be dismissed as irrelevant in attempting to understand the bent of Soviet policy. Awareness that communist universalism presented itself as a paradisaical ideal for persecuted, alienated Jews is, however, a far cry from the identification of communism as a world Jewish conspiracy.

For seventy-five years the international communist movement wrestled with the polar forces of ethnic identity and organizational centrality both in theory and in practice. Constitutional structures were devised to make "republics" out of ethnic units, paper governments that had no powers. At international assemblies there were verbal demonstrations in which the wretched of the earth joined hands. The first world congress of oppressed nationalities, which publicly proclaimed a formal communist policy of equal ethnic rights, took place in 1922–1923 in Baku, the city where seven decades later troops of the central Soviet military power opened fire to quell the internecine war of hostile ethnic enclaves whose jurisdictions overlapped. Neighboring ethnic units in Central and Eastern Europe almost invariably have clashing cartographical fantasies, because in the years after the breakdown of the empires—Turkish, Russian, Austrian, Polish—that had once held them in bondage, nationalities were shoved around like cattle as local potentates succeeded one another, leaving a record of enslavement and massacre. The linguistic map of the moment never corresponds to the illusory land maps engraved in the memories of rival groups. Self-determination through voting may turn out to perpetuate a historic crime. When tyranny begins to loosen its grip, ethnic minorities, once kept in check by fear, emerge in force. How dizzying the effect would be if maps of Vilnius and its environs representing the distribution of Poles, Lithuanians, Jews, Belorussians, in different centuries, were superimposed upon one another! Gravestones have no suffrage and exiles are forgotten.

After World War I, government authorities in Central and Eastern Europe, whether nominally democratic or communist, had treated Jews like Marx with a contempt that made a mockery of his universalist fantasy. During World War II the Jews of Eastern Europe had no choice but to side with the Russians against the Nazis advancing eastward. As the Russians pushed back the German tide after Stalingrad and reoccupied border lands, Jewish communists in the train of the Soviet army inflamed the enmity of native ethnic groups, rekindling endemic antisemitism, a hatred that outlived the extermination of millions of Jews, in which Ukrainians, Lithuanians, Latvians, Estonians, Poles, Belorussians, Hungarians, Romanians, Slovaks, and sundry other ethnic agglomerations in the region were often implicated. The schizophrenic behavior toward Jews in communist regimes or in freshly minted ex-communist regimes calls to mind Marx's incapacity to cope with his Jewish identity. Jewish communist and ex-communist leaders in Central and Eastern Europe, well into the present, have not been cleansed of their racial stigma any more than Karl Marx was when he was baptized.

Assimilation to an alien ethnic group, as Herder knew, is a long and bitter process. As ethnic consciousness is again afire in Central and Eastern Europe, a remnant of Jews who survived the Holocaust may have to emigrate to other continents. Minority rights, piously included in European treaties as far back as the Congress of Berlin in 1878, have remained dead letters. The wobbly line that distinguishes ethnic zealotry from racism is not always preserved by the devout cosmopolites of communism; atavistic drives break through.

In the Soviet Union, the flowery theory of ethnic recognition crumbled, as language rights were first granted, then rescinded with the shifting winds of policy, and in moments of danger for the Russian motherland in World War II "nations" hungry for ethnic rights were uprooted from their native soil, transported thousands of miles away, and often destroyed as enemies. With the installation of satellite socialist governments in Central and Eastern Europe in the aftermath of World War II, the doctrine of self-determination was in fact abolished and the USSR intervened with its armies to preserve the paramount interests of world revolution, identified with the Soviet Union. When in 1989 many of these oppressed nations were liberated in the course of a general restructuring of communist society, numerous ethnic enmities were left unresolved and threatening to the newly reorganized states; they could no longer be papered over with the vague general formulas Lenin had propounded in 1915. The explosive power of ethnic forces on the perimeter of the former Soviet Union has increased rather than diminished over the decades, and the end is not in sight. Freedom of speech has now allowed long-repressed resentments to find raucous expression. Deep-rooted hatreds such as antisemitism have regained the vigor of pre-revolutionary periods. Islam revived has become a powerful catalyst among millions of Soviet citizens in borderland republics whose identity was once blurred.

The failure of Marxism even to begin to appreciate the obstinate potency of ethnicity, whatever its cultural, economic, and religious origins might be, has remained one of the tragic consequences of a theory of human nature that ignored the irrational and the daemonic and tried to erase the brand markings of the historical. Not that tribes and nations relatively untouched by Marxism were any more felicitous in their mitigation of ethnic rivalries. Attempts in Africa and Asia to spring from tribalism into capitalism or communism in a variety of eclectic political forms have usually been accompanied by brutal tyrannies, irrespective of their nominal doctrinal inspirations.

In the writings of Marx, ethnic questions were subordinate, so that at first glance it seems preposterous to regard them as on the same level of significance as the rest of the communist ideology. In official histories of his thought the question of his own ethnic consciousness has often been casually dismissed; he himself had referred to it only in a few isolated passages. The *Communist Manifesto* had predicted in 1848: "National differences and antagonisms among peoples are daily vanishing more and more, owing to the development of the bourgeoisie, to freedom of commerce, to the world market, to uniformity in the mode of production and in the conditions of life corresponding thereto. The supremacy of the proletariat will cause them to vanish still faster."[3] The confidence of the *Manifesto* was misplaced. Ethnic and national rivalries and wars in the next century and a half deflated its sanguine prophecy, and communist man turned out to be as bloodthirsty as his ancestors.

=== 8 ===
Utopias:
The Approved and the Forbidden

Prometheus: I caused mortals to cease foreseeing doom.
Chorus: What cure did you provide them against that sickness?
Prometheus: I placed in them blind hopes.
Chorus: That was a great gift you gave to men.
Prometheus: Besides this, I gave them fire.

—Aeschylus, *Prometheus Bound*

Among the hundreds of disparate pronouncements on human need in modern times, two are curiously linked. The first is from *King Lear*. After the king had been mercilessly nagged by his daughter to dismiss his retainers as serving no *need* for a retired monarch, he roared with rage:

> O! Reason not the need, our basest beggars
> Are in the poorest thing superfluous;
> Allow not nature more than nature needs,
> Man's life is cheap as beast's.

The other declaration was made by that life-long admirer of Shakespeare who knew large parts of his plays by heart, Karl Marx, in a letter written to his follower Wilhelm Bracke on May 5, 1875. It was published posthumously in 1891 by Friedrich Engels, who captioned it *Critique of the Gotha Program of the Social Democratic Party*. In our time the aristocratic *Almanach* with which the city of Gotha was long associated has yielded to the *Critique*. The political circumstances that called forth the letter—Marx's attempt to supervise from his exile in London, to control from afar, the compromise draft prepared at Gotha by two hostile branches of German Social-ism, the Eisenachians (who followed Marx) and the renegade Las-salleans—are by now generally forgotten, and so is Engels' motive in dispatching the letter to Karl Kautsky's journal *Die Neue Zeit,* where it was unceremoniously followed by Max Schippel's article on "Zuckersteuer und Zuckerindustrie" (The Sugar Tariff and the Sugar Industry). Fundamentally, Marx in 1875 felt that a new party program was supererogatory; the *Communist Manifesto,* cogent and lucid, had been around for popular consumption since 1848, and the publication of another statement of principles was likely to be obfuscatory. Moreover, neither Marx nor Engels had been consulted about the new articles of union, which had come as a bolt from the blue, and the leaders of the world communist movement were angry. But since the German and international tactical situations demanded Marx's immediate intervention (he was under simultaneous attack from anarchist Bakuninists and reformist Lassalleans), the ailing patriarch of the revolution, despite his doctor's orders, laboriously wrote out line-by-line glosses on the draft, and then concluded them with a mock religious "Dixi et salvavi animam meam," a Latin version of Ezekiel 3:19.

For a time the glosses on the Gotha Program had great prestige in the communist thought of the West because they were quoted as authoritative by Lenin in *State and Revolution* and by other theore-ticians whenever party conflicts raised issues of doctrinal purity in the face of "opportunism." Among other things, the *Critique of the Gotha Program* contained a clear-cut passage on the "revolutionary dictatorship of the proletariat" as the appropriate transitional stage between capitalism and communism. By now the tactical measures and programmatic criticisms painfully spelled out in the *Critique of the Gotha Program* have become too old for usage even by the most devout European followers of Marx, though before the unification of Germany the East German official history of the German work-ing-class movement still called the hallowed text the most important theoretical document of Marxism after the *Communist Manifesto* and *Das Kapital.* It is reported that peasant communes in China during the Cultural Revolution discussed the *Critique* in their edu-cational assemblies, and faint echoes of its phraseology can be detected in the constitution of the People's Republic of China. Time has diminished the reverence for Marx's utterances, though whether the Chinese analyses of his words ever bore any kinship to their original meaning is doubtful. In the West, the centenary of the *Critique* was not marked with anything like the festive reconsiderations that accompanied the anniversary of *Das Kapital*'s appearance in 1867; but the utopian principles enunciated in Marx's letter to Bracke long continued to resound throughout the world. The banderole inscribed "From each according to his abilities, to each according to his needs" may be getting a bit frayed with age, but it is still fluttering in the winds of doctrine, belief, and hope. A full version of Marx's utopia was embodied in the paragraphs of the *Critique* where he distinguished for the first time between Phase I of communist society, during which real equality could not yet be instituted because economic and cultural resources were too limited, and Phase II, the higher plane of communism. Here Marx also included one of his very rare characterizations of the future communist world.

Both Marx and Engels on occasion had a word of approval for old utopian socialists and communists as antecedents—Thomas More, Thomas Müntzer, and the Levellers faithfully reflected the conditions of their times—but what was innocent daydreaming up to about the end of the eighteenth century could not be considered so thereafter. The later utopians, without any sense of the objective conditions of society and its historical development, were spinning purely subjective fantasies that distracted the proletariat from its destined political mission. Once Marx and Engels had come onto the world stage, any utopian survivors had to be repudiated, since they had been transcended by scientific socialism. The idea of utopia acquired heavily pejorative overtones in communist theory. As the appointed guardian of true revolutionary consciousness, Marx was obligated to combat every utopian system that raised its empty head—Owenite, Saint-Simonian, Fourierist, Blancian, Proudhonian, Stirnerian, Weitlingian, Bakuninist, Lassallean, Dühringean, in fact any deviation from the realistic and correct doctrinal position set forth in the writings of Marx and Engels. "Utopian" became an epithet of denigration to be splashed onto any theoretical opponent.

If a roundabout story is credible, Marx became more, rather than less, severe with the utopians as he advanced in years: Georges Sorel in the *Reflections on Violence* reported that, according to the economist Professor Lujo Brentano, Marx wrote the English Positivist Edward Spencer Beesly in 1869: "The man who draws up a programme for the future is a reactionary."[1]

Yet, despite the persistence with which Marx and Engels belabored contemporary utopians, essential parts of the *Critique of the Gotha Program* were the answer to a utopian inquiry that Marx himself had initiated. "What transformation will the nature of the state undergo in a communist society? In other words, what social functions will then remain that are analogous to present-day state functions?" This question could only be answered "scientifically" *(wissenschaftlich)*, he declared in the *Critique,* but some pages back a grand apostrophe had already escaped him and he was caught in the utopian web.

> In a higher phase of communist society, when the enslaving subordination of the individual to the division of labor, and with it the antithesis between mental and physical labor, has vanished; when labor is no longer merely a means of life but has become life's principal need; when the productive forces too have increased with the all-round development of the individual, and all the springs of shared wealth flow more abundantly—only then will it be possible to transcend completely the narrow horizon of bourgeois right, and only then will society be able to inscribe on its banners: From each according to his abilities, to each according to his needs [Jeder nach seinen Fähigkeiten, jedem nach seinen Bedürfnissen]![2]

Implicit in this passage was the quintessential problem of what are and what are not human needs that has always been at the core of utopian thought in the West. The question of need has been analyzed in abstract philosophical terms, as in Plato's *Philebus,* or in concrete physiological terms. Distinctions have been established between need and desire, between authentic and inauthentic needs. The relationship of needs and abilities has been probed. Marx's own interpretation of needs and abilities can perhaps best be established, not in an isolated or autonomous commentary on the brief, laconic phrases of the *Critique,* but in juxtaposition with the views of the

French utopian communists and socialists who antedated him and whose followers survived to bedevil him, and in relation to his own views on other occasions. The French utopian tradition about the future of society was the most serious body of utopian thought with which he was confronted. Though Marx had a way of defining himself by negation, he did not live by refutation alone, and the encyclopedic and synthesizing mind of this man deeply immersed in the culture of his age managed to assimilate the ideas of his enemies even while he was berating them. Marx's utopia, like so many of his provocative ideas, was the offspring of his aggressive drive, the need to demolish the last remnant of Lassallean doctrine and tactics.

In the *Manifesto of the Equals,* that primary document of the modern communist utopia, Gracchus Babeuf had given revolutionary content to Morelly's plan for agrarian communism in the *Code de la nature* (1755). Marx was aware from his reading of Philippe Buonarroti that there had also been a deliberate and momentous decision among the members of Babeuf's Conspiracy of the Equals to reject the equal, private, individual holdings of More's *Utopia* in favor of communally held property as the only feasible way to enforce equality. Equality for Babeuf presupposed a continent—almost ascetic—community, in which shirkers would be severely punished. Absolute equality, immediately proclaimed and instituted, was the paramount human need, not in its vague French Revolutionary sense, which could be twisted in almost any economic or social direction, but in plain terms: one man should not have more of *anything* than another. If there was not enough to go around, the product itself was to be eliminated. This egalitarian communism assumed the virtual replication of needs, desires, and abilities among all citizens, though it made some special allowance for children, the feeble, and the elderly. Its intolerance of any distinctions was fierce. To be equal, not to suffer the humiliation of a superior's slights or power or authority, was to set the tone of life, and all else was to be sacrificed to it. "We are all equal, is it not so?" the *Manifesto of the Equals* asked rhetorically.

"Well, we henceforth intend to live and to die equal, just as we were born; we want real equality or death, that is what we need. And we shall have it, this *égalité réelle,* no matter what the price. . . .

Woe to anyone who would offer resistance to so keen a desire! . . . May all the arts be destroyed, if need be, as long as we have *égalité réelle*."[3] The Babouvist dogma of immediate equality lived on in the popular French communist tradition that Buonarroti, a survivor of the Conspiracy, resurrected in the 1830s.

When the young Marx was exposed to Babouvism, he rejected it totally and unequivocally. His loathing for instant egalitarianism was a constant of his thought from his first appearance in the political arena. Although he could treat more tenderly the egalitarian communistic utopians of the eighteenth century whom he knew, Mably and Morelly, their identification with the consequences of their thought in the abortive Babouvist uprising caused him to sneer even at these guileless ones.

In the *Communist Manifesto* of 1848 the Babeuf type of communism was labeled reactionary. "It teaches a general asceticism and a crude leveling."[4] From the 1840s onward, Marx, who saw himself as coming to mankind in order to establish a communist system for a dynamic, world technological-industrial mechanism inherited from bourgeois capitalism, heaped scorn upon the eighteenth-century French founders of "optimum little republics" based on egalitarian principles and their nineteenth-century German imitators with their "federal republics with social institutions" and vapid egalitarian slogans. The German scribblers of the Gotha Program of 1875 had fallen into the same oratorical trap, and he would have none of them. The notes that preceded Engels' *Anti-Dühring* (whose express purpose was to distinguish authoritatively between utopian and scientific socialism) are spotted with similar jibes, witness that the two men were on the same track. "To want to establish Equality = Justice as the highest principle and the ultimate truth is absurd." Ahistorical manifestoes like the Gotha Program were drivel for both of them. "So the concept of equality itself is a product of history to whose working out the whole of pre-history is necessary," wrote Engels. "It has not existed as truth from all eternity." When Engels heard talk of a sudden communist revolution against the "existing military bureaucratic state," he could only liken such political rashness to Babeuf's attempt "to jump immediately from the Directory into communism."[5] As late as 1885, recollecting the Babouvist influence in the secret League of the Just and the League of Communists in the 1840s, Engels continued to denounce them for deriving community of property from the principle of equality rather than seeing communism as an outgrowth of the historical process.

Inequalities were inevitable in the first phase of communism as it would emerge, after long birth pangs, from capitalist society, Marx insisted in his *Critique,* and for Social Democrats in a program of unification to advertise promises of instant equality promiscuously was a base deception. Justice (he meant distributive justice), the law of a society, could not be more complete than its economic structure and the cultural level dependent upon it would permit. True equality had to await the higher stage of communism.

The idea of absolute equality, in the Babouvist sense, as a human need had become deeply rooted in certain branches of French communist thought of the 1830s and 1840s, usually among the violent direct actionists such as Auguste Blanqui. But equality clashed sharply with other utopian needs as they had been set forth by two seminal utopian thinkers and their followers who had moved in a very different direction from Babeuf: Saint-Simon and Fourier. These were men toward whose followers both Marx and Engels had to adopt a generally negative attitude, which was a utopian's due. But despite their criticism, ambivalent feelings colored their treatment. All utopian thought was inimical to scientific socialism, but some conceptions were less inimical than others. In the collected works of Marx and Engels scores of citations deal with Saint-Simon and Fourier and their adherents, and they range from contempt to praise. The writings of these utopian socialists left their mark on the banderole of the *Critique of the Gotha Program.*

In these two most original of nineteenth-century French utopians, Saint-Simon and Fourier, and among their disciples, the idea of equality had become identified with dread recollections of the Terror. In revulsion against the *égalité* of the *sans-culottes* and of Babeuf, they denounced absolute equality—Saint-Simon in the name of a new or refurbished organismic conception of society and the markedly *unequal* needs of human beings for self-fulfillment in different types of work and emotional expression, Fourier in the name of the unique and variegated psychic needs and goals of men that were totally discordant with the ideal of equality. Viewed through the lenses of Marx and Engels in the 1840s, some of these utopian ideas appeared less pernicious than the wanton egalitarian and libertarian slogans that were being hawked in the European revolutionary marketplace.

Saint-Simon and the Saint-Simonians had come to dwell on the differences in human needs in both professional and amorous self-actualization, and they totally reversed the Babouvist ideal of equality as the final utopian condition. On his deathbed, Saint-Simon reflected that if he had done anything for mankind, it was to proclaim the need for the free development of distinctive natural talents. "Talents" was his word and the Napoleonic overtones are patent; the Saint-Simonians later called them "capacities." Among members of the cult, fulfillment of capacities became the new formulation of the primary need in utopia. *Un capacité,* around the time of the Restoration, acquired the meaning of a man expert in some branch of activity as well as the expertise itself. (It had a scientific significance.) *C'est un capacité* was said of a person, of Flaubert's father, a noted doctor, for example. Utopia was no longer confined to equal access to a sufficiency of food and drink and knowledge, which, though hardly a reality in early nineteenth-century France, could be hypothetically assumed in any futurist vision of the development of great productive resources. What was now at issue was the realization of man's creative potential, his professional capacity, his innate talent, but with modern scientific, not Platonic, connotations.

Marx in his early period highlighted untrammeled creativity as the primary attribute of man under communism; his conception of creativity was tinged with the values of both French and German Romanticism and involved the expression of the unique inner self of each man. A new typology of human personality formulated by the Saint-Simonians for utopian man, though it bears some intellectual resemblance to the Platonic division of golden, silver, and brass men, has very different roots. Men needed to actualize their psychic beings in at least two major areas: creative work and ideal sexual relationships. And these, it was newly appreciated, were complex and varied, not easily subsumed under egalitarian rubrics, except perhaps such coveralls as equal access to self-actualization. Whereas Plato aimed to keep his castes as stable as possible and controlled the guardians eugenically to prevent the birth of brass children among them (Marx was always sarcastic in his references to the purported communistic systems of the ancients, especially those of Plato, Xenophon, and Plutarch's Lycurgus), the Saint-Simonians would abolish inheritance and give every newborn babe an equal chance to express its natural talent and to have it developed through education.

The Saint-Simonians divided men into three fundamental physiological types—the idea originally came from the physiologist Marie-François-Xavier Bichat—those with innate scientific capacities, those with administrative or manual capacities, and those with moral-artistic-religious capacities. Around this new triad they heaped up the slogans of their utopian propaganda. When after their internal schisms they established a religious hierarchy, the capacity to love mankind was the talent that counted most, since the need to love and be loved was the overriding human need. The function of the Saint-Simonian priest was to help adepts find their optimum situation in the hierarchy. On the morrow of the July Revolution, the Saint-Simonian Fathers issued a proclamation abolishing inheritance and setting forth the new hierarchical principle: "Each will be placed according to his capacity and rewarded according to his works." "Each according to his capacity, to each capacity according to its works," was emblazoned on the masthead of their newly acquired newspaper, *Le Globe*. In their sermons and formal expositions of the doctrine, they testified to their recognition of sexual needs with "rehabilitation of the flesh" and "emancipation of woman." They introduced novelty into the political vocabulary: "The end of the exploitation of man by man; its replacement with the exploitation of nature by man," and "Performance of the function to which a man's natural calling destines him." Other battle cries were repetitions, with minor modifications: "Each one pursuing his own capacity in order that its products may be distributed to each one according to his works"; or "To each, labor according to his calling and rewards according to his works"; or "An education and function that conform to one's natural calling and a reward that conforms to one's works."[6] The Saint-Simonians were clearly adapting religious terminology—*oeuvres, vocation*—for their program. And in his turn Marx utilized the Saint-Simonian language. Though he could never stomach Saint-Simonian religious balderdash, the *Critique of the Gotha Program* phrase "From each according to his abilities" has an unmistakable Saint-Simonian resonance. This is not to say that Marx consciously plagiarized the Saint-Simonians; but their proclamation "Each will be placed according to his capacity and rewarded according to his works" is a pretty fair statement of Marx's expectations for the first phase of communist society.

When the Saint-Simonians launched the quest for a Female Messiah and made the banking system the administrative heart of their economy, Marx ridiculed them, deriding as hypocrites the former adepts who had turned into supporters of Napoleon III and had become prosperous international financiers. Nevertheless, he and Engels continued to study the writings of Saint-Simon as they had done since their twenties. In the *German Ideology* of 1845–1846, Marx, who occasionally flaunted his pedantry, had torn to shreds *The Social Movements in France and Belgium* (Darmstadt, 1845) by Karl Grün, a leader of the "true socialists," for its misquotations of Saint-Simonian and Fourierist writings. After Marx's death, Engels and later Lenin applied words like "genius" to Saint-Simon for his insights into the conflict of classes. Abhorrent though the Saint-Simonian principle of hierarchy was to Marx and Engels, they recognized the affinity between their own and the Saint-Simonian outlook for the future world—an endlessly dynamic prospect founded upon the boundless expansion of science and technology, exploitation of the inexhaustible natural resources of the globe, and the flowering of human capacities.

In retrospect, Charles Fourier, that lonely, pinched bachelor of early nineteenth-century Paris, has emerged as the most imaginative modern utopian of human needs. He poses the problem of the other half of Marx's banderole, "To each according to his needs," with startling originality. The older utopian ideal of Western man was shifted dramatically away from calm felicity, achieved through more or less equality, to the excitement of novelty and of rich sensation as the supreme need. As men were different so did their needs vary. For Fourier, the objects of need were primarily sensate and sensual, though he impishly made provision in his phalansteries for the residual rationalist needs of moralist professors of natural law by letting them write parodies of their own works for comic relief. Individual needs were psycho-physical and innate. They were extraordinarily complex, consisting in each person of a wide range of sensory responses, unique sexual and social demands.

Fourier's utopia was based on phalansteries of about eighteen hundred persons each, because the psycho-physical needs of most humans required the presence in their proximity of that many individuals, all different, for fulfillment—we might now say optimal interaction. Individual fulfillment thus called for a communal society of great variety, an idea that would reappear in its Marxist incarnation as the need of every individual to enjoy a communal existence as the precondition for personal self-actualization. Through reflection in the other and in social action each man's being was realized. In the *German Ideology,* following Fourier, Marx wrote: "Only in a state of community with others has each individual the means to develop his predispositions in all directions; only in a state of community will personal freedom thus become possible."[7] The reaffirmation of man's social nature in utopian thought may now sound banal, but in its day it had a psychological dimension that went far beyond the old saws about man as a political animal and challenged the presumed bourgeois doctrine of absolute individualism.

If there was an implied hierarchy of values among the Fourierist needs, it was the rarer and more extravagant needs that were cherished above the ordinary and commonplace. Fourier had a predecessor in the Marquis de Sade, one of the few moralists he acknowledged as a progenitor, whose heroes were supermen precisely because of their abnormal capacity for the quick renewal of appetites for food and sex. The phalanstery would seek out these peculiar specimens, cultivate them, and search, even throughout the world, for their social complements in other persons. To the extent that there was a unitary social goal in Fourier's system, it was the multiplication of sensate needs. Danger to society and the individual was incurred only when desires were choked up—his term was *égorgement*—for then they tended to seek release in destructive channels. Though in his published works Fourier avoided discussion of homosexual needs, his manuscripts, especially the *Nouveau monde amoureux*, ranked them along with others. The multiplication of varied relationships and a capacity for rich and complicated sensory experiences were highly prized, as was the talent for imparting pleasure to others through artistic creations. Work became indistinguishable from play and erotic pleasure, as every work group in the phalanstery was bound by amorous ties of one kind or another. The needs of Fourier's phalansterians were continually changing both in the course of a single day and in the various stages of the life cycle. They were not infinite in number, but were categorizable by types and manipulable with the aid of central filing systems of each man's profile of needs. Computerized pairing and selection were approximated manually.

Like all magnificent obsessions, Fourier's system provided for virtually every contingency, and he developed intricate ceremonial institutions to take care of those situations where a specific desire, by definition equivalent to a need in his vocabulary, could not enjoy immediate satisfaction, such as two men wanting the same girl at the same time. Everything was arranged to mitigate the pain of a denial. For Fourier, the calm felicity of the pre-Revolutionary utopia had become the yawning boredom of the nineteenth-century French bourgeois family ruled in stolid silence by a patriarchal, though cuckolded, lord. In his utopia of endless stimulation, monotony— the bane of modern society—would be banished forever. Although he would allow the vestal or celibate or monogamous state for those who chose it, he doubted whether many would opt for such impoverished forms of existence.

But Fourier's utopia of maximal dynamism in action and in sensation was too far-out to be acceptable in the nineteenth century, even in radical circles. His own disciples bowdlerized his writings. Socialist thinkers of the Victorian world, like Marx, could not endure this utopia in all its nakedness; for him it reeked of the brothel. Many Fourier manuscripts were not published until the 1960s, when there was a recrudescence of interest in a utopia of the free satisfaction of all psycho-physical needs; it found contemporary parallels in such men as Wilhelm Reich, Norman Brown, and Herbert Marcuse in one of his moods. Marx was clearly exposed to Fourier's conception of needs and read his critical anatomy of the cheats of industrial civilization and the hypocrisy of bourgeois social values with an appreciative eye. But he was not ready to follow Fourier in his labyrinthine analysis of psycho-sexual needs, and he was resentful whenever the label "communist" was attached to him. Marx's own language remained properly vague and philosophical when he depicted man's relationship to the sensate world of objects, human and natural.

If in rationalist and argumentative propositions with respect to the philosophical character of communism and historical materialism Marx and Engels had no significant disagreements (*pace* those who have tried to drive a wedge between them), differences in the modes of life of the communist dioscuri may suggest differences in their attitudes toward sex and the family. Nonetheless, when they paint the family of the future, their palette is the same. Marx was brought up and remained enclosed for all ostensible purposes within the boundaries of the Western Judeo-Christian family as it had evolved into its bourgeois form by the nineteenth century.

Wherever his personal impulses may have led Marx, the destruction of the nuclear family was not an integral part of his utopia, and those societies that accepted his philosophical guidance did not tamper with the family structure beyond the verbal assertion of a measure of female equality in relationships. In the 1870s, Marx and Engels occasionally exchanged notes on the sexual customs of the medieval Welsh and passed on to each other somewhat salacious jokes about them; but in general the traditional monogamous family structure was not attacked in public. In fact, wiping out the evils of capitalism would render familial ties less constrained by economic considerations, more open, and more loving—that was a recurrent Marxist promise over the decades. In the 1840s, Marx was already quoting Morelly on the deleterious psychic effects of private ownership on marital relationships. "Interest denatures the human heart and spreads bitterness over the most tender relations. These are transformed into heavy shackles that our married couples hate, and they end up hating themselves."[8] (Self-hate was a feeling that kept bobbing its head through the crust of Marx's rationalist system in unexpected places.)

One might point, in contradiction, to a footnote in the *German Ideology:* "That the supersession of an individualist economy cannot be divorced from the supersession of the family is self-evident";[9] but this was a solitary manuscript observation of the 1840s, part of a polemic with German ideologists who denied that the family had its origin in production relations and established the "concept of the family" as a timeless absolute. In his manuscripts of 1844, though Marx continued to treat of sexuality in the same abstract terminology as need, alienation, and work, there is the prospect that in the future communal state, sexual relations will become uniquely human, transcending animality. Nothing resembling the concreteness of Fourier's understanding of sex is in evidence. The brilliantly mocking excursion on the abolition of the family in the *Communist Manifesto* patently refers to the contemporary bourgeois family.

In his brief sketch of the history of changing forms of love and sexuality Engels could write of the Greek poet Anacreon, with no more than an arched Victorian eyebrow, that "sexual love *[Geschlechtsliebe]* in our sense was of so little concern to him, even the sex of the loved person was all one to him."[10] But when Engels inherited Marx's notes on the anthropologist Lewis H. Morgan's *Ancient Society* and expanded them into a full-blown work, *The Origin of the Family,* in which he spelled out the derivation of the family from production relations, he probably stated the definitive views common to both of them on the historical transformations of the family and its possible future, views that were not always acceptable to the German Social Democrats and English "socialists" among whom he lived and died.

As Engels examined Morgan's historical hypothesis, the outrageous Fourier's stadial theory of the growth of civilization took on new meaning, and he wrote to Kautsky on April 26, 1884: "I must show how brilliantly Fourier anticipated Morgan in so many things. Through Morgan, Fourier's critique of civilization appears in all its genius."[11] But this did not imply acceptance of the bewildering multiplicity of sexual patterns prescribed by Fourier for "harmonian society." Engels' prognostication of the future of the family after the abolition of property was not indecently Fourierist. He argued that, with female equality, optional divorce when love vanished, the end of prostitution and of covert polygamy, the marital bond would become stronger than ever, since it would be the product of free choice. *En passant,* Engels delivered himself of sententious sexological opinions in the temper of the age: "The duration of a seizure of sexual love for an individual is very different for different individuals, particularly among men," or "Sexual love is by its very nature exclusive."[12] His descriptions of the contemporary bourgeois family were in the acerb Saint-Simonian and Fourierist spirit, but the communist future would nurture a loving, monogamous, and lasting relationship.

The all-around *(allseitig)* development of man in Marx's utopia is rather gingerly when it comes to sex. Herbert Marcuse's emphasis on aesthetic-sexual needs as the authentic, vital needs of a new free society, which so titillated the generation of 1968, is a leap that the Victorian Marx never made. Reading into him the validation of such needs had to await twentieth-century Freudo-Marxists. Fourier's chief innovation, the expansion of sensations and sensual capacities in all directions as superior to rational capacities, escaped Marx or repelled him. He was much more restricted in his outlook, and recognized as legitimate only reasonable, refined, and decent needs, which stopped far short of Fourier's equation of desires with needs. Marx was still too deeply imbued with the rationalist tradition of Plato and More to allow free play to all psycho-sexual desires as authentic needs. By no means was appeasement of desire necessarily salutary: English workers could be enslaved the more readily by catering to their taste for carousing in taverns. Marx's diagnosis of the function of drink among the English working classes is paralleled by Marcuse's depiction of the capitalist use of sex to dull the mass of the workers and rob them of true consciousness.

Marx refused to identify work with pleasure in Fourier's terms, and the attractiveness of labor was not bound up with erotic stimulus. Though in most of his writings he did not envisage the abolition of work, he expected that it could ultimately be reduced to a minimum number of hours. Total freedom from necessity was unlikely, though it might be possible to transcend the antithesis between free time and work time. The most famous passage on the subject appears toward the end of the third volume of *Das Kapital,* which Engels edited:

> Just as the savage must grapple with nature in order to satisfy his needs, sustain his life, and procreate, so must civilized man, under all forms of society and all possible modes of production. With his development, this realm of natural necessity is broadened because his needs become more extensive; but simultaneously the forces of production that satisfy these needs are increased. Freedom in this realm can be achieved only when communized man, the associated producers, regulate their material exchange with nature in a rational manner, when they bring it under their communal control, instead of being dominated by this exchange as if by a blind force, when they accomplish this with the least possible expenditure of their strength and under conditions that are the most worthy and most fitting for their human nature. But this always remains a realm of necessity. Beyond this realm begins a development of human powers that are ends in themselves, the true realm of freedom. This realm of freedom, however, can only flower on the foundation of the realm of necessity. The shortening of the working day is its fundamental prerequisite.[13]

In Phase I of Marx's communist world, work would no longer be dehumanizing because man would not be pouring his being into a fetish of his own making, a machine belonging to others, and he would be rewarded for the whole of the labor he invested without sacrificing a surplus to the capitalist. The same amount of labor that he gave to society in one form he would get back in another. This considers individuals only as workers. In Phase II, however, though performing equal labor, one individual might in fact receive more than another because as unequal individuals their needs differed. The division of physical and mental work would tend to be obliterated, the distortion of personality in highly specialized tasks would be eliminated, and the realm of freedom would be approached. There is a passage of the *German Ideology* in which the young Marx, despite his distaste for Fourier on sex, seems to cut a page out of Fourier's work plan—the liberated man will go hunting, fishing, shepherding, or engage in intellectual pursuits at will— though the digression in which Marx describes this free movement from one occupation to another in the course of a day, ending with after-dinner indulgence in criticism of the critical philosophy, is partly satirical, despite the fact that it has sometimes been read straight-faced by the more earnest Marxologists.

In his manuscripts, Marx is full of praise for Fourier's conception of childhood without repression and his permissive system of education. But the *Critique of the Gotha Program,* seen in its historical context of the 1870s, ignored Fourierist psycho-sexual needs and concentrated primarily on bread and butter and shelter, health insurance, and a guarantee of leisure. Marx did not have to alarm the proper Social Democrats to whom he addressed himself with the intrusion of forbidden Fourierist thoughts on free love. What Marx implied in the *Critique* was that in higher stages of communism the elementary needs of a man and his family for food and housing and care during illness would be met by society, irrespective of the quantity of social labor he was able to contribute. Marx recognized that there were differences in skills, hence his dictum: "From each according to his abilities"—that phrase with a Saint-Simonian ring; but the returns would be determined not by labor performance or labor value produced but by sumptuary needs, measured by the size of a man's family and its requirements. Beyond the work economy, Marx unfolds a vision of abundance and self-actualization, though not a utopia of absolute freedom from necessity.

The actual phraseology of Marx's utopia also approximates closely the title page of Etienne Cabet's Fourierist *Voyage en Icarie* (1840), where the formula is writ large: "To each according to his needs, from each according to his strength"; and the woolly doctrines of Louis Blanc, a potpourri of socialist and communist thought of the 1840s. Blanc, the diminutive anti-hero of 1848, whom Marx despised as much as he did any revolutionary leader— and that is no thimbleful of contempt—prefigured the Marxist formula in later editions of his *Organisation du travail,* a turgid little work that had a significance in mid-nineteenth-century France and England difficult to appreciate. Blanc pontificated that in the ultimate stages of socialism there would be true equality only when "each man . . . will produce according to his faculties and will consume according to his needs."[14]

Pierre-Joseph Proudhon took a special delight in exercising his mordant wit on the "socialist" Blanc and his followers, tearing apart the formula on capacities and needs in a perfect state of association that Marx later adapted in the *Critique of the Gotha Program.* "You say that my capacity is 100; I maintain that it is 90. You add that my need is 90; I insist that it is 100. There is a difference of 20 between us on need and capacity."[15] Thus in 1851 Proudhon, who had a strangely prophetic insight into some of the inherent tendencies of Marxist thought, was already making sport with the elements that were later combined in the banderole. Louis Blanc's formula struck roots in the French working classes, and thirty years later, on October 7, 1882, it reappeared in *Le Prolétaire,* an organ of the French Socialist Revolutionary Workers' Party, as "Chacun donnant selon ses forces recevra selon ses besoins." Marx's son-in-law Paul Lafargue was disturbed by this revival of Blanc's slogan, which carried with it a promise of instant implementation, and wrote Engels to complain. Marx, on the Isle of Wight and ailing, was silent; he was approaching the end.

Marx's banderole, with its proclamation "To each according to his needs," was a sibylline utterance that could mean all things to all men. In the mouth of a direct actionist it could become demagoguery, deluding the workers with false promises. To ordinary socialists it could mean eventual satisfaction of their plain wants and desires. And for intellectuals it was pregnant with philosophical connotations that evoked an ideal state. The phrase harked back to Rousseau and Kant, who had given voice to the true need of a self-aware man—the need for a society in which the moral worth of personal action did not derive from external constraint but was the expression of the inner being and had absolute worth in and of itself. Even today the banderole raises an image of universal psychic harmony in which the antagonisms between the individual and society are resolved under conditions that allow for the preservation of personal identity and complete self-actualization.

Isaac Newton framed no hypotheses and Karl Marx wrote no utopias; that was the official stance. But in neither case was the position maintained. If one does not restrict oneself narrowly to the phraseology of the *Critique*'s banderole and assimilates to it Marx's related pronouncements, the full dimensions of his utopian dream come into view. Though he never wrote dreary utopian stories, he encapsulated his utopia in a series of succinct, memorable phrases that have exerted an especial fascination over vast numbers of intellectuals. Their mere recitation over and over again is hypnotic, like certain rhythms of popular music.

Marx came early to utopia, and the longing never abated, though the language changed at various stages of his life. In a letter of 1837 to his father, the adolescent student first raised the curtain on his secret search for a total moral system to replace the "old gods," a pursuit that drove him to nights of relentless study and perhaps a temporary breakdown. By 1844, his manuscripts show, he had found his way with his own creed for a communist society composed of unalienated men—couched in the jargon of German Romantic philosophy. These manuscripts, prepared when Marx was twenty-six, became seductive texts for our time. The utopia achieved its clearest universal voice in the *Communist Manifesto* of 1848. What could be more in the Romantic utopian spirit than the prophecy: "The old bourgeois society with its classes and its conflicts of classes gives way to an association where the free development of each individual is the condition of the free development of all."[16]

In his late fifties, the ailing Marx, writing glosses on himself and on his enemies in the *Critique of the Gotha Program,* epitomized his vision in apothegms that were accepted as final ends for man in many parts of the world. Marx combined the underthought of German philosophy in its Hegelian version, the rhetoric of the French utopians, which, unlike German philosophy, was easily adaptable to the styles of popular expression in any country, and the rational argumentation of English economists amended and presented as science to give solidity to the whole structure. Marxists of later generations could stress one or another of these elements, transforming the whole in accordance with the passing needs of time and place. The amalgam became as flexible and plastic as the original Christian utopia of the ancient world, and for decades it enjoyed a signal success for much the same reason that Christianity and barbarism once triumphed over the Romans.

Marx's utopian formulas can be garnered from a period of more than three decades in his now published manuscripts and in printed books. They always have reference to the penultimate, higher stage of communism, called Phase II in the *Critique,* after the inadequate Phase I has been left behind. What the "highest" stage, Phase III, if there is one, would be like is difficult to discover. It has been the function of modern Marxology to bind a series of evocative phrases together into a system, but perhaps something of their original quality can be communicated by presenting them in their pristine, free-floating state: free development of the individual; development of personality; self actualization of the individual; to set in manifold motion the many-sided developed predispositions *(Anlagen)* of men. Only in community will personal freedom be possible. Men will become masters of their own socialization. Add to these the hallowed texts about freedom from necessity and the morality plays about the end of alienation that embarrassed the philosopher Adam Schaff and other sophisticated Marxologists. There are elements in this litany that are markedly Saint-Simonian and Fourierist in tone, expressive of the same Romantic temper. Other elements have counterparts and parallels in contemporary German philosophy. But whatever their source, they became part of one composite confession of faith.

The Saint-Simonians thought in terms of the progressive self-actualization of the species man, with the complete actualization of his three major capacities—scientific, emotive-moral-artistic, and manual-administrative. They avoided restricting themselves to a single capacity for each man, and provided for general education in which all three types of capacity would be nurtured until the special capacity manifested itself. Marx's *uomo universale,* too, allows for outstanding predispositions in one direction, along with the general development of all talents. And his idea of a capacity, which may be inferred from specific images and analogies in his writings, was not far removed from that of the Saint-Simonians and most other utopians of the time. Left free to himself, a man would demonstrate either artistic or scientific-rationalist excellence. Though Marx nominally rejected the Saint-Simonian hierarchy of values, he clearly had a preference, which left traces in chance conversations and obiter dicta, for the human rationalizing capacity. Paul Lafargue, who first met Marx in 1865, describes him as constantly citing a provocative Hegelian reflection: "Even the criminal thought of a scoundrel is grander and loftier than the marvel of the heavens."[17] Marx himself was committed to the tireless exercise of organized thinking, and Lafargue's later exposition of the utopian "right to idleness" would not have enjoyed his approval. Under communism the intensity of activity, a later version of creativity, would increase rather than diminish.

The Saint-Simonians were strong on the potentialities of technological development and would manipulate productive capacities to minimize manual labor insofar as possible. They did not indulge in fantasizing quite as bold as Marx's in a passage where he foresaw technological progress reaching so high a level—virtual automation—that man's relation to the machine would become purely intellectual-scientific guidance. Total technology is at the core of the Marxist utopia, its ineradicable signature.

Despite obvious differences, the Marxist slogans can be set into the Fourier-Saint-Simonian chain of filiation without violating their spirit. These nineteenth-century visionaries all inhabit the same expansive Romantic utopia of self-actualization in all directions, a boundless drive of the individual and of mankind. There was one branch of utopian thought, however, to which Marx had a profound, abiding, and unmitigated antipathy—the ascetic tradition that runs from Babeuf to Buonarroti to Proudhon and on to Bakunin (the Bakunin of theory, not of real life). They represented the false route. Their train of thought ended in an essentially static society, based upon a severe limitation of human needs; they were opposed to the expansion associated with the machine, to great productivity, to the multiplication of goods, and to the spectacular advancement of science and the arts. In a word, their ideal was reactionary, petty bourgeois. One of Marx's principal objects in writing his *Critique of the Gotha Program* was to have excised from the draft every last word of egalitarian rhetoric, in his mind generated by the constricted egalitarian communist and anarchist tradition. Looked at a century later, the compromise Marx's supporters achieved in the German

Social Democratic Party of 1875 after receiving his *Critique* is ludicrous—"Jedem nach seinen vernunftgemässen Bedürfnissen" (To each according to his reasonable needs).

Equality was Marx's eventual goal in Phase II of communism, but equality in the rich satisfaction of material and intellectual needs in a dynamic economy, not returns, equal in their paltriness, for labor expended in a primitive, artisan-like system à la Proudhon, not a holding-back of technology, not the anti-intellectualist asperities of Babeuf and of Bakunin. Irrespective of the other bases of Marx's conflict with Proudhon, there was deep antagonism to Proudhon's cramped, moralistic individualism, bounded by an artisan's horizon, whereas Marx, in the *Critique of the Gotha Program* and elsewhere in his work, opted for the free-flowing expansion of wealth in association. Marx's vision in the spirit of the Romantic utopians helps to account for its fleeting rehabilitation among the children of 1968. But they betrayed the angelic Moor by demanding utopia now and flirting with Ludditism.

Marx's utopia early became enveloped in a popular "scientific socialism," nineteenth-century style. It was a period when science achieved great prestige in European and westernized Asiatic cultures, and for Marx and Engels it replaced the religious and moral-philosophical codes that had prevailed for centuries. In the economic-philosophical manuscripts of 1844 the young Marx had already proclaimed the integral unity of the science of man with the science of nature, and the next year, in a gloss on Feuerbach, he had announced a new social mission for men of knowledge: "Philosophers have only interpreted the world in various ways, the point however is to change it"—the maxim now chiseled on the monument marking his grave in London's Highgate Cemetery. Reflections on the development of world history and sweeping schemata of periodization soon became the equivalent of laws of science. Forms of dialectical reasoning, in Hegelian terminology, were adopted as the only approved method of social science. Nineteenth-century European culture brought forth numerous theosophical, mystical, and historical-philosophical systems that lived their brief moment and died like tadpoles in a Darwinian pond. The system of Karl Marx alone survived, the fittest for the times.

At Marx's funeral in 1883 Friedrich Engels, his alter ego, encapsulated in plain language the two monumental discoveries that in his judgment made their doctrine scientific.

> As Darwin discovered the law of evolution in organic nature, so Marx discovered the law of evolution in human history: the simple fact, previously hidden under ideological growths, that human beings must first of all eat, drink, shelter and clothe themselves before they can turn their attention to politics, science, art and religion; that therefore the production of the immediate material means of life and thereby the given stage of economic development of a people or of a period forms the basis on which the State institutions, the legal principles, the art and even the religious ideas of the people in question have developed ... But not only this, Marx discovered the special law of development of the present-day capitalist mode of production and of the bourgeois system of society which it has produced. With the discovery of surplus value, light was suddenly shed on the darkness in which all other economists, both bourgeois and socialist, had lost themselves.[18]

The simple seductions of Marx's allowable utopia, which may help to account for the rapidity of its victories on the popular level, can perhaps best be illustrated by a series of articles published in 1877 in the Leipzig *Vorwärts (Forward)*. There, with Marx's approval, Engels presented the German Social Democratic Party with a comprehensive survey of the correct doctrine in all aspects of philosophy, economy, history; and despite the known objection of the dioscuri to utopian blueprints of the future state of humanity, under the aegis of "scientific socialism" he laid down the fundamental principles that would direct mankind after it made the leap from the realm of necessity into the realm of freedom. These articles, later published as *Herr Eugen Dühring's Revolution in Science* (commonly called the *Anti-Dühring*), were not weighted with the formidable scholarly apparatus of *Das Kapital*. The *Anti-Dühring* appeared in numerous editions and translations and, second only to the *Communist Manifesto,* became the canonical work of Marx and Engels adaptable to all times and places. Its only handicap was its unfortunate title, which never allowed this remarkable exercise in intellectual concision to be freed from the taint of its origin, a polemical response to the universal system concocted in 1874 by the

German professor Eugen Dühring that had sown confusion in the Social Democratic Party.

Those pages of the *Anti-Dühring* that omitted all reference to the hapless professor and ventured out on their own became texts that in their dogmatic forthrightness achieved world renown. Marx himself drafted the introduction to brief excerpts that his son-in-law Paul Lafargue published in Paris as *Socialisme utopique et socialisme scientifique* (1880), a breviary rejecting utopian antecedents in the name of the new science Marx and Engels had founded. Engels' introduction to the 1892 translation into English by Edward Aveling affirms the wide diffusion of the work and its crucial significance in the history of popular Marxism.

> At the request of my friend Paul Lafargue, now representative of Lille in the French Chamber of Deputies, I arranged three chapters of this book [the original *Vorwärts* articles] as a pamphlet, which he translated and published in 1880 under the title *"Socialisme utopique et socialisme scientifique."* From this French text a Polish and a Spanish edition were prepared. In 1883, our German friends brought out the pamphlet in the original language. Italian, Russian, Danish, Dutch, and Roumanian translations, based upon the German text, have since been published. Thus, with the present English edition, this little book circulates in ten languages. I am not aware that any other Socialist work, not even our *"Communist Manifesto"* of 1848 or Marx's *"Capital,"* has been so often translated. In Germany it has had four editions of about 20,000 copies in all.[19]

In the century following the original publication, the number of copies would have to be reckoned in the millions; a reasonable estimate would require the cooperative efforts of scholars in many countries throughout the world.

In the *Anti-Dühring*, socialist and communist theory acquired the crucial adjective, and what Marx and Engels called "scientific socialism" formally came into being. (Proudhon had at one time used the phrase, but it failed to take hold.) Engels linked Kant's nebular hypothesis and Hegel's "process of evolution of man himself" as demonstrations of the dialectic in science. When the "idealist" label was removed from Hegel and he was cleansed of the pretension to the discovery of absolute truth as the final goal of evolution, the groundwork was laid for the appearance of Marx.

The futurist promise of communism set forth in excerpts from the *Anti-Dühring,* at once scientific and utopian, could henceforward be understood by selected artisans, if not by all workingmen. "The appropriation by [the communist] society of the means of production will put an end not only to the artificial restraints on production that exist today, but also to the positive waste and destruction of productive forces and products which is now the inevitable accompaniment of production and reaches its zenith in [economic] crises." Though Engels did not call for the immediate expropriation of the rich, he reiterated in an expanded form the universal dream of human potentiality actualized that Marx had incorporated in the *Critique of the Gotha Program.* Engels went one better than the halting "higher phase" of communism: "The possibility of securing for every member of society, through social production, an existence which is not only fully sufficient from a material standpoint and becoming richer from day to day, but also guarantees to them the completely unrestricted development and exercise of their physical and mental faculties—this possibility now exists for the first time, but it *does* exist."[20]

Economic planification, the golden key to the garden, was put on display. "Anarchy in social production is replaced by conscious organization on a planned basis. And at this point, in a certain sense, man finally cuts himself off from the animal world, leaves the conditions of animal existence behind him and enters conditions which are really human." The ordinary man might have to skip Engels' exposition of dialectics, of the negation of the negation, of the nature of the medieval economy, but he could conceivably understand the assurance that the interference of the state power in social relations would become superfluous in one sphere of activity after another, and then cease altogether. "The government of persons is replaced by the administration of things and the direction of the processes of production. The state is not 'abolished,' *it withers away.*"[21] That the administration of things entails the control of men was ignored. And Marx and Engels were blind to the knotty problems of central planning and the dangers of bureaucratization and corruption.

For a while in the second half of the twentieth century Marx's words appeared to be enjoying a great triumph. Close on to half of the world's population hovered between Phase I and Phase II of communism, if official theory were accepted as reality. And there was not a political leader east or west, north or south, so steeped in reaction he would not on appropriate occasions affirm his allegiance to the principle that all men should have their needs fulfilled and natural potentialities developed to the utmost. The Constantines of the world presided at councils where Marx's utopian banderole was duly unfurled, and though slaughter was threatened over its interpretation, history assured the faithful that the correct reading would ultimately prevail. If a Diogenes redivivus should point out that such casual phrases of the *Critique* as dictatorship of the proletariat have been translated into massacres of millions of human beings, the true believer will remind him that the historical process has always been profligate of lives. There is every reason to expect that the preaching of classic communist thought in the *Anti-Dühring* will bear the same relationship to communist societies of the future—if any should be resurrected—that the Sermon on the Mount does to Christianity.

=== 9 ===
Enemies within the Gates

When you want to get an idea of the early Christian communities, look
at a local section of the International Working Men's Association.

—Engels, "On the Early History of Christianity," quoting Renan

When Marx's rage demanded a more personal discharge than
the historic battle of the classes, he fixed on individual enemies, a seemingly endless file of opponents within the gates of
his fortress, men who had once been close to him. Ideological traitors provoked the most fiery vituperation, and Marx often abandoned theoretical work to pursue and crush them. At times the
contest turned into a battle of the books, for rivals, too, came well
stocked with fantasies, and in the hand-to-hand combat of Marx
and opposing forces it was theory against theory, an incessant
shower of words. Since the bourgeoisie, the great satan of Marx's
war, paid him little or no heed, internal enemies were his standard
everyday targets.

Once Marx and Engels set forth the main lines of their doctrine
in the early years after their August 1844 meeting in Paris, they were
in possession of a touchstone by which to judge all other theories—
historical, philosophical, utopian, economical, political, and tactical.
Competitive conceptions were not appraised as mere abstractions to
be debated among fellow combatants in the revolutionary cause;
ideas were attached to specific persons, and rejection of an idea
turned those who harbored it into adversaries. To repudiate an idea
while maintaining neutrality toward the human being who espoused
it was not Marx's way. The bearer of a false view was infected with
a contagious disease and had to be quarantined, ousted from sacred
assemblies, or preferably exterminated. There were friends and there

were foes, and only for the purpose of future manipulation were some persons who differed about minor details still tolerated. Friends, sponsors, mentors, even idolaters of Karl Marx, when they strayed, could be transformed into deadly betrayers, to be thrown into the fiery cauldron of his searing sarcasm.

Marx was vengeful and rarely forgave a friend who failed to support him unhesitatingly in his personal quarrels. When the poet Freiligrath did not show enough zeal in backing Marx against Karl Vogt he earned a growl and a curse in a June 7, 1859, letter to Engels: "Between ourselves: he is a turd . . . May the devil take this whole guild of songbirds."[1] Like many others, Freiligrath refused to be locked into a "party-cage."

Marx maintained that from the dissolution of the Communist League in 1852 until the First International adopted the basic tenets of the *Communist Manifesto* in the late 1860s, he belonged to no party in the narrow sense of the term. Nevertheless it was taken for granted that wherever he stood, there was the party, and he demanded of his friends absolute allegiance. Deviations were acts of treason and lukewarm assent was perfidy. Marx's attitude toward adherents and fellow travelers was not free of a dose of hypocrisy. He took one position in the presence of those whom he needed and another in the running commentary that accompanied his reports of an encounter to brother Engels, the one person on earth to whom he virtually never lied.

Marx rarely received into his good graces as converts formerly hostile leaders even when they exposed their throats, as Bakunin did when he visited Marx in London after sixteen years in Russian prisons and exile (though Marx briefly exhibited some friendliness toward him). The infrequent absolution of penitents was usually accompanied by misgivings and an epistolary theatrical aside to Engels voicing his skepticism (often justified). Marx had studied the behavior of militant religious sectarians in Judaism and Christianity; and during his honeymoon stay at Kreuznach he had read histories of the fratricidal strife during the French Revolution, as well as Machiavelli's advice on the proper treatment of dissidents. Ostracism in the Greek manner was the least of the punishments he meted out. To demand freedom of speech, press, and assembly for one's own group while denying such liberty to any deviants within its ranks has been the practice of organized religions, nationalist movements, and political juntas throughout recorded history. Marx's denunciations of enemies within the gates of his own city were no more vicious than the tirades of antecedents and contemporaries. But though he did not have the power to destroy heretics physically, he struck moral blows that felled many a wayward sectarian.

Throughout his adult life as a revolutionary, Marx felt himself surrounded by hostile forces. A literature has grown up delineating in detail the intellectual and political differences that separated him from his antagonists, tracing his development as he jumped from one slain victim to another. Rummaging in the baggage train of his formal and journalistic thought illuminates the tone and character of his disputations and the role they played in his psychic economy, as well as their factual content. Aggression against enemies real and imaginary is a part of the human condition that is universally experienced in various degrees. When the absorption with enemies in concert becomes obsessive, modern societies have proceeded to label it a disease, to sequester the stricken, or to make attempts to alleviate their sufferings. It is unlikely that anyone engaged in revolutionary activities can wholly avoid being possessed by suspicion. To see plots and conspiracies all about one may even be a rational appraisal of the situation. By contemporary standards Marx's aggression rarely if ever assumed clinical proportions, but it surely consumed a large measure of his psychic power as he wallowed in hate.

Open aggression can partially appease a deep-rooted, enduring self-loathing. In Marx's life aggression against a host of former friends and newborn enemies was a constant preoccupation that used up as much of his energy as his study of capitalist development in the British Museum. Whether the enemies were primarily doctrinal or whether they were potential rivals for leadership of the First International, the release of affect was similar. Marx's outbursts extended from the attack on Bruno Bauer and company in *The Holy Family* through the critique of Feuerbach, Bauer, Stirner, Grün, the Saint-Simonians, Cabet, and the Fourierists in *The German Ideology*, and the derision of Proudhon's economics in *Misère de la Philosophie*. His anger culminated in the wholesale assault in the

Communist Manifesto on the entire catalogue of social doctrines—feudal socialism, petty-bourgeois socialism, German or "True" socialism, conservative or bourgeois socialism, utopian socialism, and sectarian communism. In the 1850s Marx's critical passion turned on the economists. And once the First International was established, he became entangled with reformist dissidents and anarchist trashers in day-to-day controversies over tactics. The 1860s and 1870s were spent in conflict with his two most formidable enemies, Lassalle and Bakunin. And in the last years of his life he summoned what zeal for combat he had left to berate a new generation of German Social Democrats, who were flirting with the petty bourgeoisie to garner a few votes in elections to the Reichstag.

When a rumor or a fabricated story was printed in one of the radical parish newspapers anywhere on the Continent it had to be denied and the publisher sued for libel, or the party chieftain's silence would be interpreted as an admission of guilt. As a consequence, radicals or revolutionaries devoted an enormous amount of time to acquiring local newspapers and using their influence to insert disclaimers. A misquotation of an ideological position snowballed in the course of the reprinting so that in the end a denunciation bore only a faint resemblance to the original account. These fly-by-night newspapers lived on each other's copy, creating the illusion that there was much working-class agitation when in fact most factory hands and artisans never heard of the scandals that shook their leadership. Only on rare occasions did a party member manage to get one of his libels or exculpations printed in major newspapers such as the *London Times*. Marx and Engels, who were often the objects of attack, were constantly exchanging bundles of newspapers and newspaper clippings.

When flamboyant orators like Lassalle made their progress through a German working-class province, filling halls with laborers, *agents provocateurs,* and hostile curiosity seekers, the impression was generated that a mighty working-class movement was sweeping industrial centers. Marx was not an orator, and his turgid lectures to workers' associations drew no great crowds. His carefully crafted reports on the London Council meetings of the International were read only by a handful of party members; as a consequence his own adherents delivered infelicitous renderings of his doctrinal positions, for which he was forever censuring them. Those who revered him accepted his tongue lashings and tried to mend their ways or to justify themselves, but for the vast majority of workers in France and Germany he was a mere name. It was the Paris Commune, which for a brief period resurrected the specter of communism, that was responsible for the creation in the press of a mythic figure of Karl Marx at the center of a network of revolutionary agents spread throughout the Continent.

The object of Marx's aggression did not have to be a figure of stature; sometimes a mere flea served the purpose—witness his point-by-point rebuttal of the published charges of a former radical professor, the Swiss naturalist Karl Vogt, that Marx was venal and in the pay of the Prussians. Marx gave vent to his outrage in a two-hundred page book (1860) to which he devoted months of labor, gathering evidence and testimonials in his defense from fifty correspondents throughout the world. Although Engels praised the polemical skills displayed in *Herr Vogt,* a publication that Marx had difficulty financing, a present-day reader can only look upon the absorption with Vogt's slanders as a costly aberration in the period when Marx was committed to finishing *Das Kapital.* The elaborate brief he prepared for a prominent Berlin lawyer, to whom he offered the bounty of a libel suit against German newspapers that had printed Vogt's accusations—long before the attorney had expressed the remotest interest in the case—is only one of the many egocentric illusions in which Marx constantly bathed his wounds.

In helping to prepare the attack against Vogt and the "historical vindication" of Marx and his friends, Engels had to rummage through their entire archive of biographies of radicals of various persuasions, which they had meticulously compiled and preserved. Quick to make fun of the fantasies of other men, Marx rarely faced the stark realities of his own situation. When the aggressive fury took hold of him, the honor of the movement and of his person was at stake and he proclaimed a holy war far and wide. Anyone who failed actively to rally to his defense was never forgiven. The book *Herr Vogt* passed virtually unnoticed, but after a decade Marx was vindicated among his friends: when the Communards seized the

French state archives it was reported that Karl Vogt was in the pay of Napoleon III. But the evidence, printed in a flimsy partisan newspaper, is not conclusive in the eyes of all beholders.

There was no such final resolution of Marx's troubled relations with three major heresiarchs of the revolution, two German Jews and a burly Russian—Moses Hess, Ferdinand Lassalle, and Mikhail Bakunin—each a compulsive personality with his own formula for the overthrow of bourgeois society. The three enemies, playing different roles in the life of Karl Marx, tore away at his dream of a unified proletariat of which he was the anointed leader. Hess and Lassalle represented the old and the new in the nineteenth-century reformist mode of hastening the advent of the revolution; Bakunin, the bloated scion of minor Russian aristocrats, was the unregenerate anarchist, a symbol for the ages. The personal animosity of Marx and Engels to these misleaders of mankind was bitter as long as they were alive—and often they were pursued beyond the grave. Perhaps there is a touch of remorse in Marx's letter to Hess's widow, and he shed a tear at the news of Lassalle's death; but the surviving followers of Lassalle and Bakunin were spoilers of Marx's revolution, and toward them he was unrelenting. In heaping opprobrium upon Proudhonists, Lassalleans, and Bakuninists, Engels was even more cantankerous than his partner.

Reviling the arch enemies of Marx—Hess, Lassalle, and Bakunin—did not shut off the constant flow of snarling epithets directed against other combatants with which Marx and Engels filled their correspondence. To identify the potentates on the other side of the class war with whom they had no immediate contact they invented a private language, less out of caution than as a release for their pent-up, impotent fury, and they used a vocabulary rich with scatological combinations the way ordinary workers resorted to their limited arsenal of cuss words.

Of the three secular Jewish messiahs to which the nineteenth century gave birth in Germany, Marx is now in eclipse, Moses Hess would hardly recognize the outlines of his utopia in the hard-nosed modern Israeli state, and Lassalle has survived chiefly as the protagonist in George Meredith's novel *The Tragic Comedians*.

Hess, who befriended Marx in his early political life, is an example of the rapid pendulum swings to which a young Jew born in Bonn in 1812 was subject in his emotional and social-political existence. He was the first major radical activist whom Marx encountered after he severed his ties to the young Hegelians with whom he had fraternized at the University of Berlin. Unlike Ferdinand Lassalle, Hess had been brought up in the orthodox Jewish tradition, untainted by the reform movement. His father had left him in the house of his grandfather so that he might continue his Talmudic studies in Bonn, where there was a proper Jewish school; no such institution was to be found in the city of Cologne, to which the elder Hess had moved his prosperous emporium of colonial products and his sugar refinery. In a diary entry of 1836 Moses Hess later drew a grim picture of the dismal Bonn Talmudic school, in which he was beaten to make him study more conscientiously.

After his mother's death when he was fourteen, Hess returned to his father's house in Cologne, where father and son lived together in a state of constant animosity. Though Moses Hess remembered the religious ceremonials and festive celebrations of his gentle grandfather, for whom he had a deep affection, after a short stay in Cologne he abandoned traditional Judaism and underwent a religious crisis during which he oscillated between atheism and Spinozism. He never attended a secular school, but independently began a quest for a philosophy of his own that led him to devour haphazardly the standard works of French and German culture. From this immersion in secular knowledge he came forth a devotee of Rousseau and Spinoza with only a smattering of the dominant Hegelian philosophy that, despite denials and deviations, held Marx captive throughout his mature intellectual life.

Hess fashioned himself into a socialist or communist—the terms had not yet acquired fixed parameters—and became the propagator of a new faith that was a mixture of utopian ideas derived from Weitling, the Saint-Simonians, Proudhon, and other contemporary system-makers. An autodidact who had not fully mastered the German language until he was twenty (Yiddish had been his mother tongue), he wrote *Die heilige Geschichte der Menschheit von einem Jünger Spinozas* and *Die europäische Triarchie* early in his career, and put together in Cologne a company that published the liberal

Rheinische Zeitung (Rhenish Times), whose editor Marx became. In 1842, during the same period in which he met and patronized Karl Marx, Hess for a while won Friedrich Engels over to his brand of philosophical communism.

By the next year Hess was in Paris as correspondent of the *Rheinische Zeitung,* and he became a familiar figure in French radical and German émigré circles, participating in their internal quarrels though never quite displaying the acerbity that normally characterized the battle of the systems. In 1846 he withdrew his allegiance from Marx, whom he had once idolized, and their relations grew tepid, though in Brussels in 1847 they still belonged to the same Communist League. Hess was easily outwitted by the dioscuri, who were determined to take a tough rather than a reformist stand. In their correspondence, Marx and Engels developed a scoffing jargon for references to Hess. He became Rabbi Moses or Moysi the communist rabbi, or "olle Moses"; and in the *Communist Manifesto* his brand of socialism was directly attacked. Personal denigration of Hess the Jew was added to growing theoretical differences.

Relations between the dioscuri and Hess did not improve when in 1851 Hess inherited fourteen thousand *Talers* from his father. In the 1850s and 1860s, the years of Marx's most straitened economic circumstances, Hess was a relatively prosperous man living on his income, a revolutionary who was expelled from one country after another until the Prussian declaration of an amnesty in 1861, but who did not endure the miserable lot of the other émigrés.

In 1852, when Hess's *Rome and Jerusalem: The Last National Question* appeared in Leipzig, it was revealed that he had been living a double spiritual existence, contributing articles on philosophical-religious subjects to French and German Jewish periodicals, at a time when socialists and communists almost without exception were secularists. Hess frequented Jewish scholars such as the historian Heinrich Graetz, and under the influence of the Polish, Irish, Hungarian, and Italian nationalist movements he developed a theory of Jewish nationalism that would have been anathema to Marx and Engels if they had ever bothered to read his book. The idea of the rebirth of the Jewish nation in Judaea, under the auspices of the great Western European states, combined the concept of a haven for

Jews with a revival of religious traditions. The notion of such a refuge, protected from the Bedouins by foreign powers, was so eccentric that it attracted almost no serious attention at the time. The book was not tightly reasoned and often trailed off into disconnected notes, but passages here and there were inspired by a vision of Zion as the crowning glory of all the nationalist movements burgeoning throughout the Continent. Hess, who had once preached the total assimilation of the Jews in the lands where they lived, now composed paeans of praise for Jewish rebirth and the creation of a comity of nations that had a strong Mazzinian flavor, enhanced by biblical messianic prophecy, ideas utterly repugnant to Marx and Engels.

For Hess there was no contradiction between his continuing socialist propaganda for the Social Democratic movement in Lassallean dress and his espousal of an independent Jewish national state that from its beginning would be based on the principles of communal ownership of the land and social justice. Hess did not expect Jews of the industrialized West to uproot themselves and establish their homes in the Near East; his prospective immigrants to Zion would be primarily refugees from the impoverished communities of Eastern Europe. *Rome and Jerusalem* became a canonical text of modern Zionism when Theodore Herzl updated its message toward the end of the century. Herzl's utopia of the *Judenstadt* resembled a paternalist Junker society more than the primitive cooperative system Hess had outlined—they were responding to different moments in the history of antisemitism.

For the next thirteen years, from the publication of *Rome and Jerusalem* to his death in 1875, Hess continued to lead a complicated life as both a Jewish nationalist and a German Social Democrat, a posture that now appears far less incongruous than it did at the time. He attended Workers' Association meetings in Germany and congresses of the First International, though never as a member of Marx's party; he was leery of wild Bakuninist anarchism and always opted for Lassallean reformism.

Despite their contempt for Hess, the dioscuri at one time toyed with a proposal that he translate *Das Kapital* into French. The prospect did not entirely please Engels, who was suspicious of him.

"O dear God, here comes olle Moses sucking up to us again," he wrote Marx on November 30, 1867, "and he is congratulating himself that you certified he was right when he asserted that capital is accumulated labor! . . . In my opinion, for now you could permit him to issue in the *Courrier français* a few excerpts so that we can see how he intends to handle the thing. Naturally he will sign these, and thus we shall in a certain sense qualify him as a repentant sinner. Then you could discuss the translation of the whole book that he is contemplating."[2] Marx agreed and promised to follow Engels' prescription exactly: "At all events, we must make use of the man while preventing him from misusing us."[3] The project came to naught and the task devolved upon another translator.

In Hess's last years he turned his efforts to a work he called *Dynamische Stofflehre* (Dynamic Theory of Matter), an autodidact's dream of science that was even more flawed than Engels' *Dialectics of Nature;* both were attempts to plant socialist ideas in a rock-bed of science and both were naive in their conceptions of modern science. In a competitive political world that demanded absolute, exclusive commitments, Moses Hess—who signed himself Maurice in France and Moritz in Germany—never found a comfortable niche among the ideologies; at one time he even picked up freemasonry. Marx could on occasion be kindlier to former adherents and rivals after their deaths. In 1877 he consoled the widow Hess with a promise that he and Engels would do their best to spread knowledge of the *Dynamische Stofflehre* as a "very great scientific work," a duty they would perform independently of their long relationship with Hess as *Bundesgenossen*—literally, members of the same league.

Hess's bones have been moved from Paris, where he died, to a Jewish cemetery in Deutz near Cologne (his gravestone having escaped destruction during the Nazi period because it was overgrown with weeds), to a final resting place by the Sea of Kinnereth in Israel, to which his remains were transported in 1961. Although German sources sometimes refer to him as the first Social Democrat, he has been forgotten in the land of his birth, to find a place in the Zionist pantheon. Marx, like Freud, is still kept at arm's length in the state of Israel despite the seepage of his ideas into the early political party platforms of the Left.

In 1875, the year of his death, Hess had welcomed the unification of antagonistic German workingmen's associations into a single political party, a victory for the milder and gentler and more rhetorical way to salvation, while Marx from his London exile unleashed the *Critique of the Gotha Program,* a last and ineffectual thunderbolt against the followers of Lassalle. Though Hess was not a serious contender for proletarian leadership, the scorn with which Marx treated him was typical of his conduct toward former teachers and patrons after he had abandoned radical idealism for dialectical materialism. Marx and Engels, fiercely loyal to each other, disdained minor prophets, particularly if they were Jews. (By the 1890s Engels had a change of heart: he denounced Edouard Drumont's antisemitism, protested that the most loyal comrades in the German Social Democratic movement, like Viktor Adler and Eduard Bernstein, were Jews, and even wrote a letter in which he referred to Karl Marx as springing from Jewish stock. Suddenly Engels became aware of the existence of "thousands upon thousands" of Jewish proletarians, many of them among the most exploited of the working class.)[4]

Of all the dissidents in the ranks of the revolutionaries who plagued Marx, the most difficult for him to abide was Ferdinand Lassalle, a German Jew born in Breslau in 1825, thus seven years his junior. The publication of seven volumes of Lassalle's collected works, large portions of his diary, a voluminous correspondence with his patroness the Countess von Hatzfeldt, scores of letters that passed between him and Marx, and official histories of the German Social Democratic Party, for whom he remains a heroic founding father, has not dispelled Lassalle's image as a boisterous clown intruding into a group portrait whose august central figures are Marx and Engels. Diaries of the women with whom Lassalle engaged in tumultuous amorous adventures only add to the confusion of a tale that fits more readily into a late-nineteenth-century romantic novel printed as a newspaper *feuilleton* than into a sober account of the social revolution in Western Europe. Perhaps only George Meredith caught the ambiguities of the man in *The Tragic Comedians.*

Born the son of a prosperous silk merchant, Lassalle spent his youth skipping his gymnasium classes and playing billiards. The family to which he belonged was not orthodox in the traditional sense, though his father never severed his relations with the Jewish community, and when he moved into upper-class gentile circles, where his entrepreneurial skills were appreciated, he made a point of announcing his Jewish ancestry. He acquired a son-in-law called Ferdinand Friedländer who soon changed his name to de Friedland, a clumsy attempt to cosmeticize his commonplace Jewish origin. His masquerade was aped by his brother-in-law, who turned the Lassal of his father into Lassalle, presumably a name with an aristocratic air. In Berlin the young man, well supplied with his father's money, cultivated elegant manners to match his new name, taking riding lessons and insinuating himself into a society of wealthy women from whom he learned to turn the language of love on and off as with a spigot. He dressed to fit the role and stuffed his apartment with expensive bric-à-brac. During his metamorphosis he acquired friends, mostly Jews, over whom he exercised a strange fascination, as if he were the head of a cult.

Lassalle became a rebel in search of a cause. Participation in the 1848 uprising had earned him a short prison term and the reputation of a revolutionary, which stood him in good stead for the rest of his life. When Europe in the early 1850s settled into the doldrums of bourgeois existence, Lassalle discovered a mission that suited his newly minted personality. Without much ado, he offered his services and those of two friends to the Countess von Hatzfeldt, the daughter of one of the most aristocratic and richest families in Prussia, who had been married to a noble of the same family in order to preserve the integrity of their large estates. The count turned out to be a philanderer who was consuming the fortune his wife had brought to the marriage, but her own brothers laughed at her plea for a divorce. When Lassalle volunteered his help, the countess quickly accepted the knight errant about whom she knew nothing. In her name a series of lawsuits were instituted that dragged on for almost a decade and became a *cause célèbre*. Lassalle then managed to entangle Düsseldorf trade unions in the affair on the ground that as long as one act of injustice in a society was condoned there could be no justice for any man, and the countess herself became the guardian angel of a new proletarian world order. Here Lassalle was treading on Marx's territory, a potential competitor to be watched. When the protracted suits were finally settled out of court, the countess was a rich woman again, and she bestowed a large annuity on her savior. Out of this miscegenation of a countess' action for divorce and the organization of stray groups of workers under Lassalle's direction, the General Association of German Workers was born in the early 1860s, the nucleus of a future German Social Democratic Party.

Lassalle toured the country addressing halls packed with workers who listened to four-hour harangues by their newborn hero; if he had not quite finished his oration they returned the next day for more. A workers' party was in the making that purported to rival the official opposition of the bourgeois liberals and led Bismarck to initiate clandestine conversations with Lassalle, in which the idea of the Prussian monarchy in alliance with the workers was explored. The negotiations of the Junker Bismarck and the Breslau Jew—addressed as "well-born"—speaking for the working classes turned into one of the more grotesque episodes of nineteenth-century German politics. For ten months beginning in May 1863 Bismarck met in secret with Lassalle, who was prepared to forgo the idea of republicanism if Prussia would strike out in a new direction and transform itself into a revolutionary people's monarchy.

Seventeen years after Lassalle's death, in the course of a debate in the Reichstag, Bismarck referred to Lassalle as "one of the most intellectual and gifted men with whom I have ever had intercourse,—a man who was ambitious in high style, but who was by no means a republican; he had very decided national and monarchical sympathies, and the idea which he strove to realize was the German Empire; and therein we had a point of contact. Lassalle was extremely ambitious, and it was perhaps a matter of doubt to him whether the German Empire would close with the Hohenzollern dynasty or the Lassalle dynasty; but he was monarchical through and through."[5]

In the course of his campaign to organize the workers, Lassalle was brought to trial and charged with inciting them to insurrection. He stoutly maintained that he was not provoking a riot but merely propounding a scientific theory of history, and that the Prussian constitution explicitly guaranteed freedom of inquiry. In fact, his plea was a grossly vulgarized page of Marx. His speech before the court, which Thornstein Veblen later translated as *Science and the Workingmen,* made Lassalle world famous, and he emerged from another brief prison term a twice-martyred hero. His audiences far exceeded in number the actual members of the General Association of German Workers, which had only a few thousand adherents in each of the major industrial centers, though they were still more visible than the dispersed followers of Marx.

Somewhere in the intervals between these multifarious activities Lassalle managed to compose a two-volume work on Heraclitus (Berlin, 1858), which won him election to the German Philosophical Society; a thick historical study of property law; a historical tragedy, *Franz von Sickingen* (1859); and a polemical work on economics entitled *Herr Bastiat-Schulze von Delitzsch, der ökonomische Julian, oder: Capital und Arbeit* (1864). He had traveled through the Near East in the company of his brother-in-law Ferdinand de Friedland, and participated in risky entrepreneurial enterprises. By the 1860s his amorous inclinations turned away from middle-aged Berlin society ladies, who were facile conquests, to young girls to whom he offered matrimony. An early fancy involved a Russian maiden and came to naught, though she immortalized their relationship in her diary. The final campaign ended in disaster. His pursuit of Helene von Dönniges, the daughter of a petty noble and betrothed to a young Wallachian aristocrat named Janko von Racowitza, was an admixture of farce and tragedy. Stricken by Lassalle's resemblance to a Roman emperor, she was prepared to elope with him when her family locked her up. During an intrigue that involved police authorities in Switzerland and the attempt of Friedrich Wilhelm von Dönniges to impose parental authority through force, the formally betrothed Wallachian, a mere stripling, was constrained to defend the honor of the family by accepting Lassalle's challenge. Despite the frantic intervention of the Countess von Hatzfeldt, the duel took place. Lassalle, who appears to have viewed the challenge lightly, was shot and three days later died of his wounds. In a few years Racowitza also was dead, of consumption, and Helene was in the market again, as reported by Engels to Marx with more than a touch of malice.

Lassalle's relations with Marx, one of the many murky episodes in their lives, reveal a capacity for manipulation that crosses the line into hypocrisy. As the son of a *parvenu*, Lassalle was despicable in Marx's eyes. The "Breslau wonder" had been born close enough to the Polish frontier to cast him into the category of the most despised in Marx's account book of Jews. (He had obliterated from his consciousness his own Pressburg [Bratislava] ancestry on his mother's side and his paternal grandfather's birth in Bohemia.) Once Lassalle got entangled in the judicial proceedings of the Countess von Hatzfeldt, he provided standard jokes that enlivened the Marx-Engels correspondence; but when he became associated with Düsseldorf workers and began to organize the German proletariat on a national scale, Marx and Engels were confronted with a dangerous competitor, a new type of leader, a handsome Jew who was an orator with a capacity for endurance neither of them possessed. Moreover, this character had easy access to wealthy friends, and through his Jewish relations and the countess could influence newspapers and publishers.

Marx, Mrs. Marx, and Engels treated Lassalle as a buffoon. They were amused by him, and kidded him when he raved on and on about having shaped Prussian foreign policy. The historical and phrenological dissection of his London visit in July 1862 is not to be taken too seriously; Marx liked to indulge in such fantasies to brother Engels. On July 30 he wrote: "It is now completely clear to me that, as his cranial formation and hair show, he is a descendant of the Negroes who attached themselves to the march of Moses out of Egypt (assuming his mother or grandmother on the paternal side had not crossed with a nigger [in English]). Now this union of Judaism and Germanism with a basic negroid substance must yield a strange product. The pushiness of the fellow is also Nigger-like [in English]."[6]

In the 1850s and early 1860s, Marx and Engels had been able to attract only stray adherents in Germany, which, for all the "backwardness" of its proletariat, they still considered the predestined central land mass on which the fate of the world revolution depended. Since Lassalle had sat in jail during the uprising of the forty-eighters and had been featured in a spectacular show trial, he could not be dismissed lightly. To add to their discomfiture, this popular leader had composed massive learned volumes and was ostensibly planning a great work on economics. "Baron Izzy," as they contemptuously baptized him, could not be pushed aside despite incriminating reports about his personal conduct that they carefully catalogued for future reference. After weighing alternatives they decided not to attack him openly.

To add to their dilemma, Lassalle, when the occasion suited him, declared himself a disciple of Marx, an admirer of his works. However they might differ about revolutionary tactics and in spite of Lassalle's addiction to popular programs about the future organization of workers into cooperative enterprises that they would control through the extension of the national election process, Lassalle had adopted the Marx-Engels basic version of the succession of historical economic systems—feudalism, bourgeois capitalism, popular communism—and a vocabulary that they considered a direct plagiarism of their writings. When Marx was living in London in desperate need, Lassalle gave him small sums, though he would not accept a note with Engels' signature on it that supposedly would have allowed Marx to consolidate his debts.

Lassalle's incredibly long-winded letters to Marx were megalomaniacal pleas for recognition as an intellectual equal. When Marx received page after page of Lassalle's attempt to justify the literary and philosophical theory that underlay his tragedy on Sickingen, the impoverished London exile could not bring himself to send the expected stamp of approval. Sometimes two years of silence passed, succeeded by a sudden outpouring of letters, which Marx answered with laconic acknowledgments.

A serious breach occurred when Lassalle refrained from lending his outright help against Karl Vogt's accusations, an act of abandonment that Marx never forgave. Behind Lassalle's back Marx and Engels made merry over the upstart's writings, ridiculing his philosophy, his economics, his literary capacity, and above all his relations with the countess, with whom they could not break openly because she remained, even after Lassalle's death, a financial patroness of the working-class causes to which she had been converted. Though the full details of Bismarck's overtures to Lassalle were hidden from them, they gathered enough about the electioneering politics that marked the proposed extension of the suffrage to be wary of Bismarckian ploys, though at one period Marx was under the illusion that he too was being courted by the chancellor.

After he had received intelligence from a deputation of Düsseldorf workers, Engels formed an opinion of Lassalle even more contemptuous than Marx's: Lassalle was a debauchee who in a pinch could become a turncoat in the service of the aristocracy. Back in 1856, Engels had warned his friend about Lassalle in language spiced with the common antisemitism of his class. "He has always been a man one has to watch with hellish keenness; and as a real Jew from the Slav border he was always on the ready to exploit anyone for his private ends on party pretexts. And then this drive to force his way into the upper-class world, *de parvenir,* if only for appearance's sake, to disguise the greasy Breslau Jew with all kinds of pomade and paint, was always repulsive."[7]

Lassalle's dramatic triumph in shaping a political party of sorts from the German workers was the cruelest cut of all. For Marx this flashy Eastern European Jew, the son of the merchant Heymann Lassal, was a four-flushing fool, an ignoramus who stole Marx's ideas, paraded phony scholarship, sold himself to the working classes with empty slogans, and, to cap his mountain of sins, connived with the Junker Bismarck to form an alliance between Prussian aristocrats and the proletariat against the bourgeoisie. In their private correspondence, the neglected, abandoned, rightful leaders of the European proletariat drew caricatures of Baron Itzig, but they still could not publicly denounce him because his amorous affairs, his imprisonment for subversive utterances, and his organizing energy had won him the plaudits of workers blind to the writings of Marx and Engels. Lassalle tried to charm Marx into cooperation with promises of a publisher and with occasional monetary support; but as Marx, in a rare expression of sentiment about an antagonist, wrote to the Countess von Hatzfeldt after Lassalle was killed, "Apart from all his abilities, I felt affection for him as a person. The pity is that we have always concealed the fact from one another, as if we were going to live forever."[8]

Though Lassalle was the vain creature sketched by Marx and Engels, there is something prurient in their constant dwelling on his sexual affairs and those of other émigrés. The epithets they concocted were foul—Ludwig Simon of Trier, the former leader of the Frankfurt Assembly, was the "poet or minnesinger of the female Yid, Madame Hohenscheisse-esche or-einden of Frankfurt am Main." And Lassalle's relations with the Countess von Hatzfeldt inspired a malevolent vision in Engels. He found the Lassalliads, written in Mrs. Marx's hand and preserved in the Engels archive, very entertaining. He chuckled over how "the ringleted Jewish noodle" must look atop a red nightshirt and against the "marquisian" drapery, while he moved like his usual self, the Polish Izzy. Marx's passing sorrow over Lassalle's death was not shared by Engels, who in a letter to Marx resorted to the vulgarity that was customary in their appraisal of the fallen hero of the proletariat. "Lassalle's fatal error was obviously that he did not throw the hossy [Helene von Dönniges] straight on the bed in the boarding house and deal with her appropriately, it was not his fine mind but his Jew's pizzle she was interested in. It is yet another of these affairs that only Lassalle could get involved in. That it was *he* who forced the Wallachian into the duel is deadly crazy. Old Hatzfeldt's idea that *you* should write an *apotheosis* of the latterday Redeemer is really priceless."[9]

Engels' final verdict on Lassalle seems not far off the mark, as further details about his relations with Bismarck have leaked out:

> Good old Lassalle is after all being shown up more and more as a common scoundrel. It has never been our practice to judge people by how they represented themselves, but rather by what they were, and I do not see why we should make an exception in the late Izzy's case. Subjectively, his vanity may have made the affair seem plausible to him, but objectively it was the act of a scoundrel, the betrayal of the whole workers' movement to the Prussians. Throughout, the stupid fop does not seem to have secured from Bismarck anything at all in exchange, nothing specific at all, let alone guarantees, having relied upon his own ability to shit on Bismarck, just as he was certain that he could not fail to shoot Racowitza dead. That's Baron Izzy for you.[10]

At one time there had been more ambivalence in Marx's attitude toward Lassalle than in Engels' summary judgment; Marx wrote Kugelmann that in Lassalle's letters from 1848 to 1863 he had steadfastly declared himself to be one of their partisans. But by

February 3, 1865, Marx announced to Engels that there was nothing to be done with the Workers' Association "bequeathed by Baron Izzy." Moses Hess was included in the ban, and the periodical *Social-Demokrat* was threatened with the same act of excommunication. Marx on the warpath was a formidable spectacle to behold, as he smote his enemies right and left. Even when filtered in a letter to Engels announcing *ex cathedra* what the policy of "the two of us" should be, Marx's decisions were delivered with hammer blows.

> I wrote a furious letter to Liebknecht telling him that this was the *very last* warning . . . that I cannot make it clear to members of the "International Committee" here that such things can take place in good faith out of sheer stupidity, while their gutter rag continues to eulogize Lassalle, even though they now know what perfidy he secretly contemplated . . .
>
> We have here a decent excuse for getting rid of them. In any event the air must be cleared and the party cleansed of the stench left behind by Lassalle.[11]

Despite his mockery of the prime mover of German unification, "Pissmark," Marx looked forward to a broad-based revolutionary party in the land whose citizenship he had surrendered and whose government would not reinstate him. As a consequence, he had to work through agents. Lassalle, the adventurous head of a German Workingmen's Association, though he sent money to Marx on occasion and intervened in his behalf with the government, was not amenable to his direction and management from afar. After Lassalle's death in the 1864 duel, his faction in the German party lived on to confound the London émigré, eventually provoking Marx's critique of their Gotha program, a papal bull that laid down what was and what was not permissible in the rhetoric of a party that purported to speak for the proletariat.

With Lassalle removed by the Wallachian's bullet, the role of chief villain in Marx's battle for leadership passed to Bakunin, the Russian émigré who threatened to seize control of the world revolution. In preparation for the annual congresses of the International, Marx and Engels busied themselves with co-opting delegates favorable to their side, distributing gratis membership cards and stamps that would assure them a majority, writing long letters denouncing Bakuninists as spies of the police, raging against Bakunin's authoritarianism in the Spanish, Swiss, and Italian sections of his Alliance Démocratique, exposing the lies spread by his emissary Sergei Nechayev in Russia. After the defeat of the Bakuninists in their ill-conceived seizure of the Lyons City Hall during the Commune uprising, it was easy to blame the mad Russian for the whole fiasco. Engels even indulged in the far-fetched speculation that if not for the Proudhonists and the Bakuninists, the revolution in France might have been successful.

For committed theorists like Marx and Engels, the chasm between the rival conceptions of the revolution, the Bakuninist and the Marxist, could never be bridged. Marx's primary duty as a communist was to destroy the capitalist economic system; after its downfall, the state and the institutions dependent upon it would collapse on their own. Trade-union militancy, the organization of industrial workers, the writing of a voluminous treatise setting forth the inevitability of the breakdown of capitalism because of contradictions in the process of production, were the obligations of a revolutionary.

To tackle the state frontally, attempting to grasp power through direct political-military action, was a futile exercise doomed to defeat. This Bakuninist tactic was in the tradition of Babeuf, who dreamed of the coup d'état as the only weapon against the oppressive state. Once the state was destroyed Bakunin anarchists would introduce the just society, which would rely upon man's cooperative nature. Complex economic structures were beyond their understanding. Bakunin could blithely assimilate Marx's critique of capitalist economy—he even accepted an advance payment from a publisher for his proposed translation of *Das Kapital* (one shies away from imagining the result)—though he was averse to the domineering intellectuals who tried to exclude him from the revolutionary movement. He denounced the aristocracy of intellect as "the most odious, the most despicable, the most impertinent, and the most oppressive" of all aristocracies.[12] What Bakunin and Marx differed about essentially was how to make a revolution and what to do with society on the morrow of the triumph. For Bakunin the revolution was spontaneous and imminent, and when he was addressing small clandestine groups under his spell the anarchist revolutionary predictions were sufficient unto themselves. "A little while now, two years, a year, maybe even a few months, and these two movements [the masses and the revolutionary students] will unite, and then, then you will see a revolution that will surpass, without doubt, everything that we have known of revolutions until now."[13] In present-day pre-industrialized societies, Bakuninist-type slogans, embraced in ignorance of their source, have often displaced the learned and complex Marxist theoretical analyses.

Ideological differences between Marx and Bakunin estranged them for decades, while they were being spied upon by informers so numerous they may well have exceeded the revolutionary partisans of both sides. After the establishment of the Paris Commune, the European press inflated the significance of the International and Marx became a world figure supposedly in control of millions in funds and members, an outcome that did not entirely displease Marx and Engels because it fed the illusion of strength and might draw workers into their ranks. In the end, the men in power in European societies realized that most sections of the International were empty shells.

Much of the correspondence on the Bakunin affair of 1872 that led to the dissolution of the First International was conducted by Engels. He issued advisories to Italian comrades that they should beware of all persons connected with Bakunin, because he had taught them that keeping promises was nothing but bourgeois prejudice which a true revolutionary should disregard in the interests of the cause. The defense of moral principles in political behavior sounds hollow coming from the mouths of leaders who were as skillful and as unscrupulous as other politicians in dealing with opponents. Machiavelli is not a patron saint in the Marxist calendar, nor did Marx fail to wax indignant when European ministers invoked the "reason of state" to justify their actions or to violate laws they had themselves promulgated, but Marx and Engels could always call upon the higher law of the reason of history to sanctify their own departures from bourgeois virtue.

Bakunin's cohorts were participants in a plot against Marx and his doctrine, a cabal that Marx and Engels alternately magnified as dangerous or belittled as insignificant. Engels' long communication of January 24, 1872, to Theodor Friedrich Cuno, a German engineer who organized the Milan section of the International, included an official estimate of the size of the enemy forces. "The core of the Bakunin conspiracy consists of a few dozen people in the Jura, who have scarcely 200 workers behind them; its vanguard in Italy consists of young lawyers, doctors, and journalists, who now come forward everywhere as the representatives of the Italian workers, with a few of the same breed in Barcelona and Madrid, and a few individuals here and there—in Lyons and Brussels. There are almost no workers among them; they have only one specimen here [in London], Robin [Paul Robin, a school teacher]."

Engels had a remarkable gift for compressing the differences between Marx and the Bakuninists into a capsule that avoided the legalistic paraphernalia in which Marx tended to mire his arguments. Engels was a superb pedagogue who addressed a neophyte in clear language, easily comprehensible to a convert in his twenties. "Bakunin has a singular theory," he wrote to Cuno,

> a potpourri of Proudhonism and communism, the chief point of which is first of all, that he does not regard capital, and hence the class antagonism between capitalists and wage workers which has arisen through the development of society, as the main evil to be abolished but instead the *state*. While the great mass of the Social-Democratic workers hold our view that state power is nothing more than the organization with which the ruling classes—landowners and capitalists—have provided themselves in order to protect their social privileges, Bakunin maintained that the *state* has created capital, that the capitalist has his capital only by grace of the *state*. And since the state is the chief evil, the state above all must be abolished; then capital will go to hell of itself. We, on the contrary, say: Abolish capital, the appropriation of all the means of production by the few, and the state will fall of itself. The difference is an essential one: the abolition of the state is nonsense without a social revolution beforehand; the abolition of capital *is* the social revolution and involves a change in the whole mode of production. However, since for Bakunin the state is the main evil, nothing must be done that can keep the state alive, i.e. any state, republic, monarchy, or whatever it may be. Hence *complete abstention from all politics*. To commit a political action, especially to take part

in an election, would be a betrayal of principle. The thing to do is to conduct propaganda, revile the state, organise, and when *all* the workers are won over, that is the majority, to depose the authorities, abolish the state, and replace it by the organization of the International. This great act, with which the millennium begins, is called *social liquidation.*[14]

For Marx and Engels such an absurdly simplistic theory might find favor among young lawyers and doctors in backward countries and other doctrinaires, but not among the mass of the workers, who would never deny themselves the right to participate in politics. The strategy of exclusion would drive them into the arms of the priests and bourgeois republicans. Whereras Bakunin's followers railed against the exercise in the International of any central authority, which in their minds was associated with the state and absolute evil, Engels, who believed that his party had free access to the will of the mass of the workers, was convinced they had the good sense to understand that without some authority there could be no organization. Without a unified direction and an authority of last resort, no factory, railway, or ship could run.

When forced to identify the nature of the social order that would follow the abolition of capital, Marx and Engels fell back upon generalities about capacities and needs that were no more specific than Bakunin's fantasy of autonomous sections of the International or Proudhon's cooperatives. Since utopian descriptions of future bliss were forbidden to Marxists and the elysiums of their opponents were empty of flesh-and-blood human beings, the polemical emphasis of all parties shifted to rival tactics for achieving the paradisaical condition of mankind. The competitors spent themselves in backbiting and displayed their virtuosity in the construction of networks of followers, real and imaginary.

In inventing fictitious adherents, Marx was no match for Sergei Nechayev, the youth who suddenly appeared in Bakunin's presence in Geneva in 1869, and captivated him with accounts of a web of revolutionaries in Russia. Together the two composed a *Revolutionary Catechism* and *Principles of Revolution,* which became the bible of revolutionary terror. Asked what he would do if because of the revolution he had nothing to smoke, Bakunin retorted: "I would smoke the revolution! . . . I drink to the destruction of the public order and to the unleashing of evil passions."[15]

Bakunin recognized Marx's drive to dominate any organization in which he participated, and in his turn Marx leveled the accusation of megalomania against Bakunin. In their brutal struggle for control of the First International, they drew verbal sketches of each other that are mirror images. Both were motivated by vanity, the need to be surrounded by sycophants. They pursued their enemies without restraint, slandering them, lying, using agents to infiltrate revolutionary sections in each other's territory. The record of Marx's assaults is more voluminous because of his predilection for writing and publishing long official reports. Bakunin's imaginings, especially his invention of non-existent revolutionary cells, were extravagant. He was probably impotent and his outbursts bordered on the abyss of psychosis; and yet for a time he bewitched sensible men like Alexander Herzen and recruited followers among skilled Swiss artisans in the Jura. Marx was a master of lawyer-like argument and pulled apart Bakunin's plans of action phrase by phrase, piling up the evidence of fraud and deceit as if he were conducting a trial in a bourgeois court. When Bakunin neither returned the money he had received on his promise to translate *Das Kapital* nor produced anything, Marx publicly denounced his conduct as immoral.

Bakunin was always grasping at familial metaphors—the International was the "mother"; Marx, the tsar, like his father, was hated and loved. This wild Russian anarchist supplied an element of opera buffa to his relationship with Marx. Bakunin jested: "He called me a sentimental idealist, and he was right; I called him vain, perfidious, and sly, and I was right too."[16] Their gaming, which continued to the very end, went back a long way. When the *New Rhenish Times,* edited by Marx during the Revolution of 1848, accused Bakunin of being in the pay of the tsar, he challenged Marx to a duel. The affair was called off only when Bakunin's second accepted the explanation that the story was a news report and not an editorial judgment. Marx retracted the charge after George Sand, one of the supposed sources of the pasquille, denied any role in the slander. The European bourgeoisie was deprived of the spectacle of these two heavy-set revolutionaries in combat on an open field.

Marx laid down conditions for admitting Bakunin's Alliance into the International. The central body of his organization would have to be dissolved and individual sections of the Alliance, like the Genevans, would be allowed to join as separate entities. Bakunin formally accepted these conditions of the London Council, and then proceeded to flout them. In an official report to the International, Marx laid bare the machinations of the Alliance for a seizure of power, and ridiculed its three-tiered institutional apparatus, at its summit a directorate of a hundred clandestine members—Jesuits, Marx charged, who would be controlled by Bakunin the pope. To Bakunin and his followers the publication of their secret revolutionary programs was perfidy.

There were ample policy reasons for the distrust of Bakunin that moved Marx and Engels to pursue his group until they were definitively ousted from the ruling body of the International. Bakunin envisaged a sudden uprising of the people, which after its initial success would be guided by the directors, secretly prepared in advance for their task; Marx advocated propaganda through every working-class newspaper or journal or trade union that would open its doors, and he was ready to alter his discourse to suit a particular audience so long as he did not have to depart from fundamental principles. Bakunin's intrigues and the manipulations of his emissary, Nechayev, had violated rules of honor and morality with impunity. The mission of Marx and Engels, as responsible leaders, was to raise the consciousness of workers everywhere, avoiding the apparatus of tiny cells of the elect. They never doubted, however, that they themselves were in command of what they called the "whole thing," though Marx eschewed the office of head of the International so long as his man, Eccarius the German tailor, whom he ridiculed in private, sat in the chair.

In the eyes of Marx and Engels, their entire mechanism was democratic. Important documents that set forth the position of the International on matters of procedure—above all, the acceptance into their midst of new voting sections—were drafted by Marx. Individual members of the International's Council sitting in London represented national units, but when there were no émigrés at hand and travel was impossible, a substitute was resorted to, as a consequence of which Marx might act for the Swiss, the Germans, or the Russians, Engels for the Spaniards or the Italians. Aware of the bizarre aspect of their roles, Marx once signed a private letter to Engels "Secretary for the Russians," followed by an exclamation mark. Though Marx's intellectual authority was not often challenged openly in the course of the First International's ten-year existence, there was subterranean grumbling against the location of the central office—a room in a trade union or a fraternal body—in London. The continentals, sparked by the Bakuninists and the Proudhonists, claimed that situating the Council in England placed its members under the influence of the staid English working-class movement and dampened the ardor of revolution everywhere. Marx warded off his critics and even survived the crisis of the Paris Commune, but at a price—the dissolution of the International after its transfer to New York to forestall a Bakuninist takeover.

Marx's involvement with the French radicals, for whom Proudhon remained an idol, was ill-starred. The behavior of the Proudhonists at the First Congress of the International Working Men's Association in Geneva, September 3 through 8, 1866, had cast them in the same circle of Marx's hell as the Bakuninists. Marx had carefully prepared the agenda for the meeting in the guise of Instructions for the Delegates of the Provisional General Council, which included nine mostly practical proposals, such as limitation of the working day, restrictions on child labor, organization of cooperatives and trade unions, as well as generalities on the struggle between capital and labor—all directed toward consolidating the workers of the world into a class conscious of its identity through participation in concrete political activities. Though most of his guidelines were adopted, the Proudhonists, who controlled a third of the delegates, managed to fill the deliberations with prattle, mouthing Proudhon's vapid clichés about anti-authoritarian individualism and anti-governmentalism. In rebuttal, Marx berated them as cowards who countenanced Napoleon III's despotism while preaching bourgeois economics under the cover of Proudhonian idealism.

In his account of the congress to Dr. Ludwig Kugelmann on October 9, 1866, Marx traced their behavior back to its source, his old Paris enemy of the 1840s. Proudhon himself, who had died the previous year, was responsible for the enormous harm that had been done.

> His sham criticism and sham opposition to the utopians (he himself is only a philistine utopian, whereas in the utopias of a Fourier, an Owen, etc., there is the presentiment and imaginative expression of a new world) attracted and corrupted first the "brilliant youth," the students, then the workmen, particularly those of Paris, who, as workers in luxury trades, are strongly attached, without knowing it, to the old muck. Ignorant, vain, presumptuous, chattering, dogmatic, arrogant, they were on the point of spoiling everything, for they came to the Congress in numbers which bore no proportion whatever to the number of their members. I shall have a dig at them in my report without mentioning names.[17]

Proudhonism was for Marx the perennial malady of French socialism, with a distinctive appeal to intellectuals, though he never equated it with the perils of Lassalleanism, Bakuninism, and Blanquism. The high moral tone of Proudhon's works and the rhetoric of his disciples were impediments to the diffusion in France of the tough-minded arguments in *Das Kapital*. Proudhonists remained among the enemies to be routed, though in later years they could not be classed among the prime objects of Marx's resentment. He constantly shifted his targets; heretics of the first order had to cede pride of place to newcomers, though in rhetorical excursions he might lump them all together in collective guilt.

Once communes mushroomed in France after the victory of Prussia in the War of 1870, Marx could neither ignore them nor dominate them, with Bakunin in Lyons and his own son-in-law Lafargue running wild in the south of France. As a revolutionary strategist, Marx desperately hoped to avoid a repetition of the failures of 1848–1849, but since the battle had been joined he could not refrain from offering his advice and criticizing the military bunglers among the Communards. When the massacre of the defeated began, he denounced the savage repression ordered by the French government. The Commune was Marx's last strategic fiasco. Henceforward he was reduced to action at a distance, fighting for nominal control of the German working classes, while he wrestled with the diseases that would ultimately overcome him. He lived more comfortably and gained greater notoriety, but his capacity for serious work was diminished. *Das Kapital* remained uncompleted.

At the time of the Commune, the bourgeois press brought the International to the fore of European awareness by singling out the organization as the conspiratorial agency behind the Paris uprising and identifying Marx as the secret leader of the world revolutionary movement. Having created their bewhiskered bogey, the newspapers kept it alive by sending interviewers around to Marx's house, men who were impressed by the strength of his personality when they met him in private. Marx was ambivalent about the new distinction that had been accorded him, obviously savoring his world-wide fame, while expressing contempt for the press that had promoted it and the public it purported to inform. To his Hanover correspondent Ludwig Kugelmann he wrote in January of 1874: "For the rest, don't worry at all about newspaper gossip; *still less answer it.* I myself allow the English papers to announce my death from time to time, without giving a sign of life . . . I don't give a farthing for the public, and, if my occasional illness is exaggerated, it at least has this advantage, that it keeps away all sorts of requests (theoretical and otherwise) from unknown people in every corner of the earth."[18]

By the mid 1870s Marx had survived his major antagonists: Lassalle had died in 1864, Proudhon in 1865, Moses Hess in 1875, and Bakunin in 1876. But though the old luminaries could no longer threaten to outshine him, the center of gravity of the world revolutionary movement had shifted from London to Germany, and a new generation of leaders arose who were outside Marx's dominion, though they sometimes ventured to pay a courtesy visit to the lion in his London den.

The chronically ailing Moor had been dealt a stunning blow in 1875 when he was confronted by the amalgamation of the remnant of his own followers with the Lassalleans, their outlooks fused in the Gotha program. After issuing anathemas from London for ten years, he had become an impotent old man. The intricacies of his clandestine manoeuvres among the German working-class factions now appear as crude as the details of a superannuated spy novel. What Marx and Engels bequeathed is the spirit of authoritarian rule, which manifested itself in peremptory purges of the deviationists who dared to defy the leader. His manner of manipulating the instruments of political destruction against foes and former comrades reveals a naked Marx, his body covered with carbuncles, driven by a lust for absolute power as consuming as his passion for system-building. Perhaps the excruciating carbuncles directed his *praxis* more often than the abstract theory of his economic and philosophical writings. We now know that during the final years of completing the first volume of *Das Kapital* he was stretched on a bed of pain for long periods, when he could neither sit nor bend over to place himself in a writing posture. The tendency of sufferers to strike out against presumed enemies is common enough; the same force that fueled the creation of his juggernaut against the bourgeoisie could be mustered against rivals in the working-class movement.

Marx's last major intrusion into the affairs of the German Social Democratic Party was provoked by the publication of a review of the socialist movement that appeared in July 1879, with the signatures of Karl Höchberg, Karl August Schramm, and Eduard Bernstein, in the *Jahrbuch für Socialwissenschaft und Socialpolitik*. This was a period of great confusion in the ranks of the party after the Reichstag had passed anti-socialist legislation under which the Social Democratic press was outlawed and many of its leaders arrested. The "Zurich trio," as the authors of the review came to be known, had criticized the party for adopting an abrasive tone in its propaganda that alienated educated middle-class adherents of the Social Democrats and appealed exclusively to workers. When the trio then proposed to publish a weekly in Zurich, the dioscuri could no longer remain silent in the face of a resurgent petty bourgeois ideological position against which they had fought for forty years. In high dudgeon Engels drafted and Marx co-signed a circular letter they dispatched in September 1879 to August Bebel, Wilhelm Liebknecht, and Wilhelm Bracke, Social Democrats they thought could be relied upon to follow the hallowed party line. In this document, which achieved a level of prolixity unequaled in the Marxist corpus, with the possible exception of *Herr Vogt*, they decried the open betrayal of proletarian principles and mocked the bourgeois deviationists of the united German party. "Wherever the class struggle is thrust aside as a distasteful, 'crude' manifestation, the only basis still left to socialism will be a 'true love of mankind' and empty phrases about 'justice.'"[19] A new heresy, opportunism, with a long future history had been born.

In private correspondence Marx resorted to his old antisemitic expletives, berating the "little Jew Bernstein" as a nephew of the Berlin rabbi, Rebenstein. Engels justified the views of the dioscuri in rationalist, albeit dramatic, terms: "We couldn't think of lowering the proletarian flag which we had held aloft for nigh on 40 years, still less join in the general petty-bourgeois fraternisation fantasies against which we had been fighting, again for nigh on 40 years."[20] The affair came to center around the editorial control of the Zurich *Social-Democrat* and revived quarrels that involved the political conduct of members of a Social Democratic Party faction who had been elected to the Reichstag and had supported a Bismarckian tariff law and other measures pandering to the bourgeoisie. Marx and Engels threatened to withhold their support from the Zurich publication. The new German leaders, no longer intimidated by their elders, nevertheless wanted their blessing, even though they were subjected to a dressing down in private when they appeared in London. Through the intervention of August Bebel, Eduard Bernstein went to Canossa and the dispute was papered over.

Marx had become notorious in the bourgeois world, but this generation of German socialists did not stand in awe of the doctrinal absolutes of leaders from afar who failed to appreciate the need for compromise with bourgeois elements in a party operating under precarious conditions in a parliamentary system. On this occasion the aging Marx showed a rare willingness to compromise. He was tired. After his death, Engels was revered as a figurehead and his birthdays were duly celebrated, while the rising socialist politicians allowed Marxism to become an academic subject fit for professors.

═ 10 ═
Shearing of the Beard

Of course, at a certain age, it becomes completely indifferent how one may be launched into eternity.

—Marx to Engels, June 5, 1882

L iving with Marx and his family is like being a stagehand in a Shakespearean tragedy played in Victorian costume. An ailing wife bore children in rapid succession: one was stillborn; Guido and Franziska died within a year of their birth, Edgar at the age of eight. An early hint by Jenny that they use the "French method" of intercourse apparently went unheeded. Three girls reached maturity and two outlived their father but subsequently committed suicide. The only male who survived was the maid's Freddy.

The verbal portraits of Marx by family members, political friends and enemies, life-long disciples and casual acquaintances, police spies and newspaper reporters, are contradictory, often more revelatory of the authors of the reminiscences than of their subject. That they caught him at different stages of his life cycle and in various moods accounts for contrasts that are no more extreme than those emerging from attempts to capture the inner core and outward conduct of any man. He is slim or stocky, above average height or short, violent and formidable or benign and gentle, changeable or stubbornly uncompromising. The photographs, in chronological sequence, are more of a piece; the most striking feature in all of them is his hairiness, crown and beard jet black in the beginning, growing white toward the end. An enlarged lithograph of his student days in Bonn, in which he sports a wisp of a moustache, seems inauthentic, and there is no record of the clean-shaven old man in Algiers.

Collectively the photographs convey the power of his person. Sadness creeps in with age, as hair and beard lose their color.

The piling up of detail in lengthy biographies obscures the secret of the man as much as his bushy whiskers conceal the visage. The lives of Marx have multiplied over the decades and excerpts from his copybooks will continue to be published; but even when every smidgen from his pen has been examined and deciphered, the quest for the hidden Marx will continue. This is not the last requiem for the enigmatic Mohr, who has left a paper trail that intrigues and perplexes us even as the echo of his name grows fainter. After the memoirs composed by friend and foe have been ransacked and analyzed, the question, what manner of man was Marx, remains unanswered. Any monochromatic construct of his personality is robbed of persuasiveness by individual character sketches drawn by observers with different perspectives.

Paul Annenkov, a Russian émigré who belonged to no revolutionary party, portrayed Marx in action during his Brussels exile in 1846, the period when he and Engels were seizing control of the Communist League, the embryo of future communist associations through which they hoped to direct the revolution.

> Marx himself was the type of man who is made up of energy, will and unshakable conviction. He was most remarkable in his appearance. He had a shock of deep black hair and hairy hands, and his coat was buttoned wrong; but he looked like a man with the right and power to demand respect, no matter how he appeared before you and no matter what he did. His movements were clumsy, but confident and self-reliant, his ways defied the usual conventions in human relations, but they were dignified and somewhat disdainful; his sharp metallic voice was wonderfully adapted to the radical judgments that he passed on persons and things. He always spoke in imperative words that would brook no contradiction and were made all the sharper by the almost painful impression of the tone which ran through everything he said. This tone expressed the firm conviction of his mission to dominate men's minds and prescribe them their laws. Before me stood the embodiment of a democratic dictator such as one might imagine in a daydream.[1]

Twenty years later, when *Das Kapital* was being published, Marx's daughter Laura interpreted in a different spirit a photograph her father sent the family from Hamburg. "I admire especially the eyes and forehead and expression: the first have the true 'roguish twinkle' I am so fond of in the original, and this is the only one of your shadows which unites the two expressions of a sarcasm and good nature of the substance: a stranger, I think, would consider only the last but I, who look upon it with a peculiar 'bird's-eye' of my own, spy a little maliciousness in the likeness, very pleasant no doubt to your friends but calculated to play the deuce with your enemies."[2]

Karl Marx acquired a pistol with which he once threatened a police informer. On another occasion he abruptly turned on an agent who was shadowing him, fixed him with his monocle, and drove off the creature with the sheer force of his stare. During the 1848 uprising in Cologne, as editor of the radical newspaper *Neue Rheinische Zeitung* (New Rhenish Times), he managed its policy with an iron hand. His outspoken criticism of the Prussian regime led to a charge of *lèse-majesté;* in the trial that followed he was acquitted by the jury and applauded for his daring by a crowd of partisans—a rare moment of popular acclaim that he never forgot. In such public confrontations he was a bold and courageous man. Only Engels and members of his family were privy to the moments of weakness when he succumbed to despair.

At various times in his life Marx was under detention for brief periods—on the accusation of rowdyism during his student days in Bonn, and after judicial procedures in connection with his expulsion for subversion from one country or another. Getting deported was a method that impecunious exiled revolutionaries devised for traveling between Western European capitals in order to attend party congresses. Ordinarily Marx obeyed the law, and by our contemporary standards the police were lenient with the sworn political enemies of the society they protected. When during the course of a long night of pubcrawling Marx joined Edgar Bauer in throwing stones at street lamps, the miscreants outran the London police chasing them—the closest he came to a serious breach of the peace.

Edmund Wilson attributed Marx's commitment to Armageddon to his "somber and savage" personality; yet as Engels observed to one of his correspondents, Marx was diffident, "as bashful as a young girl," when it came to spreading notices about his book. Like many other portraits of Marx in photographs and verbal sketches, Wilson's disparaging remarks reveal only partial truths. Anger, self-loathing, insatiable curiosity about matters philosophical, historical, and economic are dominant. Marx's mode of expression is ironic, often cynical, because he thinks he knows human nature and its propensity for hypocrisy and treachery. He values intellectual acumen, logic, understanding of the dialectical processes of development in nature and history, and believes in models that represent these processes; his contempt for ignorance and stupidity makes no allowance for circumstances. In his last years he began to receive visitors from the English labor movement more frequently, but though he dreaded isolation, when company appeared he was bored and wished they were gone. Outside of Engels and the family circle there is not much sympathy for human beings in Karl Marx. But while officially condemning a surrender to pathos or sentimentality as a character flaw, he himself could not always rise up from the swamp of self-pity.

Marx was sufficiently self-revealed to describe himself as an "anxious" man. In his letters to Engels, an excursion on some technical point of economic theory or an inquiry about business practices, on which Engels was the expert, intruded into an account of a personal tragedy, fortifying the impression of a cold, heartless man. A penchant for terms such as "tragi-comic" in introducing a dismal situation suggests that he is play-acting, resorting to the device of Shakespeare, through whose eyes he saw much of the world. But there was not always a role in which he could take refuge: when a beloved son died in childhood his grief was overwhelming.

Marx's playfulness with his children was reported by Wilhelm Liebknecht, and his daughter Eleanor describes his giving a penny to a ragged street urchin and patting him on the head. He invented long, fanciful tales for his young ones, and trotted them about on his sturdy shoulders. He wanted male children, but became a devoted father of his three surviving daughters. The anecdotes that capture him in changing moods modify the chiseled figure of the formidable Karl Marx. Pride alternates with self-denigration, and there are shifting winds and passions.

Marx was an introspective man whose blatant megalomania was softened with the saving grace of self-mockery. That odd digression boasting of the scholarship of *Das Kapital* in a letter to Engels as the admirable achievement not of one man but of the whole German nation was a tongue-in-cheek comment offset by the remark that the Germans were the silliest of all peoples. Marx then admits the inevitability of minor errors in detail, a confession of his fallibility. Though he suffered intermittent periods of despondency, on one occasion in 1863, four years before the publication of the first volume of *Das Kapital,* Marx composed a self-congratulatory, if stilted, summary of his life's work. "I have brought to light voluminous works in diverse and formidable areas of scientific knowledge; I have not been deterred by toil or sleepless nights in my efforts to extend the limits of such knowledge; and I can perhaps say with Horace: 'militavi non sine gloria.'"[3]

A stiff letter from Marx to Paul Lafargue dated August 13, 1866, admonishing him to restrain his creole temperament in his courtship of Laura, sounds ludicrous to contemporary ears. The young Lafargue had introduced himself to the family as a revolutionary follower of Marx. In the course of his rambling criticism of the creole's amorous ways, Marx reflected that if he had his life to live over again he would never have married; but since the damage was done, he was unwilling to expose his daughters to the deprivations that Mrs. Marx had suffered. In the stern language of a middle-class Victorian father, he demanded the suitor's credentials and an account of his financial status, present and prospective, confronting him with the ordeal of long years of chastity—a recollection of his own youth—until the medical student had established himself and the marriage could be consummated.

In a letter to Engels, Marx sounded pleased with himself in the austere posture of a *paterfamilias.* Yet the priggish Marx could copy recondite pornographic passages from old French poets that he had chanced upon when he was wearied with his usual diet of British parliamentary reports. Gossip about the sexual behavior of German émigrés and about the high jinks of Lassalle was a standard divertissement in the Marx correspondence. The self-righteous hypocrite is a character not alien to the prophet of a future state in which true love would prevail once man was liberated from the bonds of the cash nexus.

Though among his many illusions Marx fancied himself a knower of men, his meticulous examinations of pretenders to the hand of his daughters were dismal failures. Paul Lafargue, who married Laura, managed to get a medical degree and then tried his luck at photography and French post-Commune politics; Charles Longuet, Jenny's husband, was also enmeshed in Third Republic radical political affairs. Both men deeply disappointed their father-in-law. On November 11, 1882, a few months before his death, Marx voiced his exasperation to Engels: "Longuet the last Proudhonist and Lafargue the last Bakuninist. May the devil take them!" Their efforts to support his girls, the prime concern of his initial inquiries, were none too strenuous, and in politics he found the two men totally unreliable. Both were French (though Paul was a mulatto) and were never cleansed of the taint of Proudhonism. Marx railed at Lafargue when he continued to manifest traits of his "creole character," shooting off his mouth without regard for the political consequences. Marx complained to Engels: "Lafargue has the customary mark of the Negro race, no feeling of shame, by which I mean the shamefulness of making oneself ludicrous."[4] During an election campaign after the debacle of the Commune, Lafargue intimated in one of his public harangues that through the intermediary of German Social Democrats the French socialists had been informed of the intentions of the German General Staff. The fool had never for a moment considered that these careless phrases had put the German Social Democratic Party in jeopardy. Marx was outraged and demanded explanations. What Lafargue had to offer only muddled matters further.

The union of Jenny and Charles Longuet was an unfortunate one. The morose journalist constantly nagged his wife, whose misery was aggravated by a domineering mother-in-law. Marx's visits to their house in Argenteuil were not joyful, and the burden of caring for "Papa" fell primarily on Eleanor, who was herself beset with anxieties. Eleanor's anguished letter to her sister Jenny Longuet on January 8, 1882, from the Isle of Wight, lifts a veil on the unhappiness of Marx's children that saddened his last years.

> [S]eeing how anxious I am to be able to look after Papa, I was terribly afraid of breaking down altogether, as I had done before . . . (For a

long time I tried various drugs—this quite *entre nous,* and am loth to try them again—it is not much better, after all, than dram-drinking, and is almost if not quite as injurious.) *Since I have been here I have not slept six hours.* You may imagine—even without counting other things—that this is killing—and I really do fear a complete break-down—which for Papa's sake I would do anything to avoid. What I most dread is the consulting of doctors. They cannot and will not see that mental worry is as much an illness as any physical ailment could be.[5]

The two Jennies, mother and daughter, died within a year of each other. Doctors did not allow Marx to attend his wife's funeral, at which Engels delivered the oration, a stand-in for the last time. Eleanor, who later committed suicide as did her sister Laura, became active in spreading socialist ideas among Jewish immigrants from Eastern Europe in London, a dramatic reversal of her father's Judeophobia. At the time of the Dreyfus affair she announced, "I am a Jewess"; in her speeches she advertised her father's Jewish origins; and she declared herself the only member of her family "drawn to the Jewish people." In self-deprecating jest she had written to Karl Kautsky: "I unfortunately only inherited my Father's nose (I used to tell him I could sue him for damages as his nose has distinctly entailed a loss upon me) and not his genius."[6]

The editors of Marx's papers have apologetically pointed out that when he called Lafargue a "nigger," the term had none of the overtones that it acquired in later times; but a gathering of the texts, jocular and serious references alike, leaves the uncomfortable impression that Marx and Engels were as prone as their contemporaries to lapse into derogatory racial epithets. Derisive thumbnail sketches of national character have been part of the ordinary European vocabulary for centuries, and Marx innovated nothing in the psychology of peoples except to adapt the stereotypes in confused analyses of revolutionary situations. In caricaturing the nations in his published works he tended to avoid the grosser labels of popular speech, but the philosophical German, the flighty Frenchman, and the phlegmatic Englishman were commonplaces of his everyday usage.

Only a psychology undaunted by contradictions, the play of opposites, light and darkness, could untangle the web of Marx's personality. To identify a consistent, rational essence presumes to have discovered what may not exist. The deep-rooted aggressiveness in Marx's nature was a dominant drive ever on the prowl for objects, in himself or persons who crossed his path. Tracing an intellectual development that exchanged one theoretical allegiance for another illuminates one side of his face and tends to accept the formula expressed by both his father and his mother in their letters to him during his adolescence—the hypertrophy of head at the expense of heart. The dismal chronicle of his ailments recorded in his correspondence in the medical language of the day reveals his physical pain but often disguises the intensity of his psychic anguish. To measure his conduct by his philosophy, by his political manipulations in the grey world of revolutionary exiles of various persuasions, or by his abstract principles, is to force him onto a procrustean bed from which no one but a messianic robot could rise unmutilated. Marx the beggarman constantly pleading for handouts from friend and foe can be either viewed as a selfish egocentric, a model of incompetence and irresponsibility, or exalted as a savior who is above the mundane uses of this vile world.

Marx's rages in the directorial committees of the First International that met in Fleet Street pubs were proverbial. When illness forced him to stay away for a number of months he feared that on his return he would lose his temper, his irritability exacerbated by the bungling of his colleagues and by his carbuncles. Often this man had difficulty perceiving his behavior as an integrated whole, and treated his body and the temperamental explosions to which it gave rise as divided from his real self. This psychological separation, of which he was sometimes acutely aware, had its counterpart in his attitude toward the proletariat. He could dissect the working classes of the world objectively as he did his own person, and it sharpened his sense of the chasm between what they did in fact and what they ought to do in pursuit of their historic destiny. Dr. Marx scolded his proletarian patients, mocked them, unleashed his anger against them. The discordant relationship of body and mind, of which he was conscious in his own person, could be applied to the history of social classes.

Marx was not a complete narcissist, a label that a psychologist might be prone to affix to him; he slithers out of the categories that modern mental science has prepared for its patients. For a while he obeyed the orders of one or another doctor and altered his unhealthful habits, but eventually he fell back into his old ways. There were woes, public and private, that prevented him from pursuing a regimen to the end, he wrote to his friend Dr. Kugelmann. Or was the crippling disease of carbuncles, caused by bacteria that doctors today can identify and treat with antibiotics, incurable with the pharmacology then available? His temporary psychic breakdowns were probably more frequent than the written record shows. But the man rebounded, and he clung to his grand illusion until the disease-ridden body could sustain him no longer.

The voice of a university professor, the career that was closed to Karl Marx, would not be stilled, and once he embarked upon his own *chef d'oeuvre* he wrote not for laborers but for the philosophers and scientists of the Western world. His exposition became as comprehensive as an academic disquisition should be. Praise from a professor, even a Russian professor, was the kind of approval after which he thirsted; the preface to the opening volume of *Das Kapital* recalled with obvious satisfaction the accolades that his *Contribution to a Critique of Political Economy* (1859) had received from afar.

After the appearance of the first volume of *Das Kapital,* the renewed eruption of carbuncles and the public silence that enveloped the book became sources of physical and psychic pain that made Marx "fidgety"—his own description. Though he ultimately set about arranging his papers for the promised continuation of the work, he did not quite recover from the indifference of its initial reception. As a compensatory device he immersed himself more and more in the organizational details of the International. Bakunin and his Alliance replaced Lassalle as the enemy, while the Lassalleans continued to propagandize in the name of their fallen hero. Without a prime antagonist life would have been empty for Marx.

The outbreak of the Franco-Prussian War and the proclamation of the Commune filled a void for a time, when the news agencies pounced upon Marx and the International as the secret force behind the uprisings. The bogey of the *Communist Manifesto* had become incarnate in the person of Karl Marx. Twenty-three years after the revolutions of 1848, it was feared that the Continent was again on the verge of bursting into flames, with the French incendiaries in the lead. Members of Marx's family on a visit to France had been caught in the turmoil, and the archenemy Bakunin was rampant in Lyons—anxious moments for the aging theoretician. For a brief while he was on center stage again, denying bourgeois rumors, dispensing advice to the revolutionaries that went unheeded, composing "addresses" for distribution to the scraggly sections of the International in order to coordinate their policies. Though he had been opposed to the hotheads of the Commune, once the die was cast Marx refurbished his debating style and composed the last of the analytic, polemical pamphlets that became a canonical guide to action for communist and socialist parties for more than a hundred years. The *Civil War in France* had neither the bite nor the fluency of the *Eighteenth Brumaire*, but it demonstrated that his hand had not lost its cunning.

Since Marx had been trained both in the law and in philosophy, he argued as if he were in a court, aiming poisoned darts with precision at an opponent, quoting a rival's text only to demolish it. As a university student in Berlin he had devoured the works of Hegel; and the method of reasoning and turgidity of the philosopher, who had died in 1831, possessed him as they did a whole generation of young Germans. Though he entered the lists against one rival after another, from Proudhon through Karl Vogt, he never treated them as equals, and during the bitter dispute with Bakunin he draped himself in the lawyer's gown and bore down upon his adversary as if he were a prosecutor at a trial, rather than a revolutionary engaged in a power struggle with a dangerous competitor in a more or less secret society.

Whatever the particular issue Marx was debating, he dramatized it and in his polemics strove for a glittering effect. He was a master of the opening gambit—the first sentences of his manifestoes and pamphlets were always arresting. They compelled immediate attention and were fixed in the mind long after the substance of the argument had faded from memory: "A spectre is haunting Europe—the spectre of Communism. All the powers of old Europe have entered into a holy alliance to exorcise this spectre: Pope and Tsar, Metternich and Guizot, French Radicals and German police-spies" (*Communist Manifesto*, 1848);[7] "Hegel remarks somewhere that all facts and personages of great importance in world history occur, as it were, twice. He forgot to add: the first time as tragedy, the second as farce" (*The Eighteenth Brumaire of Louis Bonaparte*, 1852).[8] His tirades do not wound the observer as do Goya's drawings, but their sarcasm leaves scratches in the manner of Daumier.

In the early years of their London exile the family had lived in squalor in a hotel room or a two-room flat. In 1856 a bequest from Jenny's mother enabled them to move to larger quarters at 9 Grafton Terrace; and a legacy from Karl's despised mother allowed them in 1864 to rent a spacious villa in Maitland Park, which they exchanged eleven years later for a smaller, but still commodious house at 41 Maitland Park Road. But not until Engels sold his share in the Manchester partnership in 1870 and settled a £350 annual income on Marx was he able to lead a comfortable middle-class existence. There the suddenly notorious chief of the International, the conspirator who according to the bourgeois press had hatched the plot of the Paris Commune, gave private interviews to newspaper correspondents. One of the journalists sent his paper a description of Marx's living-room, comparing it to that of a thriving stockbroker who was beginning to make his fortune in the market. The spies and visitors to earlier rooms had suggested no such comparisons, as they sat on rickety chairs amid a hodgepodge of papers, broken crockery, and the remains of children's attempts at cooking.

The forces of order slaughtered their quota of captured Communards, and Marx effectively transferred the seat of the International to New York, saving it from a Bakuninist take-over. Marx preserved his newly acquired repute for more than another decade, sententiously counseling German workingmen's factions, receiving journalists of the popular press who published interviews with him as an object of curiosity. In conversing with them he became facile in the oral presentation of his doctrine, once buried in *Das Kapital*, as a theory of inevitable capitalist development, now divested of inflammatory rhetoric, a set of beliefs expounded by a learned, intellectual, mild-mannered Jew who was obviously no danger to anybody. He had finally won the fame that had eluded him when the first volume of his magnum opus was published. The journalists, surprised that this affable, middle-aged man had been regarded as the inspiration of a revolutionary violence that threatened society, did not understand that by then he was but a shadow of his former self.

By 1879 Marx was enough of a celebrity to capture the interest of Queen Victoria's eldest daughter, the wife of the crown prince who later became Frederick III of Prussia. After a three-hour luncheon with Marx, Sir Mountstuart Elphinstone Grant Duff responded to her inquiry with a letter praising Marx's immense learning and dry humor, and declaring him correct about the past and present, though vague and unsatisfying when he turned to the future. Nevertheless, Sir Mountstuart relayed Marx's forecasts without demurral. "He looks, not unreasonably, for a great and not distant crash in Russia." Interrogated about the possibility of armament reduction and consequent relief to the peoples of Europe, Marx replied skeptically that fears and jealousies among their rulers would prevent it, that the "burden [of the people] will grow worse and worse as Science advances, for the improvements in the Art of Destruction will keep pace with its advance and every year more and more will have to be devoted to costly engines of war." Grant Duff made a prediction of his own: "It won't be he who will turn the world upside down." The princess was to rest assured that Marx was by no means a gentleman in the habit of eating babies in their cradles— "I daresay the view which the Police takes of him." He so intrigued the seasoned English diplomat that he would gladly have resumed their amicable colloquy.[9]

A foreign journalist who called on Marx in the comfortable London house on Maitland Park Road where he spent his last years was impressed with the literature from all Western European cultures that filled the bookcases. In the record of a family game preserved by one of his daughters, Marx's preferences among writers were noted: in addition to the dramas of Aeschylus and Shakespeare, which left the deepest imprint, the prose of Diderot, the poetry of Goethe. His own style was tailored to the purpose of the work at hand and often bared his contradictory drives.

There are few descriptions of nature in the hundreds of letters Marx wrote to Engels. In reviewing a book in 1851 they had ridiculed the cult of nature; the world they appreciated was manmade, the creation of his mind and his labor. After reading a book on the history of plants and climatic changes in historic times, Marx found support for his contention that unless nature was controlled by man, wastelands were left behind in areas of once-rich vegetation, as in the Tigris-Euphrates Valley. When with advancing years pulmonary disease forced Marx to seek out benign climates during the winter—the Isle of Wight, the south of France, Algeria—he would comment on the weather, with rare reference to his physical surroundings. For the rest, he lived principally in one metropolis, London, where his home and the British Museum were located; the places he visited made no particular dent upon him—from his letters one would not deduce whether he was in Paris, Cologne, Brussels, Berlin, Hamburg, Geneva, or Vienna, the cities where he sought refuge or attended party meetings. If he looked at paintings or architectural monuments, he failed to record any significant reaction to them. Greek sculpture was admired the way an adult in an industrial society is fascinated by a child's playfulness—it did not contradict his fundamental idea that creations of high culture reflected an epoch's production relations.

Marx was a man of the word, with a command of the philosophies and literatures of the West, of political and economic thought; visual images are rare. Science was Engels' province, but few of the many contemporary writings that he recommended to Marx—Darwin was an exception—were studied with professional care. When in connection with the economic history in *Das Kapital* Marx had to acquaint himself with the technical aspects of agricultural chemistry or new mechanical inventions, Engels was available to check on his use of the information he had assembled. Marx seems to have been oblivious to the latest European movements in art and poetry, and while he pored over accounts of Russian land distribution, the Russian literature that was penetrating traditional Western European bastions went unnoticed. The ironic class portraits of Balzac and the witty writings of Heinrich Heine, the exiled Jewish convert, were his contemporary favorites, brilliant social documents. Paul

Lafargue suggests that Balzac's portrayal of the obsessed artist in *Le Chef-d'oeuvre inconnu,* which Marx admired and recommended to Engels, could be a double for his inner self.[10]

Where principles of theory were concerned Marx could be rigid and unyielding, but since he lived amid the petty cheats of the age of Victoria, white lies, convenient hyperbole, even aristocratic pretenses were permissible. He told the elder Lafargue, who was in the wine-trade, that he had once owned a vineyard; he advised his wife to use a calling card inscribed *née Baroness von Westphalen;* he allowed physicians to whom he had casual recourse in foreign countries to believe that the Dr. Marx they were treating was a member of their profession—after all, he knew more about carbuncles than they did. There is something ridiculous in the disguises Marx adopted on his travels—A. Williams in continental spas, Johnson on vacation with Engels in Ramsgate. That Karl Marx thought such pseudonyms could protect him betrays the naiveté that often possessed him in play-acting the secret agent.

Marx had sought to cure a persistent cough by fleeing to Algiers in 1882, but the weather was miserable. In March he lapsed into a "profunda melancolia"—and since he was rarely stranded without a literary allusion he added "like the great Don Quixote," a figure who with advancing years replaced the Prometheus of his youth. Sleepless nights brought back images of his past, nostalgic dreams that he could not banish. Half a century of marriage, hardly the idyl that had begun in Trier, was recalled in a rare outpouring of sensibility. To Engels he wrote in awkward English on March 1, 1882: "By the by, you know that few people more averse to demonstrative Pathos; still, it would be a lie [not] to confess that my thought to great part absorbed by reminiscence of my wife, such a part of my best part of life!"[11]

In Algiers Marx became aware of the shameless arrogance, pretentiousness, and gruesome Moloch fanaticism of the French in their administration of justice—though among the imperious races they were of course surpassed by the British and the Dutch. As a rule he was not particularly sensitive to racial persecution as an aspect of bourgeois colonialism, but his sojourn in Algiers brought forth new perceptions in the failing man. There are even descriptions of the landscape—notably the harbor of Algiers—a responsiveness to natural beauty rare in one whose eyes were riveted on persons and books, unlike his friend Engels, who had a gift for conveying the genius of places he saw on his travels.

On April 28, 1882, writing from Algiers, Marx announced to Engels with mock solemnity that because of the sun he had parted with his *Prophetenbarb* (prophet's beard), though before making this hairy sacrifice on the altar of an Algerian barber, he had himself photographed for his daughters. The small likeness that he sent to Jennychen is one of the few pictures that shows a smiling Old Nick and, if one looks closely, a twinkle in the eye. Despite the discomforts of the sirocco and the collodion tattooing to which a Dr. Stephann had subjected him to ward off another pleurisy attack, a note of self-mockery crept into his letters. Perhaps he had begun to take himself less seriously, and had surrendered his mission to save the world along with his formidable whiskers.

Marx's restless travels took him from Algiers to Monte Carlo, to Argenteuil, where his daughter Jenny lived, to Switzerland, then back again to Argenteuil, where he had spent three months in the summer of 1882. The noisy Longuet household was a strange choice for so long a stay. His grandson little Johnny ran wild, while the boy's father lay a-bed the whole morning and left for Paris each afternoon at five. Marx may have been unaware that from April on Jenny was suffering from a bladder disease, probably cancer. She was hard-pressed to care for three young children, ward off her disagreeable mother-in-law, and endure an indolent, querulous husband. She had confided to Eleanor on April 10, 1882: "The cruelest of it all is that though I drudge like a nigger [he] never does anything but scream at me and grumble every minute he is in the house."[12] Unpaid debts haunted Jenny like crimes day and night, and in her desperation she concocted hare-brained schemes, such as boarding Indian and other children from London, to bolster the family income. Jenny, the eldest of the sisters, begged advice from Eleanor, the youngest, who was herself living on the edge of a breakdown.

In a letter marked "Private and Confidential," Marx had written to Laura in June that he could no longer risk traveling alone; and that it was her duty to accompany the "old man of the mountains."[13] Laura obliged, and toward the end of August they set out for Vevey by way of Lausanne, returning to France on September 28; in the meantime, Jenny had given birth to a girl, her fourth child. This time Marx did not tarry long at Argenteuil; in the first week of October he joined Eleanor, Lenchen, and their new charge, Johnny Longuet, in London. But by the end of the month the fog and dampness had driven the ailing man off to the Isle of Wight, where Eleanor and Johnny visited him in November and where he hoped, in vain, to remain until spring.

After his futile North African trip, Marx had become painfully conscious of the steady decline of his powers of concentration. He detected signs of deterioration in his spelling, syntax, and grammar, portents that he candidly reported to brother Engels. The Stoic lingered on, consulting doctors without confidence in their healing skills, submitting to treatments he did not much believe in. Old Mohr was dying. Engels, expecting the end, for weeks made daily visits in the early afternoon, full of anxiety as he rounded the corner. On January 9, 1883, Jenny Longuet died, and two months later, on March 14, Marx himself was dead—a blood vessel had burst. In the same year Nietzsche published *Thus Spake Zarathustra*.

=== 11 ===

Vicissitudes of an Icon

Tragedies and hopes and the myths and errors of millions of people are connected to an idea on whose foundation our lives were constructed for decades.

—Alexander Yakovlev, *The Fate of Marxism in Russia*, 1994

As the countries that drew their self-justification and legitimation from Lenin, Marx's most eminent disciple in theory and practice, now appear to have turned to what they call a market economy, and as the teaching of selected texts from the Marxist canon is no longer compulsory in their schools and universities, the time may be propitious to reflect on the stamp Marx left upon the world. To single out a composite body of beliefs labeled Marxism from the welter of conceptions swarming through the past hundred years is by its very nature artificial; yet in some form Marx's thinking has pervaded the mentalities of masses of human beings whose social status ranges from peasants living in the wretched huts of a rain forest to professors pontificating from the lofty podia of university halls. No country has been immune to Marxist ideas, even when they have been savaged. To be sure, they have not always been the same ideas.

A philosophical author (his self-description to the London census-taker of 1851) who conceived of himself as the anointed raiser of proletarian consciousness, Marx was once treated indifferently by many working-class leaders in the land of his birth and kept at arm's length in England, the land of his exile. Paradoxically, his ideas were adopted in peasant Russia, the country where they seemed least applicable. At the time of its publication (1867), the first volume of *Das Kapital* in a modest printing of one thousand copies was not sold out. The three thousand copies of the translation published in Russia made a far greater impact on intellectuals in that country than the book had in England, France, or Germany. Toward the end of the nineteenth century, while accepting some of his principles, a group of German socialist political leaders arrived at the conclusion that the world revolution was not imminent—economic crises were not becoming progressively more severe—and they revised the doctrine to make it palatable to Social Democrats operating in a parliamentary system; the contempt that Marx had so often visited upon working-class parties amenable to compromise with bourgeois parties was overlooked. In the twentieth century, the Marxist heritage of precepts for socialist and communist parties has often been baneful for their standard-bearers.

If nothing preserves a theory better than the absence of empirical evidence, Marxism was virtually invulnerable. For decades it survived on apology and propaganda. With the triumph of the Bolsheviks in World War I, the techniques of revolution became the focus of interest among the leaders of the Soviet Union and in the Communist International. Texts of Marx and Lenin were repeated with the refinements customarily reserved for religious dogma. Marx's admonition to take careful account of objective transformations in societies before invoking revolutionary slogans was given mere lip-service, especially after Lenin was shot, as official theoreticians mechanically quoted examples from Marx's writings on the Revolution of 1848, Napoleon III's coup d'état, and the Commune of 1870; having mouthed the hoary proof-texts, they proceeded to act like the putschists Marx had denounced.

In the period between the two world wars, an adamant refusal to compromise characterized the official communist parties under Soviet tutelage and led them to espouse outlandish doctrines such as "worsism," which furthered the success of fascism under the illusion that the deterioration of social and economic conditions and the suppression of elementary liberties would make life so intolerable that the recalcitrant working classes would be driven to rebel against their oppressors. After Hitler's advent, communist parties made sporadic attempts to fashion popular fronts, which they effectively controlled, even as Marx and Engels had operated to persuade a handful of Paris artisans to adopt their rhetorical manifestoes.

In the 1920s Marxism became increasingly dependent for verification upon the Russian experience. Westerners descended upon the land and found what they had set out to find—heaven, hell, or purgatory. They saw the future and in their eyes it worked, or they were appalled by the constraints, the fears, the miseries of proletarian society. More distant spectators, who relied upon the latest report, either shouted hallelujah or were mortified, sometimes undergoing mood changes in the course of a year, a month, even a week. Among many thinking men who made no commitment to communist party discipline there was a sort of free-floating assent to the Soviet Union and by extension to Marxism. This atmospheric Marxism is difficult to define, since its density varied from person to person and fluctuated widely within the individual host. But it did exist, from the period of fascism's rise in Western Europe through the revelations of Khrushchev at the Twentieth Party Congress. Except for the period of the Ribbentrop pact, benevolence toward Marxism and the system it had spawned became a way of expressing repugnance to the brutal aggressions of fascism on the march.

On the international stage, communist power politics were conducted as if the Soviet world were a traditional nation-state shifting alliances and alignments in accordance with the diplomacy of the times. It became the responsibility of Western communist parties to bend and twist ideological considerations in defense of the Soviet Union. The Soviet dictator made decisions that proved to be catastrophic, and in the War of Liberation against Nazi Germany the system survived by the skin of its teeth. The war rekindled Russian nationalism, while dictatorial procedures were reinvigorated. After the war, Marxism, the official philosophy of the Soviet Union, was installed in its satellite states, while throughout its sphere of influence corrupt regimes flourished, and economic and political structures were debased.

If the tactical directives of Marx, as interpreted by Lenin, experienced only variable success in different parts of the world, Marxism as a philosophy came to be embraced with fervent devotion. When after World War I Russia had adopted the system of Soviet Republics, the writings of Marx achieved canonical status and were imposed with rigor as beliefs to which citizens were obliged to take at least a formal pledge of allegiance; rejection or deviation from them could be severely punished. With time, a Marxist vocabulary penetrated ordinary speech. This Marxist doctrinal hegemony was extended to other Central and Eastern European countries after World War II and endured until the 1980s. As recently as 1990, the works of Marx, along with those of Engels, were still an intrinsic and compulsory part of the educational system of some Eastern and Central European countries. In others, their disappearance from the curricula has been faster than the dismantling of the communist economic apparatus—words are more easily displaced than outworn machinery. China has not yet cut itself completely loose from the bonds of Marxist philosophy, but obeisance to its tenets is now hedged with caveats.

Even where there was non-observance in political practice, the penetration of Marx's thought among Western intellectual elites in the century following his death was phenomenal. The speed of its movement outstripped the tempo of advance of sculptural forms from classical Greece to Buddhist China, of the Holy Book of the Koran from Arabia to the heart of Christian Spain, of Christianity from Judaea to the whole of the Mediterranean basin. Marxist studies in the university in France and in the underground of fascist Italy were assiduously cultivated in the period between the two world wars. Marxism was slower to penetrate the United States (though Daniel de Leon, a labor leader in the early twentieth century, considered himself a Marxist). In 1936 a seminar on Marx was finally held at Harvard, conducted by Wassily Leontieff, a young émigré economist from Russia, later a Nobel laureate, and Edward Mason, an economist who came to preside over the choice of strategic bombing targets in World War II. In attendance were a young Japanese aristocrat, Shigeto Tsuru, who had learned by heart large sections of *Das Kapital* in Tokyo University, where academic Marxism was widely cultivated, and a sprinkling of English, German, and other Central European visitors. Despite conservative resistance, Marx became a fixture of academic life in the United States when a learned journal of Marxist inspiration, *Science and Society*, appeared. In the decades after World War II Marxist ideas were infused at an accelerated tempo into the intellectual atmosphere of Western Europe and America.

Revived as philosophers in the 1930s and 1940s, Marx and Engels became the revered mentors of sophisticated English scientists—Joseph Needham, John Desmond Bernal, J. B. S. Haldane—who discovered in the jejune works of Engels depths of wisdom only they would fathom. In 1940, Haldane wrote a preface to the English translation of Engels' unfinished manuscript called *Dialectics of Nature,* which had been printed for the first time in the second volume of the official communist *Marx-Engels Archiv* (Moscow, 1927). When in 1924 Eduard Bernstein had consulted Albert Einstein on the advisability of printing the original manuscript of the *Dialectics of Nature,* he replied with his usual candor that from the standpoint of either present-day physics or the history of physics it was of no particular interest, though it might contribute to an understanding of Engels' intellect. Einstein's lukewarm response in no way affected the onward progress of the diffusion of Marx's thought. Contemporary philosophers of science may now read Haldane's eulogy with a measure of astonishment at the power of political enchantment. In an overflow of enthusiasm Haldane gushed: "Had Engels' method of thinking been more familiar, the transformations of our ideas on physics which have occurred during the last thirty years would have been smoother. Had his remarks on Darwinism been generally known, I for one would have been saved a certain amount of muddled thinking . . . One reason why Engels was such a great writer is that he was probably the most widely educated man of his day . . . And he managed to accumulate this immense knowledge, not by leading a life of cloistered learning, but while playing an active life in politics, running a business, and even fox-hunting!"[1]

Bernal, establishing a direct line of affiliation from Marx and Engels through Lenin to Stalin, was no less enthusiastic: "The ideas of Marx and Engels found worthy development in the thought and work of Lenin and Stalin. With the key of the dialectic and the experience of revolutionary struggle they made the first breach in the world domination of capitalism. They succeeded because, thanks to Marx, they understood the laws of action of the social forces and above all the role of the proletariat as the leading force of the revolution."[2]

On the Continent, Marx's early writings, in print and in manuscript, were ransacked by academics and inflated into grand philosophical, economic, and moral systems. Historical and literary studies became so saturated with economic-social explanations that it was supererogatory to comment on their Marxist inspiration. Lucien Goldmann's analysis of Racine and Jansenism during a doctoral thesis defense sent tremors through the Sorbonne. Racine's *Phèdre*—when Rachel acted the lead, men of exquisite sensibility like Marcel Proust had been set aquiver—was turned by Goldmann into the plaint of the legist nobility of seventeenth-century France caught between the nobility of the sword and the rising bourgeoisie. The most sublime poesy of France, to be properly appreciated, now had to be probed to the very bottom of its economic-social substructure.

Marxist concepts were absorbed without reading Marx; often they were drawn from popular compendia. In our engrossment with economic indices of production as keys to felicity, we all became Marxists of sorts. In France, Italy, Germany, England, and the United States, the youthful manuscripts that had created a humanist Marx when they were belatedly published in the 1930s, in the 1960s and 1970s served as a secular substitute for a religious guide to a large body of American students in search of a progressist anthropology. In the eighteenth century, many a European writer's fame had been dependent on Voltaire's imprimatur. The twentieth century produced a cohort of stylish literary mandarins in France who determined the fate of writers great and small, keeping the limelight focused on themselves and their squabbles as they moved in and out of the temple of Marxist orthodoxy.

Though not as intoxicating as Rousseau's rhetoric, Marx's writings could be compressed into slogans that had a hypnotic effect. Herbert Marcuse's Freudo-Marxism found adepts in American universities among professors and their disciples, many of whom have survived long enough to forget their past. A hope theology with Marxist overtones, mediated by the German philosopher Ernst Bloch, seeped into the Protestant Church. And in Latin American countries young Jesuits became agents of transmission for a Marxist liberation theology. In China the writings of Marx did battle with the precepts of Confucius, and the mainland victory of communism in 1949 was the end of a long struggle that had begun with what Mao Zedong called the canon volley of the Russian October Revolution. Throughout Mao's reign, in Chinese translations of Russian translations, Marx was taught in Communist China's schools, where carefully selected excerpts from his works were used to indoctrinate young aspirants to political power. Marx penetrated to far corners of the earth: a traveler in Patagonia, Bruce Chatwin, found a settler reading Marx to his housekeeper.

During the Cultural Revolution, Mao's communism preserved the idea of class struggle as the primary social force to animate a bureaucracy prone to fall into the somnolence of routine; economic centralization was secondary. When Deng succeeded to the leadership, the slogans of modernization were developed along economic lines, and the pivotal role of ideology was de-emphasized. Simultaneously, intellectuals in pursuit of freedom resuscitated the writings of the young Marx, the Westerner's humanist Marx, with the concept of alienation in its multiple meanings writ large. These works became the breeding ground of the martyrs of Tiananmen Square.

Today the danger of swallowing Marx whole is recognized by Jiang Zemin, the general secretary of the Chinese Communist Party, who advised the restored Communist Party cadres to study Marxism only to the extent that it had lessons directly applicable to their positions—military teachings for army officers, educational guidelines for professors—a caricature of the *Gotha Program Critique*'s "to each according to his needs." Philosophical Marxism in China has nonetheless proved itself a useful instrument for pragmatic rulers, filling for a time the spiritual vacuum in a society that, unlike the West, does not conceal a religious gene somewhere among its chromosomes.

In retrospect, the spread of Marxism represented an amazingly fast conversion of millions of human beings to a new spiritual world belief, even though the doctrine was militantly materialist. The recent dissolution of Marxist thought has been equally swift—Marxism just faded away, as a Prague intellectual characterized his experience.

It is difficult to assess the meaningfulness of the required study of Marx in those countries where it was enforced by state mandate.

One is now told that when lectures on Marx were compulsory, students surreptitiously read novels while the lecturers droned on. Even in China, by the 1980s there was a tendency for the professor to distinguish between the relevant and the irrelevant in Marx's writings as they pertained to contemporary events. The force-feeding of Marx in many communist lands clearly led to boredom and often repugnance. One hears jokes about this indoctrination by command, about course papers churned out by friends, about examinations that nobody failed. But, after all, this is an experience familiar to those of us who have taught less doctrinaire required courses in American universities.

Most of the primitive rebellions of the dispossessed that are now erupting throughout the globe are not laden with the intellectual baggage that accompanied the Bolshevik and the Chinese revolutions and their offspring. Marx, Lenin, and Mao may still provide phrases for rallying cries in parts of Africa, Latin America, and Asia, but the sustenance of these spasmodic uprisings derives from heterogeneous sources—Christian theology, native cults, despair too profound to find hope or appeasement in frayed nineteenth-century revolutionary texts. These cries of misery, bereft of even a semblance of an organized thought system, often lead to a slaughter of the innocents when military responses are unleashed by regimes in power.

Henri Saint-Simon, the French utopian eulogized as a genius by Engels though less admired by Marx, once observed that ideas were like musk: one did not actually have to touch them to undergo their influence. If this reflection is applied to Marx in the nineteenth and twentieth centuries, his influence—flaccid term—cannot readily be submitted to known methods of measurement. How can we evaluate the role of one man's abstract ideas in the reorganization of immense territories stretching from Central Europe to the Pacific Ocean or in fateful decisions of war and peace that encompass half the people on the planet? We forthwith become enmeshed in the intricate relationships between thought systems and political structures that parade their logos, their trademarks, in the bloody arena of action.

One could take the position that there never was an inherent connection between the philosophy Marx developed in Berlin, Paris,

Cologne, and London and the economic-political apparatus imposed upon Russia and China by revolutionary leaders primarily motivated by a resolve to seize and entrench themselves in power. Perhaps, then, a dismal rehearsal of the contests of rival factions, irrespective of their nominal commitment to one brand of Marxism or another, is all that can be recounted about the history of the seventy years of communist hegemony in Russia and the forty in China. Yet the plain fact that a succession of leaders throughout the world called themselves Marxist and used terminology manifestly related to the writings of Marx cannot be summarily dismissed. The adoption of his name shaped the rhetoric of men in power irrespective of the varied cultural inheritances of the peoples they governed, which doubtless deeply colored their policies and in the end may have predetermined, at least in part, the fortunes of their Marxism. Gorbachev's fatal addiction to analysis of the development of phenomena in "phases" bore the telltale marks of Marx readings in school. In his departure speech, he touched obliquely on "ideological bias" as one of the forces of resistance to his grand project of reformation, but he still justified his policies in the Marxist mode: they were "historically correct" and everything that was done had been "prepared by the entire preceding period." Marx was not mentioned in the ceremonials of Soviet dissolution, and it is reported that Lenin in his tomb on Red Square was harangued by a lone drunk; but only those insensitive to the pervasiveness of ideas will deny their ghostly presence.

Perhaps a tricorn metaphor could relate a psychological profile of Karl Marx to the philosophic-economic theories he invented and both to the twentieth-century political movements and societies that bore him aloft as an icon. For some, this may imply cause and effect in a series that mounts from Marx the man to the revolutionary party to the first phase of the new communist world order. But the process can hardly be traced so neatly. When Marx himself was confronted by a similar, if less complicated, problem, the connection between the realm of ideas and production relations in the material world, he found refuge in stock formulas asserting that ideas "reflected" economic-social realities, or were "determined" by them. The verses from the preface to Marx's *Contribution to a Critique of*

Political Economy (1859) have been repeated like a litany by philosophical Marxists: "The mode of production in material life determines the general character of the social, political, and spiritual processes of life. It is not the consciousness of men that determines their existence, but, on the contrary, their social existence determines their consciousness."[3] Marx avoided the language of simple causation and respected the signs and forms of Hegelian dialectic. Theoretically, he eschewed any focus on the individual as irrelevant in explaining the behavior of classes or their leaders—a position from which he often departed in the heat of controversy as he hurled thunderbolts of *ad hominem* vilification against a rival revolutionary.

Das Kapital was adapted by a succession of twentieth-century commentators who brought it into harmony with new philosophic and economic thought, much of which Marx himself would not have recognized. Georges Sorel metamorphosed the theory of class struggle into a dynamic myth and freed it from the scientist preconceptions of the nineteenth century. He was followed by an array of sophisticated European Marxists who wrestled with *Das Kapital* each in his own manner. Gramsci in Italy and Lukacs in Hungary prolonged the life of Marxism by infusing it with collateral conceptions, though it had already been seized upon by communist bureaucrats who turned it into a dead official doctrine for themselves. The English economy, which had served as the living model for the work, changed so radically in the twentieth century that both the theory and its model became archaeological ruins fit for historical study. Lenin and other revolutionary leaders created a system that had a dynamic of its own, even while they retained the rhetoric and philosophical flourishes of the original creation.

In the period after World War II Marx became a darling of the intellectuals and the soil of France sprouted a plethora of Marxologists. In an attempt to resurrect the "true" Marx during a brief rebirth of French communism, Louis Althusser's *Lire le Capital* (1965), which enjoyed considerable academic prestige, regrouped Marx's writings in an unorthodox quadripartite system of periodization, distinguishing between works of "maturation" and works of "maturity." Close readers of Marx had not surfaced in France until half a century after his death; but when they finally discovered and learned to read him, French intellectuals became prime movers in the spread of his methodology in historical and literary researches throughout the world.

The nineteenth-century European revolutionaries, many of whom were Christian and Jewish apostates, had not succeeded in wholly dissolving their religious bonds. After the death of Marx and Engels, the Second International in 1897 still preserved the religious metaphor in one of its posters, albeit in an amended form: "The workers are the rock on which the church of the future will be built." The disciples of Lenin passed on to their successors the authoritarian religious temper of their childhood nurture. The transmission was easy since Stalin had imbibed a good dose of theology in the seminary where he received his early education. So deeply pervasive was the religious virus in the early years of the Russian Revolution that Lunacharsky, the beacon of universal culture in the Bolshevik party, toyed for a time with the idea of founding a revolutionary church— shades of the French Revolutionary theophilanthropic cults—in which to enthrone the Marxist ideology. Lenin, who had become an uncompromising proponent of Marxist universalism, free of nationalist or religious residues, put a quietus on the idea and sequestered the old icons in isolated monasteries; but he could not completely wipe out the religious tradition that was cherished in secret among his people.

Marxism refined and sophisticated the concept of alienation to the point where philosophers in twentieth-century communist lands raised the nettlesome question as to whether alienation in some form could still survive in a communist state. Such recondite conundrums did not burden the ordinary communist believer, who accepted the fundamentals of his faith by rote, and soon most of the grand theoreticians of Marxism abandoned overriding questions, or at least deferred their solution to a future age. A present-day observer may bemoan the disappearance of these subtleties and experience the same nostalgia that overcomes the intellectual historian who witnesses the neglect of scholastic niceties in an age of disbelief.

There is a sharp distinction between the Judaism and Lutheranism that fed Marx's early messianic vision and the philosophy of history that he developed in his mature writings. The crux of the difference lies in the role of the individual in the historical process. For all their orientation toward a future kingdom of heaven, both Judaism and Christianity promulgated precise codes of individual moral conduct that were acceptable to God. In the corpus of writings that Marx composed years after the adolescent fantasy of his gymnasium graduation essay, the significance of the individual in this capitalist vale of tears is reduced to the function of hastening or impeding the coming of the end. Hegel's world history, which permeates the Marxist ethic, is not a moral spectacle: it tramples underfoot many a noble flower in the achievement of its goal, the triumph of the Idea. By contrast, though Jehovah's ways are unfathomable, no true follower of the commandments of the God of Israel is ever destroyed with the blind indifference of the Hegelian and Marxist historical process. Though Marx may graphically depict the sufferings of a dehumanized proletariat under the factory system and the victims of bourgeois military repression in the defeat of the Paris Commune, deaths in the class struggle have no meaning except as testimony that the whole of precommunist history is a denial of man's humanity. The concept of "universal moral values" has only belatedly entered the vocabularies of some formerly communist societies, now in the throes of redefining their ethos. Rejection of individual moral absolutes on the ground that such virtues were bourgeois and a sham was one of the more treacherous legacies of Marx's philosophy.

In many ways Jean-Jacques Rousseau was a predecessor of Marx. Both unveiled the vices of their societies, Rousseau to end in the impasse of the general will, Marx to herald the dictatorship of the proletariat as a necessary transitional stage in the perfection of communist man. The executioners of the French Revolution harked back to Rousseau as their prophet, and as late as 1990 Marx remained an icon for the more ghastly police bureaucrats of communist governments. Personal commitments, rights, claims counted for nothing when set beside the spectacle of a future bliss for all mankind. It may seem heavy-handed to couple Marx with the bloodthirsty tyrants who tortured and executed millions while mouthing his shibboleths. But the regimes that spoke in his name derived their justification from the idea that the individual was of no moment in the period before the dawn of true human history, the coming age of unalienated labor; and if one Soviet state after another denied the meaningfulness of individual lives during the transition to that blessed time, Marx cannot be spared the world-historical verdict of complicity in their crimes. His sin of omission in failing to introduce into his system restraints upon the dictatorship of the proletariat, when even a madcap like Babeuf, who originally invoked the idea, had included pleas for the exercise of mercy against enemies, is more than a minor blemish.

The indigenous character of the Muscovite and Chinese empires, fashioned in the course of centuries, was still discernible in these states after they adopted Marxism; elements from their authoritarian past were fortified by the introduction of dictatorial ideas that had been embraced by the world revolutionary movement. For decades, two forces, one traditional, the other a foreign novelty, were intertwined, making it difficult to estimate their relative potency. Of late, nativist passions appear to have gathered momentum; but at the same time the rhetoric of the European Enlightenment, which China and Russia had assimilated only in a gingerly way, seems to be finding converts among some of their citizens. Since there are many chambers in the house that Marx built, the ideal of physical and psychic self-actualization as a human right, embedded in the Marxist utopia and long repressed, may yet find a place as a moral statement acceptable to both a secular and a religious humanism. And the breakup of the communist empire should not blind us to the possibility, after an interlude, of the resurgence in some new habit of Marx's universalist utopia. Nationalist intoxication is neither more nor less eternal than Marx's planetary vision.

At the moment, the fate of Marx in world politics is as unpredictable as that of other saviors. In the land where *Das Kapital* was born, Tony Blair, the leader of the British Labor Party, pointedly disavowed any relationship to Marx: "A belief in society. Working together. Solidarity. Cooperation. Partnership. These are our words. This is my socialism. It is not the socialism of Marx or state control."[4] On the other side of the globe, Madhav Kapur Nepal, the general secretary of the Communist Party in the Himalayan kingdom of Nepal, told a Western reporter on the occasion of the party's victory in the parliamentary elections: "If Marxism-Leninism is dead in Europe or not, I cannot say, but in Nepal it is the ideology of the people." Though angrily rejecting the suggestion that his party was more social democratic than Marxist, he issued a clear declaration of independence: "We don't have to go by the word of Marx or Lenin or Mao. It is we who are leaders of Nepal, and it is we who know what is best. As they used to say in Eastern Europe, 'Just because it rains in Moscow, do we have to carry an umbrella?'"[5] In other states great and small, former communist parties have sprouted names that conceal tenuous ties to Old Mohr. At the sight of these "false noses," Marx would surely have flung open the scatological floodgates, which were never tightly closed as long as he lived.

Envoi

For the sufferings of Karl Marx the exile, we can feel compassion; for his elaborate theoretical system, benign doubt and perhaps selective approval; for the abominable practices instituted in his name, loathing. A requiem for Marx cannot ignore the iniquities of his offspring—prophets and messiahs must share the blame for the excesses of their followers—but the banner that he unfurled need not be interred with his bones. Even a skeptical utopian like myself can still believe in the worth of the guiding principle: from each according to his abilities, to each according to his needs.

Notes · Index

Notes

English translations, unless otherwise noted, have been quoted from *The Collected Works of Marx and Engels,* abbreviated as *CW.* Translations from the *Marx/Engels Historisch-Kritische Gesamtausgabe,* abbreviated as *MEGA,* and from the *Werke,* are mine, as are quotations from French works. Not all volumes in the several collections have appeared in consecutive order, nor have their contents always been arranged in chronological sequence. The published texts of the *MEGA,* the *Werke,* and the *CW* do not duplicate one another in all particulars.

1. The Alien of Trier

1. "Betrachtung eines Jünglings bei der Wahl eines Berufes," *MEGA,* ser. 1, vol. 1, pt. 2 (Berlin: Marx-Engels-Verlag, 1929), pp. 164–167.
2. Marx to Engels, August 25, 1879, ibid., ser. 3, vol. 4 (1931), p. 490.
3. Marx to Arnold Ruge, March 13, 1843, *CW,* vol. 1 (New York: International Publishers, 1975), p. 400.
4. Marx to Engels, July 13, 1851, ibid., vol. 38 (1982), p. 384.
5. Engels to Carl Siebel, June 4, 1862, ibid., vol. 41 (1985), p. 374.
6. Marx, "Economic and Philosophic Manuscripts of 1844," ibid., vol. 3 (1975), p. 272.
7. Marx to Engels, February 20, 1866, ibid., vol. 42 (1987), p. 232.

2. Joanna Bertha Julie Jenny von Westphalen

1. Heinrich Marx to Karl Marx, March 2, 1837, *CW,* vol. 1 (New York: International Publishers, 1975), pp. 670–671.
2. Jenny von Westphalen to Karl Marx, 1839 or 1840, ibid., pp. 696–698.
3. Jenny to Karl, August 10, 1841, ibid., p. 709.
4. Marx to Arnold Ruge, March 13, 1843, ibid., p. 399.

5. Jenny Marx to Karl, June 21, 1844, ibid., vol. 3 (1975), pp. 576–577. The salutation quoted appears in Jenny's letter of August 11–18, 1844, ibid., p. 581.
6. Jenny to Karl, June 21, 1844, ibid., p. 579.
7. Jenny Marx to Joseph Weydemeyer, May 20, 1850, ibid., vol. 38 (1982), pp. 555–558.
8. Louise Freyberger to August Bebel, September 2 and 4, 1898, typescript, Internationaal Instituut voor Sociale Geschiedenis, Amsterdam.
9. Jenny Marx, "Short Sketch of an Eventful Life" (autobiographical notes dating to 1865), in *Reminiscences of Marx and Engels* (Moscow: Foreign Languages Publishing House, n.d.), p. 227.
10. Jenny Marx to Louise Weydemeyer, March 11, 1861, CW, vol. 41 (1985), p. 572.
11. Marx to Engels, July 31, 1851, *MEGA,* ser. 3, vol. 1 (Berlin: Marx-Engels-Verlag, 1929), p. 226.
12. Jenny Marx, "Short Sketch of an Eventful Life," p. 228.
13. Marx to Engels, September 8, 1852, *MEGA,* ser. 3, vol. 1 (1929), p. 392.
14. Jenny Marx to Engels, April 27, 1853, ibid., pp. 467–468.
15. Karl to Jenny, June 21, 1856, *CW,* vol. 40 (1983), pp. 54–55.
16. Karl to Jenny, August 8, 1856, ibid., p. 66.
17. Jenny Marx to Louise Weydemeyer, March 11, 1861, ibid., vol. 41 (1985), pp. 573–574.
18. Marx to Engels, December 9, 1861, *MEGA,* ser. 3, vol. 3 (1930), p. 48.
19. Marx to Engels, June 18, 1862, ibid., p. 77.
20. Jenny Marx-Longuet to Dr. and Mrs. Ludwig Kugelmann, May 12, 1873, *CW,* vol. 44 (1989), p. 586.
21. Jenny Marx to Engels, December 24, 1866, ibid., vol. 42 (1987), p. 576.
22. Jenny Marx to Dr. Kugelmann, December 24, 1867, ibid., pp. 578–579.
23. Jenny Marx to Engels, ca. January 17, 1870, *MEGA,* ser. 3, vol. 4 (1931), pp. 266–267.
24. Jenny von Westphalen to Karl Marx, March 1843, *CW,* vol. 1 (1975), p. 728.
25. Jenny Marx to Wilhelm Liebknecht, May 26, 1872, ibid., vol. 44 (1989), pp. 580–581.
26. Jenny Marx to Dr. Ferdinand Fleckles, ca. September–October 1880, quoted in Yvonne Kapp, *Eleanor Marx,* vol. 1 (London: Lawrence and Wishart, 1972), p. 216.

3. *The Dioscuri: Old Moor and the General*

1. Arnold Ruge to Kurt Moritz Fleischer, July 9, 1844, quoted in Auguste Cornu, *Karl Marx et Friedrich Engels,* vol. 3 (Paris: Presses Universitaires de France, 1962), p. 8, fn.
2. Elisabeth Engels to Friedrich Engels, after October 4, 1848, *CW,* vol. 38 (New York: International Publishers, 1982), p. 541.
3. Eleanor Marx, "Frederick Engels," in *Reminiscences of Marx and Engels* (Moscow: Foreign Languages Publishing House, n.d.), pp. 188–189.
4. Engels to Marx, October 5, 1860, *MEGA,* ser. 3, vol. 2 (Berlin: Marx-Engels-Verlag, 1930), p. 514.
5. Marx to Engels, January 8, 1863, ibid., vol. 3 (1930), pp. 117–118.
6. Engels to Marx, January 13, 1863, ibid., p. 118.
7. Marx to Engels, January 24, 1863, ibid., pp. 119–120.
8. Engels to Marx, January 26, 1863, ibid., p. 121.
9. Marx to Engels, January 28, 1863, ibid., pp. 122–123.
10. Marx to Engels, May 29, 1863, ibid., p. 141.
11. Marx to Engels, July 31, 1865, ibid., p. 279.
12. Engels to Marx, ca. October 8–10, 1844, ibid., vol. 1 (1929), p. 3.
13. Engels to the Communist Correspondence Committee in Brussels, October 23, 1846, ibid., p. 50.
14. Engels to Marx, November 23–24, 1847, ibid., p. 87.
15. Engels to Marx, October 25–26, 1847, ibid., p. 83.
16. Paul Annenkov, "A Wonderful Ten Years," in *Reminiscences of Marx and Engels,* p. 272.
17. Engels to Marx, October 5, 1860, *MEGA,* ser. 3, vol. 2 (1930), pp. 515–516.
18. Marx to Engels, August 17, 1877, ibid., vol. 4 (1931), pp. 473–474.
19. Marx to Engels, January 20, 1864, ibid., vol. 3 (1930), p. 164.
20. Marx to Engels, February 20, 1866, *CW,* vol. 42 (1987), p. 231.
21. Engels to Marx, February 22, 1866, *MEGA,* ser. 3, vol. 3 (1930), pp. 310–311.
22. Marx to Engels, July 7, 1866, ibid., p. 343.
23. Marx to Engels, August 17, 1877, ibid., vol. 4 (1931), p. 474.
24. Marx to Vera Zasulich, March 8, 1881, in *Karl Marx and Frederick Engels: Selected Correspondence* (Moscow: Foreign Languages Publishing House, n.d.), p. 411.
25. Marx to Engels, October 19, 1867, *MEGA,* ser. 3, vol. 3 (1930), p. 436.

4. Emigré Cannibalism

1. Engels to Marx, February 5, 1851, *MEGA,* ser. 3, vol. 1 (Berlin: Marx-Engels-Verlag, 1929), p. 142.
2. Marx to Joseph Weydemeyer, June 27, 1851, *CW,* vol. 38 (New York: International Publishers, 1982), pp. 375–376.
3. Engels to Ernst Dronke, July 9, 1851, ibid., pp. 382–383.
4. Marx to Engels, June 18, 1862, *MEGA,* ser. 3, vol. 3 (1930), p. 78.
5. Marx to Engels, August 1, 1856, ibid., vol. 2 (1930), p. 143.
6. Marx to Engels, September 22, 1856, ibid., p. 147.
7. Marx to Engels, November 4, 1864, ibid., vol. 3 (1930), p. 198.
8. Marx to Wilhelm Liebknecht, November 17, 1871, *CW,* vol. 44 (1989), p. 248.
9. Marx to F. A. Sorge, November 9, 1871, ibid., p. 241.
10. Engels to Carlo Terzaghi, January 14–15, 1872 (draft), ibid., p. 295.
11. Engels to Wilhelm Liebknecht, January 18, 1872, ibid., p. 297.

5. The Albatross: Das Kapital

1. Marx to Engels, June 18, 1862, *MEGA,* ser. 3, vol. 3 (Berlin: Marx-Engels-Verlag, 1930), pp. 77–78.
2. Engels to Marx, ca. October 8–10, 1844, ibid., vol. 1 (1929), p. 1.
3. Marx, *Capital: A Critical Analysis of Capitalist Production,* trans. Samuel Moore and Edward Aveling, ed. Friedrich Engels, from 3rd German ed. (London: Swan Sonnenschein, Lowrey, and Co., 1887), vol. 1, p. xv, author's preface to 1st ed.
4. Marx to Joseph Weydemeyer, February 1, 1859, *CW,* vol. 40 (New York: International Publishers, 1983), p. 377.
5. Marx to Engels, December 8, 1857, *MEGA,* ser. 3, vol. 2 (1930), p. 253.
6. Marx, *Capital,* author's preface, pp. xvii, xix.
7. Ibid., p. xix.
8. Marx to Engels, August 16, 1867, *MEGA,* ser. 3, vol. 3 (1930), p. 408.
9. Marx to Engels, September 30, 1882, ibid., vol. 4 (1931), p. 564.

6. The Arena of Class War

1. *CW,* vol. 6 (New York: International Publishers, 1976), p. 482.
2. Engels, *Condition of the Working Class in England in 1844,* trans. Florence Kelley Wischnewetzky (London: S. Sonnenschein and Co., 1892), pp. 132–133.

3. Marx to Joseph Weydemeyer, March 5, 1852, *CW,* vol. 39 (1983), pp. 62, 65.
4. Marx to Ludwig Feuerbach, August 11, 1844, ibid., vol. 3 (1975), p. 355.
5. Marx, *The Eighteenth Brumaire of Louis Bonaparte* (1852), trans. from 2nd German ed. (New York: International Publishers, 1963), p. 19.
6. Ibid., pp. 50–51.
7. Ibid., p. 47.
8. Engels to Marx, September 26, 1856, *MEGA,* ser. 3, vol. 2 (Berlin: Marx-Engels-Verlag, 1930), p. 151.
9. V. I. Lenin, Preface to letters from Marx to F. A. Sorge and others (April 6, 1907), in *Selected Works,* trans. from the Russian (New York: International Publishers, n.d.), vol. 11, pp. 736–737.

7. The Ambiguities of Nationhood

1. Engels to Marx, May 23, 1851, *MEGA,* ser. 3, vol. 1 (Berlin: Marx-Engels-Verlag, 1929), p. 206.
2. *CW,* vol. 8 (New York: International Publishers, 1977), p. 234.
3. *CW,* vol. 6 (1976), p. 503.

8. Utopias: The Approved and the Forbidden

1. Georges Sorel, *Reflections on Violence,* trans. T. E. Hulme (New York: Peter Smith, 1941), p. 150.
2. Marx and Engels, *Werke,* vol. 19 (Berlin: Dietz, 1962), p. 21.
3. Philippe Buonarroti, *Conspiration pour l'égalité dite de Babeuf, suivie du procès auquel elle donna lieu et des pièces justificatives* (1828) (Paris: Editions sociales, 1957), vol. 2, pp. 94–95.
4. *Werke,* vol. 4 (1959), p. 489.
5. Engels, "Materialen zum 'Anti-Dühring,'" *Werke,* vol. 20 (1962), pp. 580, 581, 587.
6. See, for example, *Le Globe,* November 5, 1831.
7. *Die deutsche Ideologie,* in *Werke,* vol. 3 (1964), p. 74.
8. Ibid., p. 517.
9. Ibid., p. 29.
10. Engels, *Der Ursprung der Familie des Privateigenthums und des Staats: Im Anschluss an Lewis H. Morgan's Forschungen,* in *Werke,* vol. 21 (1962), p. 78.

11. Engels to Karl Kautsky, April 26, 1884, *Werke,* vol. 36 (1967), p. 143.
12. Engels, *Der Ursprung der Familie,* pp. 83, 82.
13. Marx, *Das Kapital,* vol. 3, in *Werke,* vol. 25 (1964), p. 828.
14. Louis Blanc, *Organisation du travail,* 9th ed. (Paris, 1850), p. 72.
15. Pierre-Joseph Proudhon, *Idée générale de la Révolution au xixe siècle* (1851), in *Oeuvres complètes,* ed. C. Bouglé and H. Moysset, vol. 3 (Paris: Marcel Rivière, 1923), p. 174.
16. *Werke,* vol. 4 (1959), p. 490.
17. Paul Lafargue, "Karl Marx, Persönliche Erinnerungen," *Die Neue Zeit,* ninth year (1890–1891), pt. 1, p. 14.
18. The speech, delivered in English, was first published in a German translation. Quotation is from the English rendering in Franz Mehring, *Karl Marx: The Story of His Life,* trans. Edward Fitzgerald (New York: Covici, Friede, 1935), p. 555.
19. Engels, *Socialism Utopian and Scientific,* trans. Edward Aveling, with intro. by the author (London: Swan Sonnenschein & Co., 1892; New York: Charles Scribner's Sons, 1892), p. vii.
20. Engels, *Herr Eugen Dühring's Revolution in Science (Anti-Dühring),* trans. Emile Burns (New York: International Publishers, 1939), p. 309.
21. Ibid., pp. 307, 309–310.

9. Enemies within the Gates

1. Marx to Engels, June 7, 1859, *MEGA,* ser. 3, vol. 2 (Berlin: Marx-Engels-Verlag, 1930), pp. 397–398.
2. Engels to Marx, November 30, 1867, ibid., vol. 3 (1930), p. 454.
3. Marx to Engels, November 30, 1867, ibid., p. 455.
4. Engels to anonymous Austrian bank clerk, April 19, 1890, *CW,* vol. 27 (New York: International Publishers, 1990), p. 52.
5. Clement King Shorter, "The Private Life of Ferdinand Lassalle," introductory note in George Meredith, *The Tragic Comedians* (Boston: Roberts Brothers, 1892), pp. xvii–xviii.
6. Marx to Engels, July 30, 1862, *MEGA,* ser. 3, vol. 3 (1930), p. 84.
7. Engels to Marx, March 7, 1856, ibid., vol. 2 (1930), p. 122.
8. Marx to Countess Sophie von Hatzfeldt, October 16, 1864, *CW,* vol. 42 (1987), p. 5.
9. Engels to Marx, November 7, 1864, ibid., pp. 19–20.
10. Engels to Marx, January 27, 1865, *MEGA,* ser. 3, vol. 3 (1930), p. 219.
11. Marx to Engels, February 3, 1865, ibid., pp. 224–225.
12. Quoted in Arthur P. Mendel, *Michael Bakunin: Roots of Apocalypse* (New York: Praeger Publishers, 1981), p. 322.

13. Ibid., p. 321.
14. Engels to Theodor Friedrich Cuno, January 24, 1872, *CW,* vol. 44 (1989), pp. 308, 306–307.
15. Quoted in Mendel, *Bakunin,* p. 314.
16. Quoted in David McLellan, ed., *Karl Marx: Interviews and Recollections* (Totowa, N.J.: Barnes & Noble Books, 1981), p. 11.
17. Marx to Ludwig Kugelmann, October 9, 1866, in *Karl Marx, Letters to Dr. Kugelmann* (New York: International Publishers, 1934), p. 40.
18. Marx to Kugelmann, January 19, 1874, ibid., p. 134.
19. Marx and Engels, draft of a circular letter to August Bebel, Wilhelm Liebknecht, and Wilhelm Bracke, September 17–18, 1879, *CW,* vol. 45 (1991), p. 407.
20. Engels to Johann Philip Becker, September 15, 1879, ibid., p. 393.

10. Shearing of the Beard

1. Paul Annenkov, "A Wonderful Ten Years," in *Reminiscences of Marx and Engels* (Moscow: Foreign Languages Publishing House, n.d.), p. 270. The last two sentences, omitted from the *Reminiscences,* are translated from the original by David McLellan, *Karl Marx: Interviews and Recollections* (Totowa, N.J.: Barnes & Noble Books, 1981), p. 12.
2. Laura to Marx, May 8, 1867, quoted in *The Daughters of Karl Marx: Family Correspondence, 1866–1898,* trans. and adapted by Faith Evans (New York: Harcourt, Brace, Jovanovich [1982]), p. 29.
3. Marx to Engels, January 28, 1863, *MEGA,* ser. 3, vol. 3 (Berlin: Marx-Engels-Verlag, 1930), p. 126.
4. Marx to Engels, November 11, 1882, ibid., vol. 4 (1931), p. 569.
5. Eleanor to Jenny Marx-Longuet, January 8, 1882, quoted in *The Daughters of Karl Marx,* pp. 145–146.
6. Quoted in Yvonne Kapp, *Eleanor Marx,* vol. 2 (London: Lawrence and Wishart, 1976), pp. 510, 519, fn.
7. *CW,* vol. 6 (New York: International Publishers, 1976), p. 481.
8. *The Eighteenth Brumaire of Louis Bonaparte* (1852), trans. from 2nd German ed. (New York: International Publishers, 1963), p. 15.
9. "Sir Mountstuart Elphinstone Grant Duff's Account to Crown Princess Victoria," February 1, 1879, *CW,* vol. 24 (1989), pp. 580–582.
10. Marx to Engels, February 25, 1867, *MEGA,* ser. 3, vol. 3 (1930), p. 376.
11. Marx to Engels, March 1, 1882, ibid., vol. 4 (1931), p. 529.

12. Jenny Marx-Longuet to Eleanor, April 10, 1882, quoted in Kapp, *Eleanor Marx*, vol. 1 (1972), p. 240.
13. Marx to Laura Lafargue, June 1882, ibid., p. 238.

11. Vicissitudes of an Icon

1. Engels, *Dialectics of Nature*, trans. and ed. C. Dutt (New York: International Publishers, 1940), preface by J. B. S. Haldane.
2. John Desmond Bernal, *Marx and Science* (New York: International Publishers, 1952), p. 42.
3. Marx, *A Contribution to the Critique of Political Economy*, trans. N. I. Stone from 2nd German ed. (New York: International Library Publishing Company, 1904), pp. 11–12.
4. Quoted in the *New York Times*, October 5, 1994.
5. Ibid., November 21, 1994.

Index

Adler, Viktor, 191
Aeschylus, 87, 155, 222
Allen, Dr., Marx's physician, 49, 81, 84
Althusser, Louis, 236
Anacreon, 168
Annenkov, Pavel (Paul) Vasilyevich, 212, 245n16
Argyle, Archibald Campbell, Earl of, 32
Aveling, Dr. Edward Bibbins, 50, 119, 178, 246n3

Babeuf, François Noël (Gracchus), 125, 147, 159–160, 161, 175, 176, 200, 239
Bakunin, Mikhail Alexandrovich, 65, 78, 96, 97, 111, 112, 115, 128, 146, 175, 176, 182, 184, 186, 199, 200–205, 207, 208, 219, 220
Balzac, Honoré de, 22, 66, 86, 124, 223, 224
Barthélemy, Emmanuel, 90
Bauer, Bruno, 8, 17, 34, 105, 112, 183
Bauer, Edgar, 3, 213
Bebel, August, 40, 42, 209, 210
Becker, Johann Philip, 249n20
Beesly, Edward Spencer, 158
Bernal, John Desmond, 231
Bernstein, Eduard, 15, 76, 191, 209, 210, 231
Bichat, Marie François Xavier, 163
Bismarck, Prince Otto von, 116, 128, 193, 196, 197, 198, 199
Blair, Tony, 239
Blanc, Louis, 137, 171, 172
Blanqui, Louis Auguste, 112, 161

Bloch, Ernst, 232
Bracke, Wilhelm, 155, 157, 209
Brentano, Professor Lujo, 158
Brown, Norman Oliver, 166
Buonarroti, Philippe, 159, 160, 175, 247n3
Burns, Lizzy (Lizzie), 43, 65, 145
Burns, Mary, 43, 65, 67, 68, 69

Cabet, Etienne, 57, 171, 183
Chatwin, Bruce, 233
Chou En-lai, 107
Clemenceau, Georges Eugène Benjamin, 119
Confucius, 232
Cuno, Theodor Friedrich, 202

Danielson, Nikolai Frantsevich, 119
Darwin, Charles, 74, 102–103, 105, 176, 223
Daumier, Honoré, 221
De Brosses, Charles, 24
De Leon, Daniel, 230
Democritus, 14
Demuth, Helene (Lenchen, Nimm), 39, 40, 41, 42, 43, 44, 48, 68, 211, 226
Demuth, Henry Frederick (Freddy), 40, 41, 42, 211
Deng Xiaoping, 233
Diderot, Denis, 12, 22, 23, 222
Disraeli, Benjamin, Earl of Beaconsfield, 19
Dönniges, Friedrich Wilhelm von, 194
Dönniges, Helene von, 194, 198

Dozy, Professor Reinhart, 20
Dreyfus, Alfred, 217
Dronke, Ernst, 92, 93
Drumont, Edouard, 191
Dühring, Eugen, 112, 178

Eccarius, Johann Georg, 76, 205
Einstein, Albert, 32, 231
Engels, Elisabeth Franziska Mauritzia, mother of Friedrich Engels, 59, 65
Engels, Friedrich (The General), 1, 2, 3, 8, 15, 16, 19, 20–21, 25, 32, 33, 39, 40, 41, 43, 44, 46, 49, 50, 51, 52, 55, 57–75, 76, 77, 78, 79, 81, 83, 84, 85, 86, 87, 88–89, 90, 92, 93, 94, 96, 97, 98, 99, 101, 102, 103, 104, 105, 106, 107, 108, 110, 111, 112, 113, 114, 115, 116, 117, 118, 119, 121, 122, 123, 125, 126, 140, 144, 145, 146, 147, 150, 156, 157, 158, 160–161, 162, 167, 168–169, 170, 177, 178, 179, 181, 182, 184, 185, 188, 189– 190, 191, 194, 195, 197, 198, 199– 200, 201, 202–203, 205, 206, 208, 209, 210, 212, 213, 214, 217, 221, 223, 224, 225, 226, 228, 230, 231, 234, 237
Engels, Friedrich, Sr., 57, 59, 60
Ewerbeck, Hermann, 57
Ezekiel, 156

Feuerbach, Ludwig Andreas, 15, 57, 127, 176, 183
Fleckles, Dr. Ferdinand, 54
Fleischer, Kurt Moritz, 245
Fourier, François Marie Charles, 66, 105, 147, 161, 164–166, 167, 168, 169, 170, 171, 175
Frederick III, King of Prussia, 222
Frederick William IV, King of Prussia, 25
Freiligrath, Ferdinand, 70, 95, 182
Freyberger, Dr. Ludwig, 40, 41
Freyberger, Louise, 40, 41, 42, 53
Friedland (Friedländer), Ferdinand de, 192, 194

Goethe, Johann Wolfgang von, 9, 22, 23, 82, 222
Goldmann, Lucien, 232

Gorbachev, Mikhail, 235
Goya y Lucientes, Francisco de, 221
Graetz, Heinrich, 188
Gramsci, Antonio, 236
Grant Duff, Sir Mountstuart Elphinstone, 222
Grün, Karl Theodor Ferdinand, 72, 96, 112, 164, 183
Guizot, François Pierre Guillaume, 138, 221
Gumpert, Dr. Edward, 66, 80, 81, 83, 84, 85

Haldane, John Burdon Sanderson, 231
Hartmann, Eduard von, 86
Hatzfeldt, Countess Sophie von, 48, 191, 192, 194, 195, 197, 198
Hegel, Georg Wilhelm Friedrich, 9, 12, 13, 14, 21, 22, 23, 33, 102, 103, 104, 105, 133, 145, 178, 220, 221, 238
Heine, Heinrich, 36, 56, 95, 223
Heinzen, Karl, 92
Heraclitus, 194
Herder, Johann Gottfried, 142, 147, 153
Herzen, Alexander Ivanovich, 88, 115, 204
Herzl, Theodore, 189
Hess, Moses (Mosi, Moysi), 15, 16, 32, 33, 56, 59, 74, 77, 93, 95, 96, 112, 186–190, 191, 199, 208
Hess, Sibylle, 32, 93, 95
Hitler, Adolf, 228
Hobbes, Thomas, 102
Höchberg, Karl, 209
Homer, 27
Horace, 215

Irving, Henry, 53

Jehuda ben Eliezer Halevy Minz, 7
Jiang Zemin, 233
Jones, Ernest, 44

Kant, Immanuel, 9, 11, 147, 172, 178
Kapp, Yvonne, 244n26, 249n6, 250n12
Kautsky, Karl, 40, 70, 106, 149, 156, 168, 217
Kautsky, Louise. See Freyberger, Louise
Kinkel, Gottfried Johann, 92

Klings, Carl, 108
Köppen, Karl, 33
Krupskaya, Nadezhda, 118
Krushchev, Nikita Sergeevich, 229
Kugelmann, Dr. Ludwig, 51, 55, 116, 117, 198, 206, 208, 219, 244n20

Lafargue, François, father of Paul Lafargue, 224
Lafargue, Laura, 22, 32, 37, 39, 40, 42, 50, 145, 212–213, 216, 217, 225, 226
Lafargue, Paul, 22, 50, 172, 175, 178, 207, 215, 216, 217, 224
Lassal, Heymann, 192, 197
Lassalle, Ferdinand (Baron Izzy, Itzig), 15, 16, 32, 46, 48, 51, 69, 70, 73, 78, 82, 96, 108, 111, 112, 128, 184, 186, 187, 191–198, 199, 208, 215, 219
Leibniz, Baron Gottfried Wilhelm von, 8, 33
Lenin, Vladimir Ilich, 1, 2, 33, 78, 79, 104, 118, 131, 140, 141, 142, 149–151, 153, 156, 164, 227, 228, 229, 231, 234, 235, 236, 237
Leontieff, Wassily, 230
Lessing, Gotthold Ephraim, 57
Lessner, Friedrich, 40
Liebknecht, Wilhelm, 47, 52, 53, 76, 97, 99, 199, 209, 214
Lissagaray, Hippolyte Prosper Olivier, 50
Locke, John, 8
Longuet, Charles Félix César, 50, 216, 225
Longuet, Félicitas, mother of Charles Longuet, 216
Longuet, Jean Laurent Frédéric (Johnny), 225, 226
Longuet, Jenny Caroline, 32, 35, 36, 37, 42, 44, 50, 145, 216, 217, 225, 226
Lormier, Marie, 83
Louis Philippe, French king, 56
Lukács, Georg, 236
Lunacharsky, Anatolii Vasilievich, 237
Luther, Martin, 9, 10, 11, 64

Mably, Abbé Gabriel Bonnot de, 160
Machiavelli, Niccolò di Bernardo, 182, 201
Malthus, Thomas, 102

Mao Zedong, 2, 78, 233, 234
Marcuse, Herbert, 166, 169, 232
Marić, Mileva, 32
Marx, Eduard, 4
Marx, Eleanor (Tussy), 4, 32, 39, 40, 41, 42, 50, 64, 68, 119, 145, 214, 216–217, 225, 226, 245
Marx, Emilie, 4
Marx, Franziska, 39, 43, 44, 211
Marx, Heinrich (Heschel), 4, 5, 6, 7, 8, 13, 14, 18, 29–30, 42, 48
Marx, Heinrich Guido, 37, 44, 211
Marx, Henriette, daughter of Heinrich Marx, 4
Marx, Henriette, wife of Heinrich Marx, 4, 6, 13, 14–15, 18, 28–29, 35, 44, 67, 70, 71, 101, 221
Marx, Henry Edgar (Musch), 37, 44, 211
Marx, Hermann, 4, 28
Marx, Jacob, 3
Marx, Jenny, wife of Karl Marx, 4, 27, 28, 29, 30–31, 32, 33, 34, 35, 36, 37–38, 39, 41, 42–44, 45, 46–47, 48–49, 50, 51, 52–54, 55, 61, 66, 68, 69, 71, 82, 83, 92, 137, 195, 198, 211, 215, 217, 224
Marx, Jenny Caroline, daughter of Karl Marx. See Longuet, Jenny Caroline
Marx, Karoline, 4
Marx, Laura (Kacadou). See Lafargue, Laura
Marx, Luise, 4
Marx, Moritz David, 4
Marx, Rabbi Samuel, 5, 7
Marx, Sophie, 4, 28
Mason, Edward, 230
Mazzini, Giuseppe, 90, 128, 143, 144, 146–147
McLellan, David, 249nn16,1
Mehring, Franz, 248n18
Meissner, Otto Karl, 79
Mendel, Arthur P., 248n12, 249n15
Mendelssohn, Moses, 10, 15
Meredith, George, 191, 248n5
Metternich, Klemens Wenzel Lothar, Prince von, 221
Meyer, Siegfried, 101
Moleschott, Jakob, 46
Moore, Samuel, 41, 119, 246n3

Mordecai ben Samuel Halevy, 5
More, Saint Thomas, 157, 159, 169
Morelly, 159, 160, 167
Morgan, Lewis Henry, 168
Müntzer, Thomas, 157

Napoleon I, French emperor, 5, 7, 133
Napoleon III, French emperor, 116, 131,
    133, 164, 186, 206, 228
Nebuchadnezzar, 138
Nechayev, Sergei, 200, 203, 205
Needham, Joseph, 231
Nepal, Madhav Kapur, 239–240
Newton, Sir Isaac, 8, 105, 113, 172
Nietzsche, Friedrich Wilhelm, 226

Othello, 45

Pellico, Silvio, 82
Pfänder, Karl, 40
Philips, Antoinette, 19
Philips, Lion, 18, 19, 40, 70
Philips, Sophie, 18
Pieper, Wilhelm, 46
Plato, 12, 147, 158, 162–163, 169
Pompey, 124
Prometheus, 22, 53, 87, 224
Proudhon, Pierre Joseph, 56, 72, 77, 90,
    107, 110, 112, 128, 146, 172, 175,
    176, 178, 183, 187, 206–207, 208, 220
Puttkamer, Elisabeth von, niece of Otto
    von Bismarck, 66

Racine, Jean Baptiste, 232
Racowitza, Janko von, 194, 198, 199
Rameau, Jean Philippe, 23
Reagan, Ronald, 1
Reich, Wilhelm, 166
Renan, Ernest, 181
Ricardo, David, 126
Rjazanov, David, 76, 104
Robin, Paul, 202
Rousseau, Jean Jacques, 5, 162, 187,
    232, 238
Ruge, Arnold, 16, 33, 34, 56, 57, 92, 104

Sade, Donatien Alphonse François,
    Count de (Marquis de Sade), 165

Saint-Simon, Claude Henri, Count de,
    63, 105, 138, 161, 162, 164, 234
Sand, George, 204
Sazanov, Nikolai Ivanovich, 95
Schaff, Adam, 174
Scherzer, Andreas, 99
Schiller, Johann Cristoph Friedrich, 23
Schippel, Max, 156
Schmidt, Johann Caspar. *See* Stirner, Max
Schneider, Karl, 99
Schramm, Conrad, 37
Schramm, Karl August, 209
Shakespeare, William, 27, 45, 86, 87,
    121, 133, 155, 214, 222
Shorter, Clement King, 248n5
Siebel, Carl, 79, 243n5
Sieyès, Abbé Emmanuel Joseph, 123
Simon, Ludwig, 94, 198
Sismondi, Jean Charles Simond de, 138
Smith, Adam, 126
Sorel, Georges, 158, 236
Sorge, Friedrich Adolph, 98, 247n9
Spartacus, 124
Spencer, Herbert, 103
Spinoza, Baruch, 33, 187
Stalin, Joseph, 1, 2, 78, 231
Stephann, Dr., 225
Stirner, Max, pen name of Johann
    Caspar Schmidt, 105, 112, 183
Struve, Gustav, 149

Terzaghi, Carlo, 98
Tsuru, Shigeto, 230

Veblen, Thorstein, 194
Victoria, Queen, 26, 222
Victoria, wife of Frederick III of Prussia,
    222
Vogt, Karl, 107, 112, 182, 185, 186,
    196, 220
Voltaire, François Marie Arouet de, 5,
    232

Weber, Louis, 99
Weerth, Georg Ludwig, 93
Weitling, Wilhelm, 72, 77, 90, 96, 112,
    187
Westphalen, Baron Ludwig, 27, 28, 42

Westphalen, Edgar von, 27, 28, 35, 39
Westphalen, Ferdinand von, 28, 46
Westphalen, Joanna Bertha Julie Jenny von. *See* Marx, Jenny
Westphalen, Karoline von, mother of Jenny Marx, 31, 34, 35, 39, 40, 45, 46, 221
Weydemeyer, Joseph, 37, 38, 93, 109, 123, 246
Weydemeyer, Louise, 42, 47

Willich, August, 90, 92, 93
Wilson, Edmund, 213, 214
Wolff, Ferdinand (Red Wolff), 93, 94
Wolff, Wilhelm (Lupus), 19, 68, 70, 83
Wyttenbach, J. H., 9

Yakovlev, Alexander, 227
Yeltsin, Boris, 2

Zasulich, Vera Ivanovna, 85